CHURCHILL TO MAJOR

Churchill to Major

The British Prime Ministership since 1945

R.L. BORTHWICK
MARTIN BURCH
PHILIP GIDDINGS
RICHARD HODDER-WILLIAMS
J.M. LEE
COLIN SEYMOUR-URE
DONALD SHELL

Edited by
DONALD SHELL
and
RICHARD HODDER-WILLIAMS

HURST & COMPANY, LONDON

First published in the United Kingdom by
C. Hurst & Co. (Publishers) Ltd.,
38 King Street, London WC2E 8JT
© C. Hurst & Co. (Publishers) Ltd., 1995
All rights reserved.
Printed in Hong Kong

ISBNs
1-85065-147-7 (cased)
1-85065-179-5 (paperback)

CONTENTS

TABLES

PREFACE

Prime ministers are far and away the dominant figures in British government. Pre-modern history may be parcelled up according to the reigns of kings and queens. But we now talk of the Attlee years, or the Macmillan premiership, or even of the Thatcher epoch. The prime minister is the focal point of the contemporary political system. It is prime ministers who must define the strategy, direction and style of government. The media ensure that prime ministers are kept unremittingly at the centre of public attention. Media reporting of election campaigns suggests that these revolve around the choice of who should occupy 10 Downing Street, the most famous address in Britain.

For so prominent an office it is surprising to find so few scholarly books devoted to the prime ministership. There are of course many biographies of prime ministers, and a few of these are very good, not least in what they say about the exercise of responsibility at the head of government. But there are few studies of the office and role of prime minister. That is what this book seeks to be. In particular we examine how that role has changed over the last half century or so.

Since Winston Churchill took office as prime minister in 1940 ten different individuals have served in that exalted station, in two cases, as Table P.1 shows, returning there after an intervening spell in opposition. The differences in age, personality, background and style between these nine men and one woman have been considerable. The degree of success that attended their administrations has varied, and remains—certainly for some of the more recent occupants—sharply disputed.

Both Churchill as wartime premier and Clement Attlee as his peacetime successor have been generally regarded as highly successful prime ministers. The former proved a powerful leader at a time of grave national crisis. The latter was a competent manager through a period of national reconstruction. Churchill came to office when the very survival of the nation was under serious threat; Attlee did so when that dramatic external threat had been replaced by the need to win the fruits of peace, still a daunting task. Although head of an all party coalition government, Churchill had himself become leader of the Conservatives, often described as the natural party of government in Britain. Attlee led a party which had never before won an overall Commons majority. The grandiloquence of Churchill contrasted with the brusqueness of the monosyllabic Attlee.

Prime ministers since Churchill and Attlee have in many ways also

Table P. 1. PRIME MINISTERS SINCE 1940

	Period as PM from/to	Length of time as PM years/months	Age as PM
Churchill	May 1940 / July 1945	5 / 2	65 – 71
Attlee	July 1945 / Oct. 1951	6 / 3	62 – 68
Churchill	Oct. 1951 / Oct. 1951	3 / 6	77 – 80
Eden	April 1955 / Jan. 1957	1 / 9	58 – 60
Macmillan	Jan. 1957 / Oct. 1963	6 / 9	62 – 68
Douglas-Home	Oct. 1963 / Oct. 1964	1 / 0	60 – 61
Wilson	Oct. 1964 / June 1970	5 / 8	48 – 54
Heath	June 1970 / March 1974	3 / 8	54 – 58
Wilson	Mar. 1974 / April 1976	2 / 1	58 – 60
Callaghan	April 1976 / May 1979	3 / 1	64 – 67
Thatcher	May 1979 / Nov. 1990	11 / 6	54 – 65
Major	Nov. 1990		47 –

been contrasting figures. But has the job that they had to do as prime minister remained essentially the same? To put this question another way, would a Churchill or an Attlee still understand how to perform the job well if they were to return to 10 Downing Street today?

They would certainly find immense changes. When Attlee received the invitation to go to the Palace on 26 July 1945, he was driven to Buckingham Palace by his wife Vi in their Austin Seven car. She waited outside while he saw the King, and then drove him on to a victory rally at the Central Hall in Westminister. For the 1950 election campaign it was again Vi who personally drove her husband, then in office as prime minister, on a 1,300-mile election tour in their newer car, a 14-horsepower Humber. The pair stayed in convenient hotels, and travelled with one suitcase. Attlee spoke to an estimated 100,000 people, but was never once observed to use a note.

All this forms a glaring contrast with recent election campaigns. Leaders fly in chartered planes, accompanied by a posse of helpers and minders, to say nothing of police special branch protection. They use so-called 'sincerity machines' to read their speeches while looking their audiences straight in the eye. Portable telephones and fax machines keep open a plethora of communications to every corner of the kingdom and beyond.

While Attlee could profess genuine astonishment at being recognised in a hotel by a total stranger, John Major's look-alike brother has apparently been pestered by those who can hardly believe they have not just set eyes on the prime minister. In the 1940s small boys could go to the door of Number 10 and have their photo taken by adoring parents; now all they can do is peer through the tall steel gates securing the entrance to Downing Street.

Again, when Churchill gave way to Attlee, Britain still ruled a string of countries around the globe. The prestige of having led the world against Hitler, and of being accorded the status of a great power, still lay heavily upon the nation. The portfolios of almost half of Attlee's cabinet dealt with overseas matters, including defence. Developing nuclear weapons sustained the nation's right to a place at the top table, one of the so-called 'Big Three'. The contrast with today is marked. The colonies have gone. Defence forces are depleted to a fraction of their size in the 1940s. From standing loftily aloof as the European Community was formed in 1956, the United Kingdom eventually clawed its way in at the third attempt in 1973. By the 1980s Britain was struggling to maintain a place simply as a major regional power.

Changes have indeed been massive. But so too have been the continuities. The party system would still be recognisably similar to a returning Attlee or Churchill, although they would find the strength of the third party challenge disturbing, especially in so far as it required more complex considerations to be weighed in the devising of party strategy. They would both observe big changes in the manners and the norms of behaviour within their own parties. But the considerations shaping their relationships with senior colleagues would be fundamentally the same. The style of the House of Commons would startle them, but they would quickly recognise that the relationship between government and parliament remains fundamentally as it was in their day. The ability to appear at question time in the House, then—after helicopter hops and a flight on Concorde—speak at a dinner in New York the same evening might amuse or more likely irritate them. Having been taught that necessity was the mother of invention, they might protest at the extent to which invention had become the mother of necessity. Old dogs would have to learn new tricks. Churchill could not afford to refuse to appear on television, and Attlee would have to learn to answer reporters' questions with at least a sentence-long soundbite rather than a single word. But the skills which brought them success in the early post-war years would in all likelihood serve them similarly well today.

The essays in this book are primarily concerned with exploring the character of the changes that have taken place over a half-century in the British premiership. Each contributor was asked to focus on a particular area, and to consider how different prime ministers had related to that area. What changes had taken place? What continuities were evident? The opening chapter considers the development of the office, and provides an overview of the main responsibilities widely thought to belong to the office. The concluding chapter considers whether the changes that have taken place amount to a clear development, or whether they are better described simply as alterations, having given rise to no particular pattern. Is there a clear job description for the prime minister, and if so how has this altered over fifty years? Beneath the many obvious changes that can be readily identified, the question for students of politics is whether there are fundamental changes which have actually made the office of prime minister in the 1990s qualitatively different from that of the 1940s. This book seeks to provide some of the answers.

THE AUTHORS

R.L. BORTHWICK is senior lecturer in politics and formerly head of department of the University of Leicester. He is an active member of the Study of Parliament Group, has published widely on Parliament, and was joint editor of *British Politics in Perspective*.

MARTIN BURCH is senior lecturer in government at the University of Manchester. He has published extensively on British and regional politics and is completing (with Ian Holliday) a book on the British cabinet system.

PHILIP GIDDINGS lectures in politics at the University of Reading. He is editing a book on Executive Agencies and has contributed to several publications concerning Parliament and Whitehall.

RICHARD HODDER-WILLIAMS is professor of politics at the University of Bristol. He is the author of *Public Opinion Polls and British Politics* and co-editor of *Politics in Britain and the United States: Comparative Perspectives*, and has recently contributed a chapter to *A Conservative Revolution? The Thatcher-Reagan Decade in Perspective*.

J.M. LEE is emeritus professor of politics in the University of Bristol and visiting fellow in the Centre for International Studies at the London School of Economics. He was formerly an editor of *Public Administration*, and has authored a number of articles and chapters on British central administration, most recently in *Parliament and International Relations*.

COLIN SEYMOUR-URE is professor of politics at the University of Kent at Canterbury. He has published several books on the role of the media, the latest being *The British Press and Broadcasting since 1945*.

DONALD SHELL is senior lecturer in politics at the University of Bristol. He is the author of *The House of Lords*, and has contributed several chapters to other books on Parliament. He writes regularly in *Parliamentary Affairs*.

1

THE OFFICE OF PRIME MINISTER

Donald Shell [1]

No one invented the office of prime minister. No inaugural moment marks the deliberate creation or commencement of the office. There has never been any authoritative definition or delineation of the powers of the prime minister, and even today the duties that a prime minister must fulfil remain without precise definition. The essential qualifications for the office are nowhere specified, nor are disqualifications anywhere formally laid down. Appointment to the office is not for any fixed period of time and there is no limit on the length of time that a particular prime minister may serve. Nor are there clear-cut procedures by which the removal of a prime minister from office can be attained. In all these ways the office may be said to be characteristic of the uncodified British Constitution.

Potentially a prime minister is a very powerful figure. The holder of this office is heir to the prerogatives of the Crown and is also the leading figure in parliament. All the institutions of the state focus on the prime minister. Prime ministers appoint and dismiss ministers and a host of other senior servants of the state; they have the capacity to initiate policy and to shape the very structure of government itself. At least, if the prime minister does not do these things, no one else can do them. The modern prime minister is aptly described as an 'elected monarch'.[2]

While no formal constitution prescribes rules about this office, it may nevertheless be argued that the understandings about how it is discharged, about the powers that may be exercised and the limits which may be imposed upon those powers, are all quite clear. How has this come about? How has the office developed? And what duties and functions are now recognised as belonging to the office of the prime minister? These are the main questions addressed in this chapter. It begins by examining the origins and development of the office up to the twentieth century, and then considers how in modern times it is attained. Then

1 I should like to acknowledge the helpfulness of comments made by Philip Giddings on an early draft of this chapter. — D. S.
2 F.W.G. Benemy, *The Elected Monarch: The Development of the Power of the Prime Minister*, Harrap, 1965.

1

follows a brief overview of the main tasks that the prime minister carries out, so setting the scene for the chapters that follow.

The Origin and Development of the Office

In a formal sense the United Kingdom is governed by the Crown in Parliament, as it has been for some seven centuries. No limit has been placed on the legal power of the Crown in Parliament (at least until accession to the European Community took place in 1973). Here is the kernel of the Constitution. And it is not clear that the formal Constitution actually consists of anything beyond this kernel. Though all manner of other things may be said about the constitutional arrangements which now prevail, or which have at various times in the past prevailed, such statements can do no more than fill out the detail, indicating how, for the time being, the system operates. Such detail can and does change; and, when this happens, it simply happens. Constitutional change is not a matter of altering by formal process specially formulated rules. Rather it is a matter of altering the way things are done, and in so doing changing the expectations politicians and other have of the method by which the British as a people are governed.

The relationship between the Crown and Parliament has altered profoundly over the centuries. Central to that process has been the emergence of the office of prime minister, and the transfer of powers vested in the Crown from the person of the monarch to the prime minister.[3] Parliament is not and never has been an initiating body; rather, it emerged as a body through which the consent of the people, or at least that section of the public which mattered in political terms, could be mobilised. Strong monarchs could at times treat Parliament roughly or ignore it or even simply send it packing. But prudence generally dictated otherwise. And when prudence was not heeded in the later Stuart period, conflict resulted. The seventeenth-century upheavals resulted in the rights of parliament being asserted and to some degree spelt out in a Bill of Rights. The institutions of Crown and Parliament continued, but the relationship between the two had altered and were to continue to alter, as indeed was their composition. At the interface between Crown and parliament the role first of a cabinet and then of a prime minister emerged.

Perhaps some court favourites from pre-seventeenth-century days can be seen as precursors of the office of prime minister. Such figures organised support for the King. They orchestrated in his name the work of government. They negotiated on his behalf. But they owed their

---

3   See especially chapter 1 of Byrum Carter, *The Office of Prime Minister*, Faber and Faber, 1956.

position solely to monarchical favour. The seventeenth-century revolution altered that. The government remained the King's government in the sense that it was the monarch who appointed and dismissed ministers, and who by and large decided the matters upon which he wanted the advice of ministers. The old doctrine of the Divine Right of Kings may have been dead, but democracy in the modern sense had certainly not arrived, even if a monarch could never again rule with disregard to parliament. At the end of the seventeenth-century and for much of the eighteenth, those in power had little enthusiasm for defining precisely where power lay, and still less in pushing to an apparently logical conclusion the outcome of the Cromwellian revolution and the Restoration. Too much blood had been spilt, and too much danger lurked in such an exercise. Rather, people tried to work the arrangements which they had been bequeathed.

In so doing those arrangements were of course adjusted and modified. A gradual evolution took place. Incrementally power shifted, and understanding of the system altered. From the large and formal Privy Council an 'inner cabinet council' or 'cabal' emerged. This consisted of the men chosen by the King and responsible to him for the exercise of that power which was delegated to them from above, so to speak. But increasingly they were also seen as responsible to the parliament in which they sat, and the power of government which they exercised was recognised as at least partly coming up from below, from the people, mediated through parliament. It became necessary for these ministers to command the support of parliament, and that necessity thereby became a vital qualification for appointment to office. Out of that group a chief minister or a principal minister – or, as some would have it, a prime minister – emerged. He was simply the King's chief adviser.

The term 'prime minister' crept into use slowly and at least initially its sense was pejorative. Its first use in Britain is generally attributed to the great satirist Jonathan Swift who, during the reign of Queen Anne, borrowed the term already applied to France's chief minister and applied it to Godolphin and Harley. Subsequently and throughout the eighteenth century various ministers were at different times called prime minister, but the title was frequently resisted by those to whom it was applied. Walpole in the 1720s denied that he was prime minister; North and Greville both disavowed the term, while Pitt preferred to be principal minister. Only in the early nineteenth century did the title prime minister become quite inescapable, but even then – and ever since – the term has found little expression in the formal language of the state.[4]

---

4   Beaconsfield signed the Treaty of Berlin in 1878 as 'First Lord of the Treasury and Prime Minister of Her Britannic Majesty'. The first statutory mention of the office of prime minister was an incidental reference concerning salary in the 1937 Ministers of the Crown Act.

Walpole's twenty-one years in office have earned for him by general acknowledgement the title of Britain's first prime minister. Appointed First Lord of the Treasury in 1721, his position was enhanced in 1729 with the removal from office of his rival Townshend; thereafter Walpole was in full control of the cabinet. If that were one reason why he has been so widely credited as Britain's first prime minister, the second concerns the manner by which he left office, for he resigned on losing a vote of confidence in parliament. Hence: 'Whether or not he [Walpole] deserves the title no one before him does.'[5] If he is seen as the first prime minister, it would be quite wrong to imagine that during his period in office any clear understandings about the nature of the office were formulated, still less any clear rules that subsequent premiers would of necessity be required to observe. For another generation, until the appointment of Pitt in 1770, party lines in the Commons were so chaotic that no one was able to fulfil a role such as Walpole's.

Robert Blake discerns three especially formative periods in the emergence of the office.[6] The first of these was 1782-4 when the resignation of Lord North swept an entire ministry from office. Party lines were becoming clearer and it was apparent that, while monarchs might initiate the choice of ministers, they must accept from parliament a veto power over who should be appointed prime minister. It was the changed relationship between monarch and parliament that was emphasised in these years. But the government still remained in a real sense that of the King, and until the 1830s the patronage power of the Crown ensured that no government actually lost an election. However, the passage of the Great Reform Act in 1832 largely destroyed the rotten boroughs and brought in its wake the break-up of the old system of politics. This is the second of Blake's formative periods. Government henceforth had to be based on party.

But this was still party in parliament, 'parliamentary connection' in Blake's terminology, not party in a modern sense of the term at all. Between the first and second Reform Acts ministries were made and unmade by these parliamentary connections. This was the heyday of the House of Commons, the so-called golden age of parliament. The House had to meet after a general election to clarify what had been the actual outcome of the election. It was the Commons that 'chooses our president', as Bagehot put it in his brilliant description of the system, made just at the moment when the pattern he so perceptively described was ceasing to exist.[7] The creation of a mass electorate through the

5   See Robert (Lord) Blake, *The Office of Prime Minister*, Oxford University Press, 1975, p. 5.

6   Blake, *The Office of Prime Minister*, p. 42.

7   Walter Bagehot, *The English Constitution* (1st edn 1867), Collins Fontana edn 1963, p. 150.

second and third Reform Acts shifted and dispersed power away from the floor of the House of Commons. In time it was the party organisations that were to soak up the newly released form of popular power. Government based on party in parliament moved to government based on party in the country. Prime ministers assumed office because they led parties that won competitive elections; they headed armies of disciplined supporters. In the 1870s, Blake's third formative period, party government emerged as recognisably the same phenomenon as we see it today, with what he describes as the 'inflexibility of party boundaries and the predictability of the division lobbies'[8] taking over.

Any brief summary of changes such as this runs the risk of implying that a much greater degree of clarity attended these developments than could ever be perceived at the time. Political expediency, together with an understanding by politicians about what was considered possible or appropriate, shaped the developments that took place. And these developments themselves were often highly confused. Any notion that steady progress was being made towards the present state of affairs must be resisted. The fashioning of the office of prime minister under Walpole was largely rescinded under his successors. Politicians who spent their formative years in the mid-nineteenth-century House of Commons were slow to adjust to the new circumstances created by the second and third Reform Acts. For example, doubt existed over whether a prime minister had the clear right to dismiss cabinet colleagues without some obvious reason, or whether only the prime minister was empowered to summon a meeting of the cabinet.[9]

By the end of the nineteenth century all the powers associated throughout the twentieth century with the office of prime minister were on display. Through party the House of Commons was subject to control with the government having assumed a virtual monopoly of the time of the House, and having armed itself with the procedural weapons necessary to ensure the passage of its legislation. W.E. Gladstone's Midlothian Campaign of 1880 heralded the new relationship between party leader and electorate, made more obvious as the mass electorate became the target of a mass media. The party leader's election address became widely circulated and by the turn of the century was being viewed as a manifesto for all his followers.

It is platitudinous to say that the context within which government operates has changed vastly since the end of the nineteenth century. Britain has ceased to be a Great Power with an empire spanning the globe. The disposition of ministerial offices has reflected this fact, with

8   Blake, *The Office of Prime Minister*, p. 39.
9   See John P. Mackintosh, *The British Cabinet*, Stevens, 1962; especially chapter 6 headed 'The survival of former political habits' and 'The growth of new political practices'; also chapter 11.

such posts as the Secretaries of State for Social Services, for Health, and for Education appearing just as other cabinet posts withered on the vine, such as those with responsibility for India and Burma, for Colonies and for War. The size of government has expanded enormously, with the proportion of gross national product passing through the public sector rising from under a tenth to almost a half. The development of technology and communications not only set before an entire nation instant news of happenings, but the same technology made it possible for ministers and diplomats (as well as foreign exchange dealers and the moguls of big business) to be in constant touch with each other, passing documents or holding televisual conferences, ensuring immediate and simultaneous response to unfolding events.

Such changes have not only brought on to the agenda wholly new problems that government must tackle, but they have also altered the way that all governments operate. Ministers, including the prime minister, spend their time differently from their predecessors of fifty or 100 years ago. They have had to learn new skills. It is far more important that they can speak convincingly in the television studio than it is that they can handle a public meeting of 5,000 or even 500. Developing the wit and skill and verbal dexterity to cope with the televised prime minister's question time is more vital than the stamina and passion and moral fervour displayed by Gladstone at the Commons Despatch Box. What prime ministers must do, and how they do it, has changed; their functions within the political system have altered. But in constitutional terms the job of the prime minister has remained essentially unchanged for the past century.

Attaining the Office of Prime Minister

I begin by stating the obvious. The prime minister must be invited to assume that office by the monarch. The monarch for his or her part must invite the person who appears best placed to command a majority in the House of Commons. All the fifty-two individuals who from Walpole onwards have held the office of prime minister have been appointed by the monarch, but the personal discretion that monarchs exercised in the eighteenth century, and less in the nineteenth century, in making that choice has all but disappeared in the twentieth century. The choice became the individual whom the monarch thought would make the best prime minister rather than the individual most congenial to the monarch. Thus in 1894 Queen Victoria could have chosen either Lord Harcourt or Lord Rosebery, and the choice fell on Rosebery because Victoria thought him the best available man for the job. In the twentieth century an element of discretion may have remained with the monarch:

for example, in 1931 when King George V's preference for Ramsay MacDonald as leader of a coalition government was made known, and in 1940 when the view of King George VI was certainly weighed by the political leaders who met to decide on Neville Chamberlain's successor. But the exercise of any personal judgment on prime ministerial qualities had by then given way to the over-riding necessity for the monarch to choose the person most likely to command the support of the Commons.

For that reason it seems self-evident that the prime minister must be a Member of Parliament. Yet there have been circumstances in which this simple condition has not been fulfilled. Before the relegation of the House of Lords to clear subordinate status by the 1911 Parliament Act, prime ministers could be drawn from the upper House, as indeed was Lord Salisbury until 1902. Because nothing in the Parliament Act itself ruled out the possibility of a premier in the Lords, ambiguity on this point continued. The failure of Curzon to be appointed prime minister in 1923 was thought to be the consequence of his being a peer, although there were other cogent reasons for the choice of Baldwin. In the wartime emergency of 1940 the possibility that Lord Halifax might succeed Chamberlain received some consideration, but in the event Churchill was considered the best man for the job for reasons other than Halifax's membership of the Lords. By 1963, when the retiring premier Harold Macmillan advised the Queen to send for the Earl of Home as his successor, the newly-enacted Peerage Act afforded to peers the possibility of escape from the Lords, an opportunity which Home instantly took, and without which his nomination as prime minister would not have been made. He became prime minister on 19 October, but was not elected to the House of Commons (in a hastily procured by-election) until 7 November.

This episode demonstrated that there is no insuperable constitutional obstacle to a prime minister not actually being in parliament at all, although Lord Home could only become prime minister because it was confidently anticipated that he would quickly become a member of the Commons. Had he lost the by-election, it is inconceivable that he could have continued as prime minister. If a prime minister or leader of the Opposition were to lead his party to election victory, yet at the same time lose his own seat, then it is at least possible that the individual concerned could still assume office as prime minister so long as a fellow MP in a safe seat were willing to resign and create an opportunity for an immediate by-election.[10] But any party leader

---

10   In 1964 this, route was taken to create a vacant seat for the defeated Patrick Gordon Walker, who had become Labour's Foreign Secretary. However, he went on to lose the by-election in the so-called safe seat where a vacancy had been created. At this point there was considered to be no alternative to his resignation from office. This

put in this position would be exposed to such unwelcome ribaldry that it seems an unlikely course of action.

Is it now impossible for a prime minister to sit in the House of Lords? Politically it may appear so given the contemporary predominance of the House of Commons. But it is worth noting that in 1955 Eden considered it impossible to appoint a foreign secretary in the Lords,[11] yet a few years later Macmillan did just that and, though Labour protested, no serious problem resulted (and in 1979 Margaret Thatcher made Lord Carrington her foreign secretary). Many would have agreed with Anthony Eden in 1955 that the foreign secretary must be in the Commons, just as most would now assume that a prime minister in the Lords is impossible. But who is to say that circumstances might not arise in which this again became a possibility, however unlikely that may seen at present?

If it is assumed that the prime minister must be a member of the House of Commons, this means that, like all MPs, he – or she – must be aged over twenty-one and a United Kingdom citizen, and cannot be an undischarged bankrupt, a felon, or a priest in the Church of England.

Between 1940 and 1993 there have been twelve occasions when a change of prime minister has occurred. As Table 1.1 shows, six of

Table 1.1. CHANGE OF PRIME MINISTER

	Without general election	As result of general election
1940	Churchill	–
1945	–	Attlee
1951	–	Churchill
1955	Eden	–
1957	Macmillan	–
1963	Home	–
1964	–	Wilson
1970	–	Heath
1974	–	Wilson
1976	Callaghan	–
1979	–	Thatcher
1990	Major	–

these have been as a result of general election defeat, and the other six consequent upon the resignation of a prime minister and his replacement from within the ranks of his own party.

Although the processes of party choice may produce unexpected

---

precedent does not therefore offer any encouragement for attempts to bring a defeated minister immediately back into the House in this way.

11   See Anthony Eden, *Full Circle*, Cassell, 1960, pp. 273–4.

results (just as general elections may), there has not been any serious doubt or difficulty for the monarch in deciding whom to appoint as prime minister at any of the dates shown in the accompanying table. Before 1965 the Conservative Party had no clear electoral mechanism for choosing a leader. When a vacancy occurred, soundings were taken within the party by senior figures; the monarch was entitled to seek advice from the outgoing leader and such other senior figures as she decided. In 1955 Churchill advised Queen Elizabeth II to send for Eden, the man whom in 1941 he had advised King George VI to appoint if he – Churchill – were to be killed in the war, and who ever since had been recognised as the heir-apparent. When Eden resigned in 1957, as well as taking advice from the outgoing prime minister, the Queen summoned both Salisbury and Churchill; the former had polled the cabinet and, although the public expected Butler to be appointed, in the event Macmillan was sent for because soundings taken within the senior ranks of the Tory Party favoured him, and this was reflected in the confidential advice received by the Palace.

When Macmillan resigned in 1963, consultations again took place within the party, and this time a good deal more widely than before. On the basis of these Macmillan as outgoing prime minister advised the Queen to send for Lord Home. Again this choice caused public surprise, and on this occasion the party was quite unable to conceal the deep and bitter divisions which accompanied the decision.[12] Because of the disarray within the party Lord Home did not immediately accept the commission to form a government, but undertook to try to do so on 18 October, and only returned to the Palace the following day to indicate that he had been successful, having secured in particular the agreement of Butler to serve under him. The confusion evident on this occasion made it imperative that a new method for appointing a leader be adopted, if only to ensure that the monarch could in future act with the impartiality considered incumbent upon the office.

In 1965 an electoral mechanism was introduced based exclusively on the parliamentary party. This was first used when Sir Alec Douglas-Home resigned the leadership while the party was in opposition in 1965, and resulted in the election of Edward Heath. Then in 1975 the procedure was adapted slightly to allow for it to be used not only to choose a leader when a vacancy occurred, but to allow for a challenge to be made to a sitting leader. This happened in 1975, again when the party was in opposition, with Margaret Thatcher displacing Heath. In 1989 and then again in 1990 Thatcher while prime minister was

---

12 See Randolph Churchill, *The Fight for the Tory Leadership*, Heinemann, 1964; also Nigel Fisher, *The Tory Leaders*, Weidenfeld and Nicolson, 1977; Robert T. McKenzie, *British Political Parties* (2nd edn), Heinemann, 1965.

herself challenged, the first time any party leader had faced an open contest for the leadership while serving as prime minister. She was forced to resign in the 1990 contest, which saw John Major elected party leader, leaving the Queen with the duty of appointing him as prime minister.[13]

In the Labour Party a mechanism for electing a new leader has been in existence throughout the history of the party. As Table 1.1 shows, Labour has only once changed leaders while the party has been in office. This was in 1976 when Harold Wilson resigned and the Parliamentary Labour Party (PLP) chose James Callaghan to succeed him. In 1981 the party decided that, instead of the PLP alone choosing the leader, this task should be carried out by an electoral college in which MPs held only 30 per cent of the votes (with constituency parties having 30 per cent, and the trades unions 40 per cent). This electoral college has so far only operated while Labour has been in opposition; in 1983 Neil Kinnock was elected leader and in 1992 John Smith was chosen as Kinnock's successor. By 1993 changes in the composition of the electoral college were being mooted, but it was still likely to remain a body in which MPs would have a minority representation.

The adoption of this method for choosing the leader brought with it the possibility of the monarch finding some element of personal discretion inescapable. In 1981 the former prime minister Callaghan was reported as saying that, if the Parliamentary Labour Party wished, it could choose as leader someone different from the choice made by the electoral college, and that, if this occurred, the monarch would be obliged to send for the individual chosen by the PLP rather than the individual chosen by the electoral college. Given that voting in the college is by open ballot, it was certainly possible that the product of the electoral college's choice would be publicly recognised as being the choice of only a minority of MPs.[14] However, to prevent the scenario envisaged as a possibility by Callaghan arising, the PLP in 1982 introduced a Standing Order stipulating that it would accept as leader whoever was chosen as leader by the party as a whole; in other words, by the electoral college.

Given that all parties, including the Liberal Democrats, have an electoral mechanism by which a leader is chosen, it would seem that in the event of a prime ministerial resignation the monarch need have no fear about having to exercise discretion as to whom to appoint prime

---

13   On the detailed results of party leadership elections, see appendix A; for further discussion of this subject, see R. Malcolm Punnett, *Selecting the Party Leader*, Harvester Wheatsheaf, 1992.

14   As very nearly happened in respect of the deputy leadership election in 1981, when Denis Healey won by a whisker in the electoral college as a whole, but by an overwhelming majority within the PLP.

minister; she only need await the outcome of a party election. If the office of prime minister became vacant at a time of grave national crisis it might be desirable to speed up the process by which the governing party chose a successor. In 1976 the Labour Party took four weeks, and that was when only the parliamentary party was involved! On that occasion, however, having announced his retirement, Wilson remained in office until his successor was chosen.

When resignation has been precipitated through the governing party being defeated in a general election, the monarch's duty is to appoint as prime minister the leader of the party which appears most likely to command a majority in the Commons. Only once in post-war Britain has an election resulted in a House of Commons in which no party had an overall majority. That was in February 1974 when Labour gained a majority of four over the Conservatives, but thirty-eight seats were in the hands of minor parties. The Conservative prime minister who had called the election, Heath, did not immediately resign. Instead, he explored the possibility of Liberal Party support for the government, but this was not forthcoming. No agreement could be reached, and indeed the political circumstances of the time made the possibility of securing such an agreement appear a forlorn hope, thus adding to the controversy surrounding the whole exercise. Heath resigned four days after the general election. But although his action in remaining in office over the weekend had rendered him subject to the criticism that he had acted in an unconstitutional manner, this criticism seems unfounded. In doing what he did Heath was exercising a perfectly legitimate right accorded to a sitting prime minister. As soon as it had been made clear that any government headed by him was likely to have less support in the House of Commons than a government headed by Wilson, the leader of the Opposition, Heath resigned.

Indeed his action was helpful in clarifying the situation in which various people would subsequently have to discharge their constitutional responsibilities. For if a minority Labour government had suffered an early defeat on an issue of confidence and then advised the monarch to dissolve parliament, the argument might well have arisen that the monarch should first send for the Conservative leader to see if he could enter into some sort of pact or coalition arrangement with another party, and thus form a government, without the need to resort to another general election so soon after the previous election. By doing what he did Heath demonstrated in advance that the Queen would not have to face such an argument.[15] An important point to recognise in all this

15   In 1974 there was in fact discussion exactly along these lines; the Conservatives threatened to vote against the new Labour government's Queen's Speech. Wilson let it be known that if such a vote were carried he would seek an immediate dissolution; some Conservatives responded by saying that the national interest would require the

is that the dissolution of parliament does not create a vacuum in government; all ministers, including the prime minister, remain in office throughout an election campaign and beyond until they resign.

When a prime minister does resign, for whatever reason, the whole government is deemed to have resigned too. If the change is between two prime ministers of the same party, then the new occupant of 10 Downing Street may choose simply to confirm many ministers in their posts, but technically all offices are placed 'at the disposal' of the new prime minister.

The Parliamentary Experience of Prime Ministers

Incoming prime ministers have generally had substantial parliamentary experience. Table 1.2 shows this, although it is noticeable that the two most recent prime ministers have had less experience than those of an earlier generation.

In choosing a party leader one important criterion MPs employ is proven ability at the Despatch Box in the Commons; hence some years spent on the front bench is to be expected. MacDonald was the last person to become prime minister (in 1924) without having previously held any ministerial office; that was in the special circumstances of a new political party rising to major party status. It is worth noting that Neil Kinnock had never held ministerial office, although he had served on the Labour Opposition front bench from 1979 until his election as party leader in 1983. Attlee came to the leadership of the Labour Party almost by accident in 1935; his previous ministerial experience had been slight, but during the all-party wartime coalition he served in very senior ministerial roles and deputised for Churchill when the latter was not available.

John Major is unusual in never having sat on the Opposition benches in the House of Commons, which he first entered in 1979, becoming prime minister eleven and a half years later. But by then he had held two of the three great cabinet offices, namely chancellor of the exchequer and foreign secretary (albeit briefly). Thatcher had held only one cabinet post before becoming prime minister, and that a post not regarded as being of major importance, namely secretary of state for education and science. In opposition she had served as a spokesman on Treasury

---

Queen to invite the Conservative leader to try to form a government rather than go straight to a general election. Palace sources let it be known that the Queen would grant Wilson's request, whereupon the Conservatives decided not to vote against the Queen's Speech. This whole episode indicates the importance of political circumstances rather than formal rules in determining outcomes.

Table 1.2. PARLIAMENTARY EXPERIENCE OF PRIME MINISTERS

	Date and age of entry into Commons (years in House before PM)		Ministerial posts held before appointment as PM
Churchill	1900 (38)*	25	PU/S Colonies 1906–8
			Pres. Bd of Trade 1908–10
			Home Secretary 1910–11
			1st Ld Admiralty 1911–15
			Ch. Duchy of Lancaster 1915
			Min. of Munitions 1917
			S/S War and S/S Air 1918–21
			S/S Colonies 1921–2
			Chancellor Exchequer 1924–9
			1st Ld. Admiralty 1939–40
Attlee	1921 (24)	38	PU/S War 1924
			Chancellor Duchy of Lancaster 1930–1
			Postmaster General 1931
			Lord Privy Seal 1940–2
			S/S Dominions 1942–3
			Ld President of Council 1943–5
Eden	1923 (34)	26	PU/S Foreign Office 1931–3
			Lord Privy Seal 1934–5
			Min. without Portfolio 1935
			Foreign Secretary 1935–8
			S/S Dominions 1939–40
			S/S War 1940
			Foreign Secretary 1940–5 and 1951–5
Macmillan	1924 (30)*	30	PU/S Min. of Supply 1940–2
			Min. Res. in N. Africa 1942–5
			S/S Air 1945
			Min. for Housing 1951–4
			Min. of Defence 1954–5
			Foreign Secretary 1955
			Chancellor Exchequer 1955–7
Douglas-Home	1931 (15)†	28	PU/S Foreign Affairs 1945
			M/S Scottish Office 1951–5
			S/S Commonwealth Relations 1955–60
			Foreign Secretary 1960–63
Wilson	1945 (19)	29	PU/S Min Works 1945–7
			Sec. for Overseas Trade 1947
			President Bd of Trade 1947–51
			(Chm Public Accounts Cttee 1959–63)
Heath	1950 (20)	34	Ld Commr Treasury (Whip) 1951–2
			Deputy Chief Whip 1952–5
			Chief Whip 1955–9
			Min of Labour 1959–60
			Ld Privy Seal 1960–63
			President Bd of Trade 1963–4
Callaghan	1945 (31)	33	PU/S Transport 1947–50
			PU/S Admiralty 1950–1
			Chancellor Exchequer 1964–7
			Home Secretary 1967–70
			Foreign Secretary 1974–6
Thatcher	1959 (20)	34	PU/S Pensions & Nat Ins 1961–4
			S/S Education & Science 1970–4
Major	1979 (11)	36	Ld Commr Treas (Whip) 1983–5
			PU/S Social Security 1985–6
			M/S Social Security 1985–7
			Chief Sec. Treasury 1987–9
			Foreign Secretary 1989
			Chancellor Exchequer 1989–90

S/S: Secretary of State; M/S: Minister of State; PU/S: Parliamentary Under Secretary of State
* Denotes interrupted membership of the Commons.
† Excludes twelve years' membership of the House of Lords.

and Environment matters, but she had no experience in foreign affairs. Callaghan by contrast had held all three major posts, as chancellor (1964-7), home secretary (1967-70) and foreign secretary (1974-6).

Heath was appointed a whip within twelve months of being elected to the Commons, and he remained in the whips' office for nine years; this undoubtedly gave him a very good knowledge of the Party, but whether it really was an effective preparation for premiership seems doubtful. Apart from anything else, whips are traditionally silent in the Commons, and Heath therefore lacked the opportunity to develop personal skills associated with effectiveness at the Despatch Box; his Commons speaking style has by general consent improved greatly since he lost office. After leaving the whips' office Heath had experience both in the Foreign Office, when he served as Lord Privy Seal in charge of negotiations for Britain's first application to join the European Community, and then on the home economic front as secretary of state for prices and regional development and president of the Board of Trade.

After becoming the youngest cabinet minister of the century in 1947, Wilson became almost the youngest cabinet minister to resign in 1950 when he left Attlee's government along with Aneurin Bevan in protest at the introduction of prescription charges. In opposition he was for four years chairman of the Public Accounts Committee, a role which purportedly gives a unique insight into the workings of Whitehall. Douglas-Home was unusual in that he was an MP from 1931 to 1945, when he lost his seat; however, in 1950 he re-entered the House, but the following year inherited an earldom which perforce took him off to the House of Lords. In the upper chamber, however, his ministerial experience broadened and deepened until in 1963 he became prime minister and returned to the Commons. After stepping down as leader of the Party in 1965 he served under his successor, completing a further spell as Foreign Secretary from 1970 to 1974, before retiring from the Commons, and once more entering the Lords, this time as a life peer.

Macmillan was a party rebel in his early days in the Commons. But the Second World War brought with it the opportunity for ministerial office and, although he too lost his seat in the 1945 Conservative débâcle, he quickly returned to the House and, when the Conservatives returned to office, was accorded accolades for his success in boosting house building to the rashly accepted target of 300,000 houses a year, set at the Conservatives' 1951 party conference. His time as foreign secretary was very brief, and as chancellor he earned the epithet of being 'first in and first out' in regard to Suez; in other words, he gave ready support to Eden's policy initially but, when the United States refused to support the country's currency, quickly shifted tack in order to avoid looming financial disaster.[16] Eden had long ministerial experience but almost entirely in the field of foreign affairs, and perhaps even more of a handicap was the fact that, before he became prime minister, he had waited as heir-apparent for some fifteen years. This probably contributed to the excessive confidence his colleagues placed in his ability to handle foreign affairs safely. For sheer length of experience Churchill easily outdistances all other prime ministers. But it is worth noting that the eleven years immediately before he became prime minister had been spent on the back benches. It was of course this fact which made him particularly suitable for appointment in the dark days of 1940.

Since 1940 the age of prime ministers on first appointment has varied between forty-seven (in John Major's case) and sixty-five (in Churchill's). The oldest occupant of the office of prime minister was also Churchill, who eventually retired in 1955 some months after his eightieth birthday. According to Robert Blake, the average age of the first twenty-four prime ministers (Walpole onwards) on first assuming office was forty-seven; for the next twenty-five up to Heath – it was fifty-nine. But four of the most recent five prime ministers have been younger than that, and John Major at forty-seven was one year younger than Wilson when he first became prime minister in 1964. The average tenure for all premiers up to Heath had been five years and two months. Thatcher remained prime minister from May 1979 until November 1990, the longest continuous period for anyone to hold the office since Lord Liverpool in the early nineteenth century.

Harold Wilson headed four different administrations as prime minister, totalling just under eight years; Churchill was prime minister for slightly longer, and Macmillan for almost seven years. Wilson, like Major, started young; his sudden resignation in 1976 caused surprise and indeed aroused suspicion as to its true motives. His own explanation, that he was simply tired after 'working 12-14 hours a day seven days a week for at least 50 weeks every year', sounds plausible enough.[17] Being prime minister is arduous. Churchill remained in Downing Street having suffered serious illness, ironically continuing to hold office for a time on medical advice because his doctor considered that resignation would have an adverse effect on his health.[18] But he was exceptional, if not unique. It seems very unlikely that a prime minister could now remain in office through any serious illness. Running the country can no longer be considered a form of therapy!

---

16 See Alistair Horne, *Macmillan 1894–1956*, Macmillan, 1988, chapter 15.
17 See Philip Ziegler, *Wilson*, Weidenfeld and Nicolson, 1993, chapter 23.
18 See Lord Moran, *Winston Churchill: The struggle for survival*, Sphere, 1968 edn, p. 407.

The Work of the Prime Minister

Before analysing in outline form the main tasks which fall upon the prime minister it is well to make two related points. First, as already indicated, there is no formal list of duties pertaining to the office. This is because the office itself has no formal definition, as might be provided by a written constitution. A search of the Statute Book will yield only a few scattered and unhelpful references to the office of prime minister. There are certain duties that prime ministers must carry out, but beyond that the job is very much what they make of it – and what their colleagues allow them to make of it. Hence the second point: that a great deal of flexibility surrounds the office. Different prime ministers have approached it in very different ways; indeed, as political circumstances have altered the same prime minister has perforce had to change to adapt to new conditions.

Macmillan commented that the prime minister has 'nothing to do'.[19] In making this remark he was no doubt in part simply expressing his customary cultivated nonchalance. But he was also contrasting his experience as prime minister with his earlier experience as a busy departmental minister. Callaghan reflected, that after becoming prime minister, once he had completed his list of ministerial appointments, 'I sat back and realised I had nothing to do'; while in previous departments 'private secretaries arrived as soon as I set foot in the door, bearing piles of official papers to read and files with urgent problems for immediate decision', no such experience greeted him as prime minister: 'For a brief period I savoured the suspicion that as everyone else was doing the government's work, I could be the idlest member of the administration if I was so minded.'[20] This does make the point that, whereas departmental ministers have a constant stream of decisions which they must make, the same is not true of prime ministers. Acts of Parliament typically lay statutory duties on specific Secretaries of State, for example to make appointments, to approve or otherwise planning appeals; to determine grant levels, or whatever. Prime ministers have virtually no such statutory duties. On the one hand, they can choose to become 'workaholics', attempting to inform themselves about everything and intervening in as many decisions as possible. The opportunity is there for them to behave in this way. Ministers and officials can be summoned from any part of Whitehall; information can be sought and ministers can be persuaded, cajoled or bullied into decisions on pain of dismissal. On the other hand, a prime minister could conceivably sit back and let ministers get on with reaching decisions, while as prime

19   Keith Sainsbury in John P. Mackintosh (ed.), *British Prime Ministers*, vol. 2, Weidenfeld and Nicolson, 1975, p. 122.
20   James Callaghan, *Time and Chance*, Collins, 1987, p. 403.

minister simply fulfilling a head of government role, making ministerial appointments and chairing cabinet.

Both Wilson and Thatcher cultivated reputations as workaholics. But in Wilson's case there was a significant difference between his pre-1970 and post-1974 attitude. In 1964 he headed a government very few of whose members had any previous experience of ministerial office. As a result, he wrote: 'I had to occupy almost every position on the field, goalkeeper, defence, attack – I had to take the corner-kicks and the penalties, administer to the wounded and bring on the lemons at half-time.' A reading of his memoirs covering the period 1964-70 underlines his love of frenetic activity. By contrast, after 1974 he sought to be 'a deep-lying centre-half...concentrating on defence, initiating attacks, distributing the ball and moving up-field only for set-piece occasions.'[21] Callaghan in 1976 no doubt felt like Wilson in 1974 that he headed a very experienced team of ministers.

There was no reason why Thatcher should not have felt the same in 1979; Wilson had fourteen former cabinet members in 1974; Thatcher had eleven in 1979. But her attitude was different. She intervened everywhere because she saw her government as a crusade. Passion and ideological commitment drove her on. Politics was not a team game where you simply sought to score more goals than your opponents; for her it was a battle in which she sought to annihilate her opponents. She worked frenetically, ensuring that throughout her time as prime minister she dominated the government.

Some commentators have discerned a growth or at least an accretion of power in the office of prime minister. Whereas prime ministers used to be *primus inter pares*, the leading member of the cabinet wherein the power of government lay, they have now become elected chief executives, surrounded by a team of of appointed advisers. Whereas collective responsibility used to mean the responsibility of all ministers publicly to support the policies upon which they had collectively agreed, it has become a means by which prime ministers bind their colleagues to support the policies they have stipulated. Many people, both scholars and politicians, have argued that the prime minister has become in effect a president.[22]

But it is not at all clear that such a change has occurred. Strong prime ministers have dominated their cabinets, and weak ones have been sharply constrained by their cabinets. A senior minister serving under Margaret Thatcher may have jokingly said 'we don't have cabinets

21 Harold Wilson, *Final Term*, Weidenfeld and Nicolson, 1979, pp. 17–18. See also Harold Wilson, *The Labour Government, 1964–1970*, Weidenfeld and Nicolson, 1971.

22 See, for example, R.H.S. Crossman, 'Introduction' to Walter Bagehot, *English Constitution*, Collins Fontana, 1963; John P. Mackintosh, *The British Cabinet*, Stevens, 1962.

any more'.[23] But the same could have been said and very nearly was said under Lloyd George. There is an ebb and flow about such arguments. It is the essential continuity of the office over the last 100 years that is far more impressive than any discontinuity. No prime minister has acted as presidentially as Lloyd George. Churchill's famous dictum that 'all I wanted was compliance with my wishes after reasonable discussion' implies a presidential style of domination. In seeking to theorise about the pattern of government, scholars have at times developed models which mislead because they pretend to a far greater precision than the facts and circumstances they are seeking to explain, taken over a period of time, properly allow.

The functions of the prime minister can be summarised under three broad headings: namely, those arising out of the prime minister's position as head of government, those consequent upon being party leader, and those which flow from being leader, or first citizen, of the nation. But, given the flexibility of the office, and the lack of any authoritative list of duties, it is helpful to try to distinguish between those tasks which prime ministers must perform, their duties so to speak, and those to which no clear constitutional obligation attaches. No precise categorisation is possible, but thinking in terms of a continuum, from the undoubtedly required to the clearly optional, is helpful.

But while doing this one must recognise that requirements can arise from political as well as from constitutional necessity. And, of course, given the variability of political circumstances, the range of tasks prompted by political necessity not only changes over time, but is subject to a good deal of conflicting interpretation. Furthermore, in discharging some responsibilities a prime minister may be both acting according to clear constitutional criteria, while at the same time engaged in what may be a delicate task of political management.

The Prime Minister as Head of Government

As head of government prime ministers must maintain a ministerial team. It is their duty to appoint (or, technically, to recommend to the monarch for appointment) fellow-members of their cabinets. However obvious some of these appointments may be, and however little choice a prime minister may feel in practice about the matter, the choice technically is theirs. Newly-appointed prime ministers who take over from a predecessor of their own party in effect inherit a ministerial team, but all offices are placed at their disposal; ministers, if they are not to be dropped or re-deployed, must be confirmed in their posts. Prime ministers who come to power as a result of victory in a general election

---

23   Quoted in Peter Hennessy, *Cabinet*, Basil Blackwell, 1986, p. 99.

bring with them a 'shadow cabinet'. A Conservative leader in opposition also appoints all members of the shadow cabinet, but on the Labour side the equivalent body is elected by the Parliamentary Labour Party (PLP). Hitherto no incoming prime minister has been obliged to translate shadow appointments into actual appointments, although in practice a high degree of continuity has been normal. However, from 1981 onwards the standing orders of the PLP have stipulated that an incoming Labour prime minister must appoint those previously elected to the shadow cabinet (provided they have retained their House of Commons seats).

In the early post-war period senior ministers sometimes made their own appointments to junior posts within their departments. But today the scope of prime ministerial power to appoint extends to all ministerial offices. A prime minister may consult with the senior minister in a department before filling a junior ministerial post, and the chief whip is now invariably consulted when ministerial reshuffles are being planned. Other senior ministers may urge the prime minister to make certain appointments, but the actual decisions clearly belong to the prime minister. Even the appointment of unpaid parliamentary private secretaries, who are not strictly members of the government, and do not have ministerial responsibilities, must be approved by the prime minister.[24]

Having once appointed the government ministerial team a prime minister could thereafter limit further appointments merely to replacing those who choose to resign. But in practice such a hands-off strategy is not practicable. Resignations and retirements are inevitable. When a senior minister goes, that vacant post is almost invariably filled by promotion, with a consequent ripple effect throughout the government. Particularly in recent years the most favoured route into Conservative governments has been through the whips office. The age of the professional politician has resulted in ministerial posts being seen very much as a career hierarchy. This requires the prime minister to be a sort of career development manager. Junior ministers are in effect on probation; if they do well they can anticipate promotion (though never tenure!) but, if they fail to satisfy, then they will be returned to the backbenches. Those who aspire to become stars in the party firmament need varied experience in different departments. For all these and other reasons regular reshuffles of ministers are commonplace. The average time spent

---

24   In 1976 Callaghan vetoed for some months the appointment of Brian Sedgemore as Tony Benn's PPS, and subsequently had him sacked for quoting from a government document while cross-examining the chancellor Denis Healey on a parliamentary select committee (see Brian Sedgemore, *The Secret Constitution*, Hodder and Stoughton, 1980, Chapter 9). In 1967 Wilson insisted or firing seven PPSs who abstained in a division on Britain's application for EC membership, even though the division was won overwhelmingly.

in the same post has declined markedly compared with the pre-war period.[25] Mid-term reconstruction of the government has given way to annual ministerial shuffles. Media attention focuses on such activity, which may be one reason why recent prime ministers have appeared to relish the task. Moving ministers around is a very visible exercise of power; it gives an appearance of purposeful activity, of governing, perhaps especially valuable when the substance is lacking.

Hence, alongside the responsibility to appoint ministers is the right to dismiss. In the twentieth century there has never been any real doubt about the right of the prime minister to request any minister's resignation and, if this is not complied with, to have them dismissed. Macmillan sacked seven cabinet ministers at once in 1962, and Thatcher dismissed a long line of ministers from her cabinet in ones, twos and threes rather than by massacre. Of course there are all manner of political constraints on the exercise of this power. Whether it is politically wise or personally advantageous for a prime minister to dismiss any particular minister is a different question from whether the prime minister has the right to do so, a point taken up by Philip Giddings below.

The prime minister chairs the cabinet and this involves determining the agenda for meetings, the time and frequency of meetings, overseeing the flow of papers and such matters. The minutes of cabinet meetings are issued on the authority of the prime minister. How a prime minister fulfills these responsibilities is a matter of both political circumstances and personal style. A prime minister may be no more than the chairman of a cabinet meeting, taking the views of colleagues on an issue and then summing up the discussion, perhaps even without declaring their own view at all. Alternatively, prime ministers may use cabinet simply to announce decisions that they have already made, and in effect confront their cabinet colleagues with the challenge to disagree; if disagreement is sustained a prime minister may threaten to resign rather than back down.[26]

While it is no doubt possible for prime ministers to manipulate the organisation of business to suit their own wishes, and so, for example, delay consideration of some items while speeding that of others, or despatch some to cabinet committees and keep others for full cabinet, any suggestion that by this means some subjects can be kept indefinitely off the cabinet agenda seems misplaced. All the normal opportunities that accrue to the chairman of a committee are available to the prime minister; ministers can be called into the discussion in the order the prime minister wishes and it is the prime minister who sums up discussion.

25 See Richard Rose, *Ministers and Ministries*, Clarendon Press, Oxford, 1987, p. 83.
26 As apparently was the case when ministers discussed entry to the Exchange Rate System in 1985; see Lawson, *The View from No. 11*, Bantam Press, 1992, p. 499.

But their position is something more than that usually held by a chairman of a committee in that they have direct power over the membership of the committee.

The prime minister also decides the terms of reference and the membership of cabinet committees. given that most cabinet decisions are made through such committees, rather than in full cabinet, deciding on the membership and chairmanship of such committees is an important task. Prime ministers have clearly varied a good deal as to the use made of cabinet committees. Some, notably Thatcher, have apparently preferred to use *ad hoc* meetings of ministers more frequently and officially constituted cabinet committees less so.[27] The prime minister chairs the more important cabinet committees. When in May 1992 the membership and terms of reference of cabinet committees was for the first time officially published, it was revealed that John Major chaired nine of the sixteen standing committees.[28] So-called 'kitchen cabinets' have sometimes appeared. How a prime minister actually operates varies considerably, but whatever methods are chosen it is the prime minister who must oversee the cabinet machine.

Prime ministers also carry overall ministerial responsibility for the civil service, although generally they are assisted by another minister who bears the day-to-day responsibility for managing the service. This means that prime ministers have to decide on the structure of government departments. They may of course be quite happy to perpetuate the structure they inherited, but many prime ministers have in fact brought modifications to that structure. This can be done simply by Order in Council. In 1964 Wilson created three new departments in his first twenty-four hours in Downing Street. Sometimes such alterations have been primarily to accommodate changes in the scope of government activity, such as the amalgamation of separate departments for the armed services into a single Ministry of Defence. Sometimes substantial experimentation has been attempted, as for example with the creation of a Department of Economic Affairs in 1964 (followed by the abolition of the same Department in 1968), or the integration of Trade and Industry and then their separation, and the same for Health and Social Security. Many changes have been made, and for various motives. The need to create a particular niche for a powerful colleague may weigh more heavily than criteria pertaining to sound and efficient administration.

The prime minister is responsible for senior appointments in the civil service. In deciding these the nominations of a senior appointments board are put to the prime minister, and until Thatcher there was probably

27   Peter Hennessy, *Cabinet*, pp. 99–101.
28   See press reports for 20 May 1992; see also *Dod's Parliamentary Companion*, Dod's, 1993, pp. 816–27.

a tendency to let the machine run itself, so to speak. But she definitely adopted an interventionist approach, though accusations that she did this according to party partisanship seem wide of the mark. Rather it was part of her wish to stir up and alter the culture within Whitehall.[29]

The prime minister is also responsible for a host of other appointments including ambassadors, the higher judiciary, Church of England archbishops and bishops and certain other clergy, the governor of the Bank of England, and chairmen of such major public bodies as the BBC and the IBA. The advice of other ministers is available – for example, that of the lord chancellor for judicial appointments and that of the foreign secretary for ambassadorial appointments – but the decisions are made by the prime minister. Again how activist a role the prime minister undertakes is a matter of choice and circumstance. Lord Melbourne's infamous remark: 'Damn it! Another Bishop dead' implied that the choice of bishops was burdensome to nineteenth-century prime ministers. Other priorities have clearly taken the attention of twentieth-century prime ministers, although not until the late 1970s was the Crown Appointments Commission set up through which advice could be formally tendered to the prime minister on the appointment of bishops, while still leaving the final decision with the prime minister. In regard to many other appointments, which are formally made by various secretaries of state, the prime minister is free to intervene, and it can be assumed most senior ministers in making such appointments are ready to seek prime ministerial advice and give way to any clear expression of the prime minister's mind.

Prime ministers are responsible for advice to the crown on the award of almost all honours, and it is through their office that the twice-yearly honours lists are prepared. Again, how active a prime minister chooses to be in overseeing this process is a matter of choice. Conservative prime ministers have always made some awards for 'political and public services', whereas Wilson and Callaghan avoided self-styled political honours.[30] In 1993 John Major announced that the honours system would be reformed to make it more classless, and he encouraged the public to write in with their suggestions.[31] But the first honours list prepared under these new arrangements appeared very little different from earlier lists. Honours include the award of peerages and the concomitant right to a seat in the upper chamber of Parliament. Suggestions for awards are invited from many sources, and it is customary for leaders of the opposition to decide who within their party should be nominated, but

29 See Peter Hennessy, *Whitehall*, Secker and Warburg, 1989, chapter 15.
30 On the varied announcements made by successive prime ministers, see House of Commons *Debates*, 27 Oct. 1966, col. 1301; 10 Nov. 1975, col. 205; 19 Mar. 1974, col. 870; and 26 Nov. 1979, col. 880.
31 See House of Commons *Debates*, 4 Mar. 1993, cols 453–63.

it is for the prime minister to decide on the total number of awards that are available to other party leaders.

The prime minister appoints the chiefs of staff who in turn have the right to appeal to the prime minister in person concerning defence expenditure. The prime minister may choose to preside at the chiefs of staff meetings. As wartime premier, Churchill also assumed the office of minister of defence, an arrangement he repeated, though only for four months, after becoming prime minister again in 1951. Thatcher did not do this at the time of the Falklands conflict, but she did preside at a specially convened committee of the cabinet, as did Major at the time of the Gulf conflict and Eden at the time of Suez. The overall direction and supervision of the security services is the responsibility of the prime minister.

As head of government the prime minister has certain parliamentary duties. Not since before the Second World War has the prime minister served as leader of the House (the minister responsible for arranging the business of the House). But as the leading member of the government the prime minister must speak regularly in the House; for example, during the debate on the Queen's Speech at the beginning of every session, and whenever a motion of confidence in the government is moved. Prime ministers are expected to speak in other major debates, and they also make Statements to the House, notably after summits or other international conferences they have attended. During the period under review in this volume the arrangements for prime ministers answering questions in the House have altered substantially, reflecting the much greater public interest in such questions. In Chapter 3 below these developments are discussed and the point is made that recent prime ministers have made fewer speeches in the Commons than their predecessors. On the other hand, the attention given to prime minister's question time is vastly greater than used to be the case. The changed pattern of prime ministerial participation again reflects the theme of flexibility, though whether the fact that prime ministers make fewer speeches in the House while having to give much more attention to questions indicates any decline in accountability to the House is a moot point.

As head of government of the prime minister is the monarch's principal adviser. Every week, while Parliament is sitting, the prime minister has an audience with the Queen. It may be assumed that prime ministers have sometimes appreciated the opportunity to talk about affairs of government with so close and well-informed, yet totally detached an observer.[32] At other times a formal submission of advice must be made,

32   Nigel Lawson remarks: 'I recall telling the Queen, the one person to whom I could unburden myself in complete confidence,...that I thought the 1988 budget would be my last, because the prime minister was making the conduct of policy impossible'; Lawson, *The View from No. 11*, p. 799. When Callaghan was considering whether

and as a constitutional monarch the Queen has no choice but to follow advice of this kind. The prime minister has the right to request a dissolution at any time, although it is the Sovereign who proclaims the dissolution of Parliament. Since the First World War the decision to call a general election has been recognised as belonging to the prime minister personally; cabinet colleagues may be consulted but the decision, and hence the responsibility for whatever consequences it brings, belongs to the prime minister alone. For all practicable purposes the monarch must follow the prime minister's advice; where this is clearly a matter of great controversy (as would have been the case had Wilson's government been defeated on the Queen's Speech in March 1974, and had he then requested an immediate dissolution) it is likely that such controversy would only be magnified in a way damaging to the monarchy if the Queen were to decline or even to delay the grant of a dissolution.

Trustee of the Constitution: Collective responsibility

Lord Home once described the prime minister as 'trustee of the Constitution'. Certainly it is the prime minister who must accept responsibility as the chief guardian of the constitution. It is the prime minister who is ultimately answerable to Parliament, and to the public, for the way the government conducts its business. There will always be occasions when this is controversial, not simply in a political sense but also in a constitutional one, and the question 'Have constitutional conventions been broken or not?' will be given conflicting answers. A brief discussion of the doctrine of collective responsibility illustrates this point. Broadly this requires all ministers to offer public support to all government policies. Sharp differences may be expressed within government, but these are in theory within the privacy of the cabinet room and within government departments. Of course in practice the press is often able to discuss such differences in a very well-informed way, not least because of leaks from ministers themselves. What is considered important, however, is that ministers do not publicly oppose each other on matters of government policy. If differences become public knowledge, it is up to the prime minister to decide at what point the expression of differences demands removal from office and on what mechanisms are necessary to maintain at least the appearance of a united front. For Labour this can present particular problems when ministers sit on the party's National Executive Committee (NEC). Wilson issued a memo

---

to take a new initiative in relation to the regime led by Ian Smith in Rhodesia in 1976, he discussed the matter with the Queen, and subsequently received a letter from her, and recalled 'The Queen's opinion was enough to tip the scales'; he went ahead with the initiative. See Callaghan, *Time and Chance*, p. 380.

on this point in 1969 when Callaghan voted against the government's proposed industrial relations legislation at a NEC meeting, and in 1974 he sought written assurances from all ministers when Benn as a NEC member was opposing policies put forward by the cabinet, of which he was also a member.[33]

If the prime minister so decides, the doctrine of collective responsibility may be set aside. In the period covered by this volume this was done on two occasions, first during the referendum campaign in 1975 on the issue of continued membership of the European Community, and second on the manner of election to the European Community Parliament in 1977. On this second occasion Margaret Thatcher challenged the prime minister to define the circumstances in which the convention of collective responsibility would be set aside; Callaghan simply retorted that collective responsibility applied unless he as prime minister decided otherwise. No doubt to Mrs Thatcher as leader of the Opposition this reply was unsatisfactory, but it was a perfectly fair summary of the formal constitutional position.

In 1975 the Wilson government officially recommended acceptance of the re-negotiated terms for British membership of the European Community, but Wilson faced a clear and unbridgeable split among his ministers. The alternative to an 'agreement to differ' would have been the resignation of several members of the cabinet. Hence the doctrine of collective responsibility was set aside. But having accepted that ministers could publicly campaign for or against a 'yes' vote in the referendum, Wilson did impose definite rules on the way the debate was to be conducted.[34] For example, while free to speak in the country and the TV studio against government policy, ministers were not allowed to do so within parliament itself, and for breach of this injunction Eric Heffer was sacked from his post as Minister of State at the Department of Industry. Public disagreement had to be confined to the issue at stake in the referendum, and the moment the referendum was over collective responsibility was once again enforced. Reimposing this discipline was accompanied by the immediate demotion of Tony Benn, the most prominent cabinet minister to campaign for a 'no' vote.

It is the prime minister who must decide to what extent and by what means this convention should be enforced. In deciding whether or not to sack a minister for breach of the convention of collective responsibility the prime minister must clearly weigh the political situation. This involves balancing various considerations, chiefly the embarrassment and adverse publicity associated with open disagreements among

---

33   For the text of this, see Harold Wilson, *The Governance of Britain*, Weidenfeld and Nicolson, 1976, appendix 1.
34   See Wilson, *The Governance of Britain*, appendix 3.

ministers against the danger of not only emphasising but actually deepen-
ing divisions within the party if a minister is sacked.

The Prime Minister as Party Leader

As party leader a prime minister's tasks are much less capable of precise
definition. At the very least prime ministers must accept that they are
their party's figurehead. As such they are incessantly the object of
media attention. What they do and how they appear to the public is
the single most important factor in defining their party's public image.
At election time especially, they are the focus of public debate. But
all this is more in the way of responsibility that must be accepted
rather than tasks which must be fulfilled.

As to the latter, Conservative prime ministers must appoint their
party chairman, undoubtedly one of the single most important appointments they make. Thereafter a Conservative prime minister can leave
the running of the party very much to the chairman, although regular
discussion between the two can certainly now be expected, and as an
election approaches a Conservative premier will typically take a much
closer interest in the activities of the party organisation. But Conservative
prime ministers can distance themselves from their party organistion
if they so wish. Conservative leaders before Heath tended to do this,
but Heath, Thatcher and Major have all become more regularly involved
in the party organisation than their predecessors. Heath was the first
Conservative leader to attend the party conference, in 1965, and since
then all leaders have attended throughout the conference. The party
now clearly expects this, and in practice the leader must now attend
a variety of other party gatherings too.

Labour prime ministers are, as party leaders, *ex officio* members
of the party's National Executive Committee, the body elected annually
by Conference and responsible for running the party organisation. While
prime minister they are still expected to attend the monthly meetings
of the NEC, where on occasions they may find themselves over-ruled
by their party colleagues – for example, over key party appointments.
Labour leaders have always attended their party conferences, and have
frequently made more than one major speech there. Again this meant
with both Wilson and Callaghan that they were at times defending
government policies against which their party had declared its opposition.
The extent to which a Labour prime minister becomes actively involved
in managing party affairs has varied greatly. Sometimes it has apparently
seemed best to ignore the party as much as possible, as for Wilson
in the late 1960s. More usually Labour prime ministers have shown

themselves watchful and, like Conservative prime ministers, intervened in party management matters, but only in a relatively minor way. An important task is the composition of the party manifesto. The parties differ in relation to the leader's responsibility here, although it is probably easy to exaggerate the extent in practice of these differences. Conservative prime ministers, as party leaders, carry the final responsibility for the content of their party manifesto, although parliamentary colleagues and other sources may, and usually have been, drawn on for advice. On the Labour side the National Executive Committee is the custodian of conference decisions from which the programme of the party, and the manifesto, are supposedly drawn. A joint meeting between the National Executive Committee of the party and the cabinet (or shadow cabinet) has been responsible for the manifesto. But a Labour leader in office as prime minister can have a dominant role in deciding the manifesto, even if at times this has had to be asserted robustly.[35]

Prime ministers need to retain the confidence of their parliamentary parties or face the danger of dismissal from the leadership, and hence the premiership. This requires prime ministers to take good care not to jeopardise their support too seriously. Conservative MPs expect the prime minister to attend the 1922 Committee (of all backbench MPs) once or twice a year. Labour prime ministers may attend the weekly meeting of the parliamentary Labour Party, and in practice they have generally done so fairly regularly. Prime ministers are well advised to listen carefully to their parliamentary parties.

The Prime Minister as National Leader

Finally, the prime minister is leader, or first citizen, of the nation. Allusion has already been made to the relationship between the prime minister and the monarch. Certain symbolic roles must be fulfilled by the prime minister on occasions of national importance; for example attendance at a royal wedding. When disasters occur prime ministers are expected to send messages of sympathy to the bereaved; whether they visit the scene of a disaster or not has been a subject of some controversy, because this can be a distraction to rescue efforts, although no doubt it can also be justified as one way of showing sympathy and as an encouragment to rescue workers.

Of much more significance is the prime minister's activity representing the United Kingdom at many international gatherings, such as the Commonwealth, NATO, the European Community and the Group of Seven,

---

35 Notably in 1979 when as prime minister Jim Callaghan threatened resignation if he were over-ruled on the contents of the manifesto; David Butler and Dennis Kavanagh, *British General Election of 1979*, Macmillan, 1980, pp. 147–9.

to name but a few of the more significant. The European Council has developed the habit of meeting at least every six months; G7 meets annually at heads of government level and the Commonwealth biannually. As Chapter 7 below shows, the demands made on the prime minister over the management of international affairs have not diminished with Britain's decline in status; global integration has if anything led to an increase in such demands. The extent to which a prime minister does spend time on the international circuit varies. Such activity can be a means of escaping from mundane and frustrating domestic chores. At any rate the extent of international activity increases with the length of time a prime minister has been in office. As leaders gain seniority in the heads of government league, so their penchant for travel and their feeling that they have something special to contribute to international diplomacy increases.

Although head of government, the prime minister, it is often said, is not a chief executive.[36] In a formal sense that is correct because ministers remain responsible directly to parliament for the actions of their departments. No provision within the Constitution charges the prime minister with directing the activity of government, or setting the major lines of policy, an important and significant contrast with many other leaders such as, the American president and the German Chancellor.

But perhaps too much can be made of this point. Although formally the prime minister is not a chief executive, in practice prime ministers have increasingly been seen in that way. The role has been forced upon them. Public attention focuses on the prime minister as the person at the top, both of party and of government.[37] A general election is seen as conferring a mandate on a particular prime minister, who in turn feels empowered by election victory to asert authority over party in parliament and throughout government. Because prime ministers can appoint and dismiss colleagues, they tend to be seen as responsible for what those colleagues do. For example, Nicholas Ridley, who served in Thatcher's cabinet for seven years, wrote: 'The prime minister alone carries the responsibility of the executive, just as the president of the USA does...An error by a minister is the prime minister's responsibility just as much as the minister's...cabinet ministers have no status or independent positions: they are there to help the prime minister and at the prime minister's pleasure.'[38] Clearly many people, including many

36   See, for example, Richard Rose, 'British Government: The job at the top' in Richard
       Rose and E. Sulieman (eds), *Presidents and Prime Ministers*, American Enterprise
       Institute, 1980, p. 32.
37   On this theme, see especially Michael Foley, *The Rise of the British Presidency*,
       Manchester University Press, 1993.

of Ridley's colleagues, would sharply contest that view. But its expression indicates a model of government held by a very senior participant.

The extent to which prime ministers have become *de facto* chief executives is a theme on which the reader is invited to reflect while perusing these essays. The British Constitution is a living, evolving instrument. Maybe it has permitted this change to take place already. Maybe not. The chapters that follow should help the reader to decide the answer to that question.

38   Nicholas Ridley, *My Style of Government*, Fontana, 1992, pp. 27–8.

2

PRIME MINISTER AND CABINET

Philip Giddings

Since 1945 prime ministers have always been leaders of their parties and, with two short exceptions in the 1970s, that party has had an overall majority in the House of Commons. For so long as they retain the confidence of their parties, therefore, prime ministers are secure in office. That basic fact is fundamental to an understanding of the evolution of prime ministers' relationships with their cabinets in the postwar period. The prime minister is the Sovereign's first minister, chairman of the cabinet (according to Haldane, 'the mainspring of all the mechanism of Government'[1]) and leader of the majority parliamentary party. With the flexibility, even fluidity, of Britain's constitutional arrangements, those roles (and others treated elsewhere in this volume) frequently intermingle. A prime minister's discussion with the chancellor of the exchequer may also be the party leader's discussion with a principal rival. The cabinet's discussion of the programme for the next parliamentary session may also be the party leadership's discussion of the preparations for the next general election. An analysis of 'prime minister and cabinet' must always take into account the perspective arising from these other roles.

'Cabinet' is both a particular institution – the 'full cabinet' which meets under the prime minister's chairmanship – and a network which provides the institutional and personal framework for British government decision-making. That network has its institutional expression not only in the cabinet itself but also in the series of cabinet committees, sub-committees, ministerial groups and meetings of ministers, formal and informal. Equally important are the personal networks of relationships between ministers, individually and collectively, and their key officials and advisers. A prime minister's relationship with the cabinet is more than how the weekly cabinet meeting is handled. It extends through the institutional network of committees, sub-committees and other meetings to the personal relationships with individual cabinet ministers, both one-to-one and in groups. It is political as well as administrative. And

1   *Report of the Machinery of Government Committee*, Cd 9230, 1918, para. 5.

a prime minister's task is to manage this network of relationships so as to produce a coherent set of government policies which will advance the party's political objectives and so enable it to win the next election. Hence, in this analysis of 'prime ministers and cabinet' we shall be as much concerned with how prime ministers have related to individual cabinet ministers as with their dealings with 'full cabinet', since the two are so closely intertwined.

The reality that any prime minister has several roles is the context within which the powers of the prime ministerial office are exercised. Much debate on prime minister and cabinet has been obscured by a failure to distinguish between the powers vested in the office and the ability to exercise those powers. Constitutionally, a prime minister *qua* prime minister has the power (by recommendation to the Sovereign) to appoint and dismiss all other ministers, including cabinet ministers. How much freedom of action a particular prime minister has in exercising that power is very much the product of the political context of the moment. Constitutionally, a prime minister as chairman of the cabinet has the power to determine its agenda, to define its conclusions, to make and unmake its committees and determine their composition. But when such decisions are more than routine, the prime minister's freedom of action is as much a political as a constitutional matter, affected by personalities and policies as well as by rules and conventions, as we see later when considering some examples of policy-making.

With a prime minister exercising several roles and with the powers of the office critically affected by political and personal circumstance, the perceptions prime ministers have of their cabinets are bound to vary. And, since that perception is itself a significant element in the leadership style which has in recent years played an important part in the prime minister's electoral image, testimony concerning it must be treated with caution. One person's 'firm leadership' is another's 'autocratic style'. As John Major discovered over replacing the poll tax in March 1991, what some welcomed as a collegial style of decision-making, others bemoaned as a lack of strategic direction.[2] Prime ministers will want to present their cabinet style in the best possible light, both at the time and in their memoirs, and their critics (from within their own party as well as the opposition) will be equally keen to present a contrasting picture. It should not be surprising, given the flexibility of the office, that both critics and plauditors should find evidence to support their views.

Every prime minister since 1945 has seen the cabinet as a group

2   E.g. Nigel Lawson's remark 'To appear to be unable to choose is to appear to be unable to govern' (HC Deb, 25 March 1991, vol. 188, c. 637; and Neil Kinnock's attacks at Question Time on 19 and 26 March (HC Deb vol. 188, cc. 158 and 761).

of party colleagues, the collective leadership of the majority party. Five
– Attlee, Churchill, Wilson (twice), Heath and Thatcher – came to Number 10 as election winners, the other five came to office between elections,
although three of them (Eden, Macmillan and Major) did subsequently
lead their parties to victory at a general election. For some prime ministers,
such as Attlee, Heath and Thatcher, the cabinet is seen primarily as
the executive instrument for delivering the party programme; the
socialism of *Let Us Face the Future*, the 'quiet revolution' of *A Better
Tomorrow* or the free enterprise of the 1979 Conservative Manifesto.[3]

For other prime ministers – Macmillan, Wilson, Callaghan and Major
– the cabinet has been primarily viewed as an instrument for maintaining
(and in some instances, as in 1957 and 1990, restoring) the cohesion
of the parliamentary party and containing the potentially disparate forces
within it. To an extent collective agreement – staying together – becomes
an end in itself, buttressed by the overwhelming psephological evidence
that nothing damages a party's electoral prospects more than the appearance of disunity. Disarray over Suez (1956–7), Europe (1961–2,
1967–8, 1975, 1989, 1993), industrial relations (1969) or public expenditure (1976) has to be corrected. No prime minister can be indifferent
to party disunity. A cohesive cabinet makes a significant contribution
to the overall objective of maintaining a united party. But there are
different ways of preserving cabinet cohesion: to preserve unanimity,
potential dissidents can be mollified by compromise, or they can be
excluded. The former tactic runs the risk that sustained opposition attack
will reveal it as merely papering over cracks which will open up again.
The latter tactic runs the risk of turning the cabinet into an unrepresentative faction of the parliamentary party with backbench dissent, fuelled
by dissident ex-ministers, constantly threatening to embarrass if not
defeat the government. Former cabinet ministers, particularly those who
have been dismissed, do not have the same incentive to be responsive
to the entreaties of the whips.

The incentive to unity is not merely electoral; it is also constitutional.
The convention of collective responsibility requires that all ministers
are seen and heard to be supporters of the policies of Her Majesty's
Government. In principle, while governments are made up from a single
party, this ought not to be too difficult to achieve, since what unites
ministers (party allegiance) is likely to be more significant than particular
policy differences which divide them. In practice, however, the potential
for ministerial disagreement is a reality which cannot be ignored, and
the cabinet provides the ultimate forum for its *private* reconciliation.
The important constitutional (and political) point is not who wins or

---

3   Labour Party *General Election Manifesto*, July 1945. Conservative Party *General
     Election Manifesto*, June 1970.

loses in cabinet, but whether those who lose are prepared to accept their defeat and remain in the government as supporters of a policy with which they disagree. The prime minister's task is normally to minimise the dissent, both qualitatively and quantitatively, so that, when disagreement occurs, it need not be forced to the point of resignation.

Thus a prime minister is constantly engaged in the business of managing the cabinet. This involves balancing the requirements of speedy and effective executive decision-taking against those of cabinet cohesion and balancing the requirements of political unanimity against those of representative leadership of the party. In this balancing task, one of the prime minister's main tools is patronage, the power to appoint and to dismiss ministers.

Cabinet Formation: Prime ministerial patronage

The first postwar cabinet was formed in unusual circumstances: the leading members of the Labour Party had recently held office in Churchill's wartime coalition and therefore provided Attlee with an exceptionally experienced team. It was, however, a team which included some very strong personalities (Herbert Morrison, Ernest Bevin, Hugh Dalton, Aneurin Bevan and Stafford Cripps, whom Harold Wilson later described as 'five headstrong horses'[4]) whose peacable management needed considerable care and attention. The need to avoid friction between Bevin and Morrison led Attlee to keep their spheres of responsibility separate, with Bevin going to the Foreign Office and Morrison having charge of 'the home front' as Lord President. Attlee was also well aware (not least from his dealings with Harold Laski) of the need to maintain a political balance between right and left within the cabinet. Yet he demanded the highest standards of probity and efficiency in his ministers, as those who were 'not up to it' discovered when they lost office.[5] Attlee's position within the cabinet has often been seen as dependent upon Bevin and the inability of possible challengers to the leadership to agree. Be that as it may, Attlee's leadership was not formally challenged (attempts in 1945 and 1947 to mount a challenge quickly collapsed[6]) and he emerged with a formidable reputation as an efficient administrator and, more significant in the patronage context, a good butcher.

Churchill's 1951 administration was deeply influenced by the prime minister's experience as war leader and his desire to effect some rapprochement between Britain, the United States and the Soviet Union.

---

4   Harold Wilson, *A Prime Minister on Prime Ministers*, Michael Joseph, 1977, p. 291.
5   Kenneth Harris, *Attlee*, Weidenfeld and Nicolson, 1982, p. 407.
6   Ibid., pp. 263–7 and 347–9.

His cabinet formation after the 1951 election victory saw a generous but rejected offer of the Ministry of Education to the Liberal leader, Clement Davies, and a number of highly personal appointments. In making these appointments 'the prime minister was very much his own man, yielding to no pressure and revealing to no Minister, not even to Eden, all his thoughts on the subject'.[7] His desire for a broadly-based government, several times referred to in the election campaign, resulted in the appointment of a number of men not initially from politics (Lord Cherwell, an Oxford scientist, Lord Ismay, a general, and Lord Leathers, a colourful industrialist, and several others). Yet Seldon points out that 'though there have been few cabinets that owed so much to the prime minister's personal choices, the composition of the Government as a whole bore a notable similarity to the officers of the Party's Parliamentary Committees.'[8]

This was the cabinet of the ill-fated 'overlords' experiment, with Churchill's wartime colleagues Cherwell and Leathers having co-or-dinating responsibilities, which kept the initial membership down to sixteen. (With the ending of the experiment and other changes it had risen to nineteen by September 1953.) While such appointments show the breadth of the prime minister's discretion when forming a government, the subsequent limitations are apparent in the succession of minor reshuf-fles which followed. Eden as Foreign Secretary could not be moved against his will and was in any case 'heir apparent'. The growing rivalry between Eden, Macmillan and Butler required careful management. Churchill was criticised at the outset for having appointed too many peers and too many old hands. Yet Seldon comments that Churchill 'imprinted his persona on the ... government by giving precedence in appointments to supporters of a moderate empirical conservatism over the 'right' of the Party. Thus four representatives of moderate con-servatism gained key positions in the cabinet: Eden, Maxwell-Fyfe, Butler and Macmillan.'[9] The prime minister's patronage may not have been unconstrained, but his discretion was shown to be very wide.

It is interesting to contrast Churchill's 1951 administration with two others returning from opposition: Harold Wilson's 1964 government and Margaret Thatcher's in 1979. In 1964 the Labour Party had been in opposition for thirteen years. Of its parliamentary leadership only Griffiths, Gordon Walker and Wilson himself had previously been cabinet members, although Brown and Callaghan had also held junior ministerial office at the end of the Attlee government. Unlike Churchill in 1951, Wilson in 1964 could not draw on experience.

7	Anthony Seldon, *Churchill's Indian Summer: The Conservative Government, 1951-1955*, Hodder and Stoughton, 1981, p. 76.
8	Ibid.
9	Ibid., p. 81.

Wilson's 1964 cabinet contained twenty-three members (almost half as many again as Churchill's in 1951) but only one 'outsider', Frank Cousins, general secretary of the Transport and General Workers' Union. Two major new departments of state were created – the Department of Economic Affairs (DEA) and the Ministry of Technology – and the Welsh Office acquired a separate identity and its own secretary of state with a cabinet seat. Early crucial economic decisions were taken by Wilson, Brown (DEA) and Callaghan (chancellor) and these three, whether in agreement or disagreement as in 1966, dominated the first half of the government's life.[10]

Wilson, no doubt with the painful experience of the Labour Party's divisions in the 1950–63 period in mind, was always conscious of the need to maintain party and government unity and to do so as far as possible by incorporating potential critics and applying checks and balances in appointments.[11] The classic instance of this was the economic duumvirate, the DEA and Treasury, headed by Brown and Callaghan; it was also to show itself on the delicate question of EEC entry as well as the more general left-right/revisionist-fundamentalist tensions. Wilson's own background on the left of the party (he resigned with Bevan in 1951 and stood against Gaitskell for the leadership in 1961) made him both sensitive to left-wing concerns (hence his personal closeness to Crossman and Castle) and also acutely aware of the dangers of divisions, plots and cabals.[12]

Although far from being a butcher in the Attlee style, Wilson used his patronage power to maintain the balance of his government and bolster his position as leader. Initially, as the leader who had taken the party to two election victories after three successive defeats, his position was strong. But within months of the second victory in 1966, the political and economic difficulties of the government were so great that the possibility of a change of leader was openly canvassed,[13] while the deputy leader George Brown contemplated resignation over the July economic measures. After devaluation in November 1967 and major party divisions over incomes policy in 1968 and industrial relations reform in 1969, Wilson's position became very weak.[14] At that stage he depended heavily on the chancellor, Roy Jenkins, and the Home Secretary, Callaghan (who had opposed the prime minister's industrial

10   See Harold Wilson, *The Labour Government, 1964-1970: A personal record*, Weidenfeld and Nicolson, 1971; compare Richard Crossman, *Diaries*, Hamish Hamilton and Jonathan Cape, 1975, vol. 1, p. 582.
11   See Ben Pimlott, *Harold Wilson*, HarperCollins, 1992.
12   See Dennis Healey, *The Time of My Life*, Michael Joseph, 1989, p. 331.
13   David Butler and Michael Pinto-Duschinsky, *The British General Election of 1970*, p. 11; Crossman, *Diaries*, vol. 1, pp. 567–83; Wilson, *The Labour Government, 1964-1970*, pp. 332–40.
14   See Healey, *The Time of My Life*, p. 341; Crossman, *Diaries*, vol. 3, p. 528.

relations proposals). Wilson's room for manoeuvre was now limited; his biographer describes him as 'lonely and isolated'.[15]

The 1979 election brought to power an experienced cabinet with an inexperienced prime minister. Margaret Thatcher had surprisingly defeated Edward Heath in the Conservative leadership election of 1975 and came to Number 10 with only her experience as education secretary in the 1970–4 government to guide her. Her election as leader owed more to a rejection of Heath than to positive support for her or her policy preferences, which were at that stage little known and certainly not (even by 1979) shared by a majority of the shadow cabinet.

Cabinet formation in May 1979 was therefore not easy and Thatcher approached it in what King calls an 'unusually collegial manner'.[16] Wiliam Whitelaw, the deputy leader but more significantly the candidate she had defeated in the final round of the leadership election in 1975, Lord Carrington (leader in the Lords) and Humphrey Atkins, the Chief Whip, were closely involved in the making of the appointments. Thatcher filled the key economic positions with those she believed shared her policy preferences: Geoffrey Howe as chancellor, Keith Joseph at Industry, John Nott at Trade, John Biffen as Chief Secretary. Elsewhere those who were strong Heath supporters, or agnostic at best about a monetarist stance, were dominant: Carrington himself at the Foreign Office, James Prior at Employment, Chrstopher Soames leading the Lords and Norman St John Stevas leading the Commons, Whitelaw at the Home Office and Mark Carlisle at Education. As Thatcher later commented, 'I knew the hardest battles would be fought on the ground of economic policy. So I made sure the key economic ministers would be true believers in our economic strategy ... Otherwise, it seemed prudent in the light of our effective performance in Opposition and the election campaign to maintain a high degree of continuity between Shadow cabinet and cabinet posts.'[17] This hardly amounted to the famous description she had given a few months before taking office of her preferred approach to cabinet making:

'If you're going to do the things you want to do – and I'm only in politics to *do* things – you've got to have a togetherness and a unity in your cabinet. There are two ways of making a cabinet. One way is to have in it people who represent all the different viewpoints within the party, within the broad philosophy. The other way is to have in it only the people who want to go in the direction in which every instinct tells me we have to go.'[18]

15 Pimlott, *Harold Wilson*, pp. 544–6.
16 Anthony King, *The British Prime Minister*, Macmillan, 1985, 2nd edn, p. 103.
17 Margaret Thatcher, *The Downing Street Years*, HarperCollins, 1993, p. 26; see also Peter Riddell, *The Thatcher Government*, Blackwell, 1985, p. 42.
18 *The Observer*, 25 February 1979, quoted in Hugo Young, *One of Us*, Macmillan, 1989, p. 149.

This was the basis on which, in an oft-quoted phrase, she promised 'not to waste time having arguments'.[19] It was to be a conviction cabinet. Yet, as Hugo Young has commented, 'Her first cabinet was not merely representative of the different viewpoints within her party, it was dominated by men with a different viewpoint from hers.'[20] She later remarked of her appointment of Peter Walker as minister of agriculture: 'His membership of the cabinet demonstrated that I was prepared to include every strand of Conservative opinion in the new government, and his post that I was not prepared to put the central economic strategy at risk.'[21] In the choosing of her cabinet, in the exercise of her power of patronage in 1979, Thatcher had shown that the prime minister was not entirely free; and a major task for her in the ensuing years was to widen that freedom and create the kind of cabinet she wanted.

It is well known that in the cabinet reshuffles of January and September 1981 and June 1983 Thatcher did gradually mould the cabinet more to her liking. She dropped 'wets' like St John Stevas, Carlisle, Soames, Ian Gilmour and even the recently appointed foreign secretary Francis Pym; and she moved Prior to the fringe as Northern Ireland secretary. In their place she promoted supporters like Norman Tebbit, Leon Brittan, Nigel Lawson and Cecil Parkinson. There is no doubt that these moves did alter the balance of the cabinet and prevented a recurrence of the 'revolt' of July 1981 when the cabinet rejected a proposal from the then chancellor, supported by the prime minister, for further expenditure cuts. To this extent Thatcher was able, by use of her appointing power, to capture her own cabinet and ensure she had a majority within it. As she herself commented later, 'The whole nature of the cabinet changed as a result of these changes. After the new cabinet's first meeting I remarked ... what a difference it made to have most of the people in it on my side.'[22]

But two features of this are significant. First, even in 1981 some of her 'loyalists', such as Biffen and Nott, were ranged against her, demonstrating the fragility of any policy test approach to appointments. Secondly, it is noteworthy that all four of the 'supporters' she promoted were sooner or later to leave her government, three of them after political disagreement. Thatcher discovered that it is one thing to be rid of a critical, obstructive or dissenting colleague, but quite another to be sure that the replacement will not prove in time to be just as troublesome.

Moreover, while dismissals may be of the prime minister's choosing, resignations are often not. After the Falklands invasion Carrington had to be replaced by Pym (but not for long); after the crisis over the

19   Young, *One of Us*, p. 149.
20   Ibid., p. 149.
21   Thatcher, *The Downing Street Years*, p. 28.
22   Ibid., p. 152.

Westland Company, Brittan had to be replaced as Home Secretary by Douglas Hurd (previously Heath's political secretary); and in 1989 after Nigel Lawson's resignation as chancellor he had to be replaced by John Major, whom Thatcher had really wanted at the Foreign Office in place of Howe. Indeed, she would have liked to have appointed Nicholas Ridley as chancellor but recognised that 'under these difficult circumstances Nick's scorn for presentational niceties might well have compounded the problem.'[23] And that reshuffle, which involved moving from the Foreign Office after only three months her apparent favourite whose original appointment in place of Howe had led to much criticism of her within the Conservative Party as well as outside, showed the limited room for manoeuvre a prime minister can have. She herself explained the limitations like this:

Planning a reshuffle is immensely complex. There is never a perfect outcome. It is necessary to get the main decisions about the big offices of state right and then work outward and downward from those. Nor is it always possible to give the best positions to one's closest supporters. Not only must the cabinet to some extent reflect the varying views in the Parliamentary Party at a particular time; there are some people that it is better to bring in because they would cause more trouble outside. Peter Walker and, to a lesser extent, Kenneth Clarke are examples ....[24]

That reflection from 1993 contrasts interestingly with her *Observer* interview approach, given in February 1979 whilst still in Opposition.

After Lawson's experience in 1989, the word 'unassailable' is difficult to use in the context of cabinet membership.[25] But the prime minister's re-dispositions of that year placed Hurd and Major in positions of very considerable strength, positions which were enhanced when Ridley resigned in July 1990. Thatcher's room for manoeuvre with cabinet appointments *at this stage* was very limited. When, just before Ridley's resignation, she told Major that she would not resist the pound joining the Exchange Rate Mechanism (ERM), she reflected:

Although the terms I had laid down had not been fully met, I had too few allies to continue to resist and win the day. There are limits to the ability of even the most determined democratic leader to stand out against what the cabinet, the Parliamentary Party, the industrial lobby and the press demand.[26]

This position of isolation was compounded by a widespread awareness of the weakness of the government's, and her own, position in the (opinion) polls and the possibility of a further challenge to her leadership.[27] When that challenge did come in the autumn of 1990, the extent

23   Ibid., p. 717.
24   Ibid., p. 418.
25   Nigel Lawson, *The View from No. 11*, Bantam Press, 1992, p. 970.
26   Thatcher, *The Downing Street Years*, p. 722.
27   For an account of the previous challenge (in 1989 by Sir Anthony Meyer) see Philip

of her weakness within the parliamentary party became apparent. Undoubtedly the manner of her handling of her senior ministers, particularly Lawson and Howe, contributed to that weakness, as did the extent of the Labour Opposition's lead in the opinion polls and dramatic by-election reversals in Mid-Staffordshire and Eastbourne.

Yet the weakness of a government's electoral position is not always a constraint on the prime minister's appointing power. In the most dramatic exercise of that power in the postwar period, Macmillan dismissed seven members of his cabinet, including the chancellor of the exchequer and the lord chancellor. He was reacting, in part, to a series of by-election reversals and policy difficulties over the Common Market and economic management. The 'July massacre' became an infamous example of prime ministerial power.

Macmillan himself subsequently recognised that he made 'a serious error' in combining a change of chancellor on policy grounds with a general reconstruction of the government designed to bring forward new and younger men.[28] It is often argued that this episode seriously weakened Macmillan's personal position, but this is difficult to prove either way. In the Commons censure motion which followed there were no Conservative votes against or abstentions, and the impact of such subsequent events as the Cuban missile crisis, the Profumo affair and the illness which led to Macmillan's resignation obscure the ultimate significance of the July reshuffle. Nevertheless, there is little doubt that, having made the reconstruction in such a dramatic way, Macmillan was a prisoner of the choices he had made, at least until the ensuing general election (by which time he was no longer prime minister).

A prime minister's power of patronage is constitutionally unfettered (saving the Sovereign's formal consent and the need to retain the confidence of the House of Commons) but politically constrained. The extent to which political constraints impinge upon a prime minister's freedom of action has varied according to the political circumstances: a newly-won general election enhances that freedom; a divided and unpopular government restricts it.

The challenge of prime ministerial leadership is to maximise freedom of action so that selections are made for genuine motives, and not forced by circumstances. Given that postwar governments have typically included between seventy and eighty members of the House of Commons, or about quarter of a majority parliamentary party, and that some MPs will be non-starters because they are too new, too old or not interested

Norton, 'Choosing a leader: Margaret Thatcher and the parliamentary Conservative party', *Parliamentary Affairs*, July 1990, pp. 249–59. Compare Meyer's account in his *Stand Up and Be Counted*, Heinemann, 1990, pp. 149–67, and Thatcher's, *The Downing Street Years*, p. 830.

28 Harold Macmillan, *At the End of the Day*, Macmillan, 1973, p. 92.

in office, the pool from which a prime minister actually selects is not very deep. And then there is aptitude and competence to consider. Prime ministers therefore have to limit their instinctive preferences. It is possible to exclude one, or perhaps two, major figures: Churchill had himself been excluded in the 1930s; Barbara Castle was excluded by Callaghan; Heath (and later others) by Thatcher. But this cannot be taken too far. Wilson and Callaghan kept Benn within the cabinet; and Thatcher, while excluding Heath himself, included Walker, Prior, Hurd and Whitelaw, Heath's closest political associates. Similarly, it is possible for prime ministers to ensure that their policy preferences are shared by appointees to particular offices (Thatcher's economic appointments in 1979, Macmillan's on Europe in 1960), but fulfilling these preferences may mean accepting others which may not be so welcome (in 1979 Carrington at the Foreign Office, Prior at Employment, Carlisle at Education). The politics of patronage are the politics of choice.

Cabinet appointments are the prime minister's prerogative, but it is now usual to consult other senior party figures, in particular the chief whip and the party chairman. Such consultations do not bind the prime minister; they are sources of information and advice, of more significance in relation to more junior ministerial appointments than to cabinet membership. It is clear that Callaghan had consultations with Michael Foot, whom he had defeated in the Labour Party's leadership contest, before making his first cabinet appointments;[29] it is equally clear that, while Foot was able to choose his own post (Leader of the House) and successfully recommended some members of the Tribune Group for others, he was unable to prevent Castle's exclusion, hard though he tried.[30] It is also amply clear that Thatcher did not consult the person she defeated in her party's leadership election, but in September 1981 and 1985 she did consult Whitelaw and the chief whip before making her reshuffles, and Lawson records that he, Whitelaw and John Wakeham discussed the post-election reshuffle with her in June 1987.[31] Attlee felt it essential that a prime minister should pick the ministers himself and played his cards very close to his chest in the July 1946 reshuffle (Harris writes that Dalton, Bevin and Morrison were all equally in the dark) whereas Wilson records that he consulted Michael Stewart and George Brown about his 1967 reshuffle.[32]

The interplay of the prime minister's constitutional prerogative to appoint and dismiss cabinet members and the political constraints upon

29 James Callaghan, *Time and Chance*, Collins, 1987, p. 401.
30 Ibid., p. 402; Barbara Castle, *Diaries*, Weidenfeld and Nicolson, 1980, p. 725.
31 Thatcher, *The Downing Street Years*, pp. 151, 418; Lawson, *The View from No. 11*, pp. 707, 710–13.
32 King, *The British Prime Minister*, p. 73; Harris, *Attlee*, p. 330; Wilson, *The Labour Government, 1964-1970*, pp. 544–5.

exercising that prerogative has remained a constant feature of post-war politics. A variable has been the personality and style of individual prime ministers, which has become more significant as British electoral politics have become more presidential in the television age. The focus upon the party leader has considerably strengthened the power of prime ministers who have successfully led their party to electoral victory, and this has enhanced their freedom of manoeuvre in making appointments (Thatcher 1983 and 1987, Major, 1992). On the other hand, the degree of exposure given to a leader has meant that, when governments have become deeply unpopular and electoral defeat looms, the prime minister's personal position comes under threat and freedom of manoeuvre is correspondingly reduced. Wilson experienced this in 1969, as did Thatcher twenty year later. Each of them knew both dominance and weakness.

Cabinet Organisation: Prime ministerial management

The composition of a cabinet needs to reflect the requirements of balanced representation, shared expectations from the party, political circumstances and the prime minister's personal preferences. In practice these requirements have produced cabinets which have been too large for effective debate of policy options. Before the Second World War cabinet size in peacetime averaged nineteen.[33] Attlee felt his first cabinet, which numbered twenty, was really too big for effective decision-making; he favoured sixteen at most[34] – coincidentally, the size of Churchill's 1951 cabinet. Wilson's 1964 cabinet numbered twenty-three, and Heath's first cabinet eighteen; in October 1970 he reduced it to seventeen with the creation of the two 'super-ministries' of Environment, and Trade and Industry. However, by the time of the first 1974 election, the creation of new departments for Energy, Northern Ireland and Trade and Consumer Affairs and the inclusion of the Paymaster-General had increased the size to twenty-one.

Given such numbers, the cabinet has increasingly become the forum for registering and promulgating policy decisions which have been initiated and prepared elsewhere in the government machine, notably cabinet committees and other meetings of ministers. The cabinet receives, reports and approves decisions; it is, as it were, the place to register rather than to formulate decisions. A body as large as a cabinet needs clear-cut, well-defined options so that its decisions can be precise and conclusions formulated in a way which provides clear directions for

33 David Butler and Jennie Freeman, *British Political Facts*, Macmillan, 1968, 3rd edn, p. 57.
34 Harris, *Attlee*, p. 402.

government departments to operate. Those are the requirements of efficient and effective administration. But they are not always practical politics, nor do they take account of the loquacity of politicians (and prime ministers in particular: Attlee could be terse, Churchill was prone to rambling monologues, Macmillan could be infuriatingly discursive).

As the pressure upon the agenda of the full cabinet has grown, reflecting the increased responsibilities of governments in the post-war era, so more business has had to be dealt with elsewhere. There has been much discussion of cabinet committee structure[35] (prompted in part by the official determination until 1992 to keep it secret lest collective responsibility be impaired[36]) and certainly committees have been used by successive prime ministers to deal with regular business.

Attlee took the view that when the cabinet had approved a line of policy, its execution could be left to the minister or to a cabinet committee.[37] In a similar way the Eden government's Middle East policy in 1956 was implemented through the Egypt Committee. Mackintosh comments that Eden 'withdrew the main decisions to a cabinet committee not to override the full cabinet or for fear of contradiction, but simply for convenience. A majority of the cabinet was told most of the facts and all but three agreed with the actions taken.'[38] Similarly, Wilson appointed a Rhodesia Committee to deal with Ian Smith's unilateral declaration of independence[39] and Thatcher used what was formally a sub-committee of the Overseas and Defence Policy Committee of the cabinet to conduct the response to the Argentine invasion of the Falkland Islands in 1982.[40] She also set up a small cabinet sub-committee to deal with the crisis in the Gulf in 1990.[41]

Cabinet committees are neither a new nor a static device. The evolution of the system (if that is not too strict a term) of committees has reflected the personal style of each prime minister and, no doubt, the cabinet secretary of the time. There is a conventional distinction between the

35 See John Mackintosh, *The British Cabinet*, Stevens, 1968, pp. 510–18; Patrick Gordon Walker, *The Cabinet*, Collins, 1970, chapter 3; Hennessy, *Cabinet*, Blackwell, 1986, *passim*; Hennessy, *Whitehall*, Secker and Warburg, 1989, Chapter 8.

36 John Major announced details of the names and membership of standing ministerial committees, sub-committees and working groups for the first time in answer to a Parliamentary Question on 19 May 1992; HC Deb vol. 208, WA cols 110–18.

37 The Labour Government's decision to extend self-government to India and Burma as rapidly as possible, which nevertheless required complex and detailed negotiations, was implemented through the India and Burma Committee and the prime minister, since Attlee himself had a long-standing personal interest in Indian affairs, having served on the Simon Commission. Mackintosh, *The British Cabinet*, p. 496.

38 Ibid., p. 500.

39 Walker, *The Cabinet*, p. 42.

40 Hennessy, *Cabinet*, pp. 118–19; Colin Seymour-Ure, 'British war cabinets in limited wars', *Public Administration*, vol. XX, 1984, p. 187.

41 Thatcher, *The Downing Street Years*, p. 822.

more permanent cabinet committees (such as those dealing with home and social affairs, legislation, overseas and defence policy, economic policy) and *ad hoc* committees on particular items, such as incomes policy or some foreign policy issue.

The logic of such committees is to bring together the ministers most directly concerned, either to pre-digest the issues or to sort out the detail. Undoubtedly this is an essential device for dealing with complex questions and a useful way of coping with controversial ones. It is also a useful management tool for the prime minister whose responsibility it is to decide which committees shall be established, what shall be referred to them and, perhaps most crucially of all, who is to serve on them and by whom they will be chaired.

Thus, when Wilson set up a cabinet committee on prices and incomes in 1967, the chancellor (Jenkins) and the employment secretary (Castle) both laid claim to the chairmanship; Wilson decided in favour of the chancellor.[42] When a cabinet committee took over the drafting of the white paper on industrial policy from Benn in 1974, Wilson took the chair himself.[43] Ministers who find themselves in a minority often feel that the committee has been 'stacked' against them, as, for example, Thatcher's economic committee was stacked against the two 'wets', Prior and Walker, in 1979–81.[44] Similarly, Callaghan is reputed to have stacked the membership of the cabinet committee he set up in 1976 to consider reform of Section 2 of the 1911 Official Secrets Act 'to ensure that freedom of information did not get a look in'.[45]

Thatcher's use of committees and small groups of ministers evoked much critical comment. Reflecting on his own experience of her administration, Lawson states that she used such means to

fragment any dissident voices. What had started off as a justified attempt to make effective decisions in small and informal groups degenerated into increasingly complex attempts to divide and rule. More and more, decisions were effectively taken in very small groups in which she had hand-picked the balance of membership to ensure the outcome she sought.[46]

But Lawson also notes that such a method has its attractions for ministers as well: 'Most of the time it is comforting for them to feel that all they need to do is to strike a deal with the prime minister, and not have to bother overmuch about persuading their other colleagues.'[47]

42 Walker, *The Cabinet*, p. 42.
43 Wilson, *Final Term*, Weidenfeld and Nicolson, Michael Joseph, 1979, p. 33.
44 Keegan, *Mrs Thatcher's Economic Experiment*, Allen Lane, 1984, p. 136; Thatcher, *The Downing Street Years*, pp. 26–8.
45 Hennessy, *Cabinet*, p. 89.
46 Lawson, *The View from No. 11*, p. 128.
47 Ibid., p. 129; N. Ridley, *My Style of Government: The Thatcher years*, Fontana, 1992, p. 29.

That is fine as long as the prime minister can be persuaded. Where a prime minister is difficult to persuade (as Lawson and Howe found over the Exchange Rate Mechanism) or wrong (Lawson's prophetic criticisms of the poll-tax were brushed aside), the results can be very damaging.[48]

As with appointments, so with committees: the prime minister's freedom of action is not wholly unconstrained. Clearly, it is difficult to exclude the relevant departmental ministers, but the art of management lies in the selection of others, and especially the chairman. This may be the prime minister or one of the senior non-departmental ministers such as the lord president or the lord privy seal, who are better placed to 'referee' inter-departmental disputes, such as the running conflict between the Treasury and the Ministry of Agriculture over agricultural price support in the 1960s.[49]

Difficulties arise for individual ministers who have 'lost' in committee if they wish to 'appeal' to the full cabinet. Wilson introduced a procedure whereby issues could not be re-opened with the agreement of the chairman of the committee.[50] but in such instances reliance cannot always be placed on rules. Serious dissent has to be dealt with, especially if it is shared by several ministers. To deal with that dissent is a political necessity, whatever the rules of tidy administration may say. One wonders whether Michael Heseltine would have felt it necessary to resign over the Westland affair in 1985 had he been able to bring his case before all his cabinet colleagues earlier.

Peter Hennessy has shown that Thatcher made less frequent use of meetings of the full cabinet and of formal cabinet committees than her post-war predecessors.[51] She rarely held more than one full cabinet a week, which works out at about half as many as were called annually by Attlee and Churchill. At the end of 1986 Thatcher had about 30-35 standing committees and just over 120 *ad hoc* groups. This compared with Attlee's 148 and 313 for a similar time-span and Churchill's 137 and 109 in his 1951–5 administration. Wilson seems to have used 236 *ad hoc* groups in his first administration (of similar length to Thatcher's by 1986) and Callaghan used 160 *ad hoc* groups in his three years.[52]

Too much can be made of such figures. Not all committees which are 'on the books' are active. Periodically there is a deliberate cull as prime ministers, or cabinet secretaries, seek to cut back some of Whitehall's administrative undergrowth. When Burke Trend retired as

48 Lawson, *The View from No. 11*, chapters 71–6, 45–6.
49 Mackintosh, *The British Cabinet*, p. 503.
50 Walker, *The Cabinet*, p. 44.
51 Hennessy, *Cabinet*, pp. 100–1.
52 Ibid., p. 101.

cabinet secretary in 1973, Heath promptly halved the number of committees.[53] Sometimes ministers prefer to do business by correspondence, as happened in 1981–2 over the Falklands.[54] Some prime ministers, like Thatcher, prefer to supplement the formal cabinet committee structure with ad hoc 'meetings of ministers', which are nevertheless still part of the process of collective deliberation which characterises cabinet government. The precise organisational preferences reflect on the individual style of each prime minister. Major, for example, has reverted to the more traditional and collegial emphasis on committees.[55]

The particular forum in which deliberation hardens into decision may not be as crucial as constitutional purists might think. What matters in practice is whether the decision which emerges will carry the assent of the majority of the cabinet. Often, given the membership of the committee or group in which the decision has hardened, full cabinet assent can be taken for granted. For this reason membership may include senior ministers who carry weight within the cabinet or the parliamentary party, which accounts for Whitelaw's inclusion in the Falklands 'inner cabinet'.[56] Problems arise in a system of collective responsibility for cabinet members who are not members of these policy-making committees. For instance, Tebbit was upset not to have known about the use of British bases for American bombing of Libya in 1986, although the cabinet's Overseas and Defence Committee had been involved and Thatcher had felt it was 'important to ensure that senior members of the cabinet backed my decision'.[57] Vital decisions will require ratification, as did the launching of the Falklands Task Force, the response to the Peruvian peace proposals, the San Carlos landings and the assault on Port Stanley in 1982.[58]

Thatcher's mode of operation raised the issue of the precise difference between cabinet committees, meetings of ministers and other forums of discussion like ministerial seminars. In principle procedures for clarifying the mind of a prime minister ought to be distinguished from those which are part of the cabinet system of collective decision-taking. But such a distinction is more easily made in theory than in practice. One particular complication is that prime ministers may not confine their consultations to their cabinet colleagues. Most prime ministers have had their own personal advisers, although their existence has not always

---

53 Ibid., p. 78.
54 See *Falklands Islands Review*, Cmnd 8787, para. 291; Hennessy, *Cabinet*, pp. 113–14; Hennessy, *Whitehall*, p. 313.
55 See Wakeham, *Cabinet Government*, Brunel University, 1993.
56 Seymour-Ure, 'British war cabinets in limited wars', pp. 186–187.
57 Thatcher, *The Downing Street Years*, pp. 446–7.
58 Ibid., pp. 193–94; Hennessy, *Cabinet*, p. 119. The use of British bases for the Libyan raid in 1986 was also ratified by cabinet (Thatcher, *The Downing Street Years*, p. 447).

been publicly acknowledged. The development of the Number 10 Policy Unit clearly demonstrates this prime ministerial need.[59] It is also clear that some prime ministers have relied heavily on advice from particular officials (Churchill from Norman Brook, Heath from William Armstrong). The process by which prime ministers prepare themselves for meetings may be more significant in determining the decision-making outcome than the meeting itself, especially in policy areas on which the prime minister is taking the lead, or in which the prime ministers' personal contribution may be decisive because colleagues' opinions are divided or uncertain.

Thus, with cabinet organisation as with patronage, there is flexibility. A prime minister has considerable, though not unlimited, freedom of action to manage the process of consultation and deliberations by which government decisions emerge. The administrative structure is there to facilitate the conduct of government business efficiently and in an orderly manner. It enables different prime ministers with different preferences to proceed differently. In this regard prime ministerial style does vary, and it does so in a way which reflects how different prime ministers perceive their relations with their colleagues.

Attlee was impressed by the need to balance guidance and co-ordination. He said:

'A prime minister's got to be even more of a co-ordinator than a cabinet Minister ... you can't ride rough-shod over a cabinet unless you're something very extraordinary. What you generally do is give guidance. A prime minister ought to keep his hand on the pulse and know how ministers are doing ... but he mustn't go and interfere and overrule a minister, he must always work through a minister.'[60]

And on the specific issue of cabinet organisation he said: 'I think it's necessary to have a committee system in which, under the guidance of senior non-departmental ministers, you can get coordination.'[61] Hence, he asked Arthur Greenwood to cover the social services, and Morrison the economy, legislation and the nationalisation programme.

While Eden had the reputation of being interventionist, Macmillan's style was, outwardly at least, more relaxed. He used the cabinet committee structure as a filter for business, although he chaired very few committees himself, except when he was particularly interested in an issue (such as reflation in 1958).[62]

Wilson, wanting to present an image that contrasted with previous Conservative governments, referred to Number 10 as 'a power house,

59   See chapter 4 in this volume.
60   Quoted in King, *The British Prime Minister*, p. 71.
61   Ibid., pp. 75–6.
62   Hennessy, *Cabinet*, p. 59.

not a monastery'. His style was 'to know all that is going on and to intervene when necessary', at least while in office during the 1960s.[63] This did not find favour with all his colleagues. 'The trouble with cabinet,' Castle recorded, 'was not that Harold ran it through little cabals, but that there was no focal point of decision-making at all. Harold operated purely bilaterally, ringing up some Ministers on some things and others on others'.[64] Denis Healey has commented on the change of style in Wilson's 1974–6 administration: '[He] took a much more relaxed view of his responsibilities.... He interfered much less in the work of his ministers and was no longer plagued by the demons of jealousy and suspicion which had tormented him in his first two Governments.'[65]

Wilson was particularly sensitive to issues which might threaten the cabinet's, and the party's, unity; of these membership of the European Communities was a prime example. In 1967 he personally chaired a cabinet committee on the issue, but soon decided that a wider forum was necessary. A collective discussion was held at Chequers (the prime minister's official country residence) involving ministers and civil servants, which Wilson likened to a 'second reading debate' but which made no decisions. There then followed a long series of cabinet meetings at which decisions were eventually made, 'a gradual cabinet decision'.[66]

Heath's style was different again, although like Wilson he was influenced by a determination to be seen to be different from the previous regime. His approach was essentially managerial. His 1970 White Paper *Reorganisation of Central Government*[67] sought to rationalise the process of central decision-making by reducing the number of departments, and in 1973, as clearly mentioned, he took the opportunity to halve the number of cabinet committees. His managerial cast of mind is reflected in a radio interview he gave in 1977.

'The cabinet is always grateful if the prime minister can give an analysis which sets out clearly first of all what has happened, secondly what the problems are, and thirdly what the options are for solutions. If a PM is able to do that and his colleagues respect that he's being fair ... I think they are immensely grateful for it. I used to try to do that as often as I could'.[68]

Certainly Heath was exceptionally well briefed and his mastery of detail was formidable. Whitelaw's testimony is that, rather than leading from the front, he always wanted to hear every side of the case argued

63 Quoted in King, *The British Prime Minister*, p. 9.
64 Castle, *The Castle Diaries, 1964-1970*, p. 347.
65 Healey, *The Time of My Life*, p. 388.
66 King, *The British Prime Minister*, pp. 112–13.
67 Cmnd 4506, 1970.
68 Interview with David Dilks, 'Politics No', BBC Radio Four, 24 February 1977, cited in J. Campbell, *Edward Heath*, Jonathan Cape, 1993, p. 486.

out before he revealed his own hand.[69] By contrast, Hennessy cites
an unnamed colleague who was less impressed: 'In cabinet he would
sit there glowering and saying practically nothing. The colleagues would
watch him to see what impression their words were making. Then he
would come down one way or the other and that was it.'[70] Heath also
recognised that as prime minister he had to be selective: 'The job of
a prime minister is to decide himself in which spheres he is going
to concentrate' ... It's then up to him to limit those and so organise
himself that he can deal with it.'[71] And, while he was happy to delegate
other matters, within the areas in which he chose to concentrate Heath
was 'unquestionably dominant, even autocratic'.[72]

Similarly, Thatcher's style has been characterised as presidential,
if not monarchical. Hennessy quotes one insider as saying: 'Temporarily
we don't have cabinet government ... we have a form of presidential
government in which she operates like a sovereign in her court.'[73] Such
quotations make good copy and doubtless exaggerate the phenomenon,
but there has been plenty of testimony from former cabinet members
like Prior, David Howell, Heseltine, Kenneth Baker and Lawson on
Thatcher's propensity to lead from the front and the singular way in
which she operated meetings.[74] Lawson put it this way:

Her conduct of meetings also became increasingly authoritarian .... Margaret, ...
when there was an issue on which she had already formed a firm view, would start
with an unashamedly tendentious introduction of her own, before inviting the
responsible and sometimes cowed Minister to have his say.[75]

On the other hand, Ridley strongly approved of Thatcher's presidential
style and had no complaints about the way she ran her cabinet. Unusually,
he took the view that

... cabinet ministers have no status or independent positions: they are there to help
the prime minister, and at the prime minister's pleasure ... She was prime minister,
she knew what she wanted to do, and she didn't believe her policies should be
subject to being voted down by a group she had selected to advise and assist her.[76]

Most prime ministers initially hold their hand in cabinet discussions.

69   Campbell, *Edward Heath*, pp. 485–6.
70   Hennessy, *Cabinet*, p. 77.
71   Interview with David Dilks, 'Politics Now', BBC Radio Four, 24 February 1977,
      cited in Campbell, *Edward Heath*, pp. 486–7.
72   Campbell, *Edward Heath*, p. 486.
73   Hennessy, *Cabinet*, p. 99.
74   James Prior, *A Balance of Power*, Hamish Hamilton, 1986, chapters 7 and 8; Hennessy,
      Cabinet, chapter 3; *The Observer*, 12 January 1986; Kenneth Baker, *The Turbulent
      Years*, Faber and Faber, p. 255; Lawson, *The View from No. 11*.
75   Lawson, *The View from No 11*, p. 128.
76   Ridley, *My Style of Government*, pp. 28, 30.

The ministers most immediately involved take the lead, and ideally a consensus emerges reflecting the preparatory work done in earlier consultations. If prime ministers need to intervene to secure agreement on a particular line, they usually do so in the latter stages of the discussion, after calling upon other ministers to speak. Thatcher, reflecting her conviction style and perhaps her somewhat isolated position politically in the early years of her first administration, operated differently. According to King:

> She states her views at the outset, or lets them be known. Often, unusual in a prime minister, she thinks aloud. She interrupts ministers with whom she disagrees and insists on standing and fighting her corner ... she does not merely chair cabinet discussions, she is an active participant in them. More often than not, she dominates them.[77]

Other prime ministers have sought to influence cabinet discussion by carefully choosing which ministers to speak when, or by lobbying individual ministers beforehand; these were Callaghan's tactics on the International Monetary Fund (IMF) loan . Thatcher preferred more direct methods, seeing herself very much as the chief executive, 'the boss', and other cabinet members as 'her' ministers rather than colleagues.

Little hard evidence has yet become available about John Major's style. The impression given initially was of a much more relaxed collegiality than existed under Thatcher. But Norman Lamont's resignation statement and Major's less than complimentary remarks about three of his 'Euro-sceptic' cabinet colleagues after the parliamentary battles over the Treaty of Maastricht suggest strong underlying tensions.[78]

The flexibility of Britain's cabinet system can contain such differences of prime ministerial style. It also enables the business of government to adapt to the variety of circumstances which occur in a fast-changing world. But the system cannot be more efficient than the ministers and officials who operate it. It cannot manufacture decisiveness, certainty or knowledge where there is hesitation, doubt or ignorance, although, with the connivance of ministers and officials, it can present the latter as if it were the former. Here, in short, is a tool for a prime minister to use and like all tools its effectiveness depends on the operator's skill and the malleability of the material: the people and the issues.

---

77 King, *The British Prime Minister*, p. 117.
78 HC Deb vol. 2266, cols 279–83, 9 June 1993; *The Times*, 26 July 1993, reporting Major's conversation with ITN's political editor, Michael Brunson, when he described them as 'bastards'.

The Prime Minister and Cabinet Policy-making

A British prime minister is party leader as well as cabinet chairman. Some party leaders have distinct policy preferences, perhaps amounting to a personal ideology, which they will want to be reflected in the decisions of the government they lead. This is not invariable; some party leaders are – or have to be – content with the task of maintaining the cohesion of the government and demonstrating its general competence, allowing ideas and policy initiatives to emerge from elsewhere. Sometimes the policy preferences of leaders will be known when they are elected, as was Heath's commitment to Europe. In the case of others, such as Thatcher, they will emerge during their period of office, as will their style of leadership.

Precisely how the relationships between prime minister and cabinet operate will depend on many factors. This simple fact is well illustrated by looking in some detail at a series of case-studies (to which reference is frequently made in this volume): two foreign policy issues, two economic policy issues and two problems posed by individual ministers. Each pair is concerned with a very similar problem, but the difficulties were resolved in different ways by the prime ministers of the day. In part, this reflected the style of the prime ministers, in part the political realities of the day.

Suez and the Falklands. The Suez and Falklands affairs were both 'limited wars'[79] and cases in which the government had to respond to outside events instigated by another state. A second common feature was the lack of mutual confidence between 10 Downing Street and the Foreign Office. Eden's vast experience of foreign affairs meant that he wanted to run foreign policy himself. His foreign secretary Selwyn Lloyd could match neither his expertise nor his familiarity with key international players. Thatcher's deep suspicion of the Foreign Office is clearly expressed in her memoirs.[80] So in both cases, Suez and the Falklands, the prime minister of the day put a very personal stamp on the government's policy. But the outcomes were strikingly different.

When he first learnt of President Nasser's nationalisation of the Suez Canal, Eden convened a meeting of senior ministers, the chiefs of staff

79   Seymour-Ure, 'British war cabinets in limited wars'.
80   At the beginning of the Falklands Crisis she writes: 'I received advice from the Foreign Office which summed up the flexibility of principle characteristic of that department' and later she speaks of 'the Foreign Office where compromise and negotiation were ends in themselves' and of 'the habits which the Foreign Office seems to cultivate – a reluctance to subordinate diplomatic tactics to the national interest and an insatiable appetite for nuances and conditions which can blur the clearest vision'; Thatcher, *The Downing Street Years*, pp. 181, 309.

and the French ambassador and the American *chargé d'affaires*. The following day the Egypt Committee was set up. Thus Eden did not follow the Korean war precedent of using the cabinet's defence committee to manage the crisis.

The Egypt Committee had a fairly fixed inner core of members: the prime minister, the chancellor (Macmillan), the foreign secretary (Lloyd), Lord Salisbury (Leader of the Lords), Home (Commonwealth secretary) and the defence minister (initially Walter Monckton, later Anthony Head). Butler was not originally included, but hec simply attended and no one objected. Several other ministers attended from time to time; indeed, sixteen different ones attended at one point or another. The committee was not given precise terms of reference but was effectively responsible for managing the crisis, initially through diplomatic means, and ultimately by war.[81]

In his memoirs Eden described the Egypt Committee's task as 'to work out plans day by day to put our policy into effect'.[82] 'Our' policy was the prime minister's personal policy and it was contrary to the advice of the Foreign Office. Nevertheless it was a policy whose objectives had broad support within the Conservative party in the House of Commons and in the cabinet. The use of the Egypt Committee was not a device for circumventing opposition in either the full cabinet or the defence committee, for there was very little opposition (as was evident when the full cabinet was asked to endorse the line of action the Egypt Committee was taking) but an efficient and practical method of managing responses to the crisis on a day-to-day basis.

The committee, which met frequently and often at length, exercised executive authority from the outset (e.g. imposing economic sanctions against Egypt). During the parliamentary recess Eden decided that no regular cabinets needed to be held, but that the Egypt Committee would continue to function; if emergency decisions had to be taken, the cabinet would be recalled. Cabinet endorsed the committee's reluctant acceptance of Dulles' proposed Canal Users' Association: it endorsed the plan that Britain and France should intervene to protect the canal if Israel attacked Egypt; and at the end of October it approved the committee's initial decisions on British action following the Israeli crossing into Sinai. The final decisions to proceed with the invasion and to call a ceasefire were taken by the full cabinet. Consulting the cabinet was a means of receiving endorsement of decisions which could not easily be countermanded, practically or politically. But, as Seymour-Ure observes: 'When it came to the moment of greatest political pressure,

81   Seymour-Ure, 'British war cabinets in limited wars', p. 184.
82   Anthony Eden, *Full Circle*, Cassell, 1960, p. 432.

the cabinet did indeed have the opportunity to do more than be simply consulted.'[83]

The policy pursued was thus both the prime minister's personal policy and the one which had general support within the cabinet. Although Macmillan was, if anything, initially even more hawkish than Eden, Butler was sceptical about the use of force and Monckton actually resigned over it. In summary, Eden had decided on a line of policy and was determined to see it through; the Egypt Committee was the instrument of that policy line and the cabinet (and parliament) its legitimator. Had Butler been at Number 10 instead of Eden, it is unlikely that the *instruments* of policy-making would have differed significantly, although the policy might not have been the same. Structure is determined by need; policy is coloured by a prime minister's judgement.

In a crisis prime ministers must lead the government's response and they need the assistance of a small group of senior ministers, able because of their political weight more or less to guarantee party and government support. Although the decisions may be taken by a small group of individuals, they are made with the knowledge that decisions thus taken have to be accounted for to their colleagues in the full cabinet, to parliament and, ultimately, to the electorate. And, among that trio, the cabinet is very much the most important. Seymour-Ure comments: 'To keep the cabinet happy was essential; the party, important; parliament as a whole, useful but not essential; and the public? Well, the day of reckoning at the next general election would be some way off.' This triple perspective is the context which determines all such policy choices.[84]

In many ways the Falklands crisis tells a similar story. Before the invasion, the forum for policy discussion was the occasional meeting of the cabinet's defence committee, supplemented (and for a crucial period replaced) by ministerial correspondence. As the possibility, and the actuality, of Argentine invasion emerged, Thatcher followed the precedents and appointed a small group to handle the crisis. Although this group was formally constituted as a sub-committee of the cabinet's Overseas and Defence Committee, it reported direct to cabinet and actually included two members, Parkinson and Whitelaw, who were not members of the Defence Committee and omitted one senior minister, the Chancellor, who was.[85] The 'war cabinet' comprised the prime minister, the foreign secretary, the defence secretary, Whitelaw ('my deputy and trusted adviser') and Parkinson ('who not only shared my political

83   Seymour-Ure, 'British war cabinets in limited wars', p. 192.
84   Ibid., p. 182.
85   According to Thatcher, this reflected advice from Harold Macmillan that the Treasury should be kept off the committee in charge of the campaign, so that military necessity rather than finance would predominate. Thatcher, *The Downing Street Years*, p. 188.

instincts but was brilliantly effective in dealing with public relations').[86] The latter two were obviously included for political rather than ad-ministrative reasons, to add a wider perspective than the departmental views of the Foreign Office and the Ministry of Defence, but also, and more significantly, to maintain links with the Conservative Party in the House of Commons and the country. This latter consideration was particularly important given the catastrophic policy failure the Ar-gentine invasion represented and the vulnerability of the government's political position, as shown in the Commons emergency debate on the Saturday after the invasion which Margaret Thatcher later described as the most difficult she never had to face.[87]

As with Suez, the policy followed – to restore the islands to British administration – was a reflection of both the personal political com-mitment of the prime minister *and* the general view of the government and the party, an instinctive response to what Carrington described as a national humiliation. Given Thatcher's style, it was inevitable that hers would be the dominant role in the 'war cabinet', but the inclusion of Parkinson, with his special rapport with the party, and of Pym, with whom she had extraordinarily little in common, underlines the fact that even as dominant a personality as Thatcher needs support. The process of decision-making was collective, even within the 'war cabinet', because everyone knew that the government's political future, and espe-cially the prime minister's, was riding on the outcome.

A crisis blew up when Pym returned from America with a set of peace proposals suggested by the US Secretary of State, Alexander Haig. To Thatcher these were totally unacceptable since they would rob the Falklanders of their freedom and Britain of her honour and respect. But Pym disagreed and, despite Thatcher's strong reservations, recommended acceptance of these terms to the war cabinet. Thatcher records that she could not have stayed as prime minister had the war cabinet accepted Pym's proposals but would have resigned. Having persuaded Whitelaw of the correctness of her views, she won the support of the war cabinet and the crisis passed. The conflict was repeated when the US/Peruvian peace proposals were considered on 5 May and when the UN Secretary-General's proposals came forward on 20 May, but in both instances the war cabinet and full cabinet agreed with the prime minister rather than the foreign secretary.[88]

Ministers not in the 'war cabinet' were content with the way that the crisis was managed. The full cabinet was given an outline of the military options at the end of April, although it is believed that Thatcher

86 Thatcher, *The Downing Street Years*, p. 188.
87 Ibid., p. 183.
88 Ibid., pp. 206–8, 217, 224.

was initially reluctant to do this for security reasons. She herself has recalled that, although the war cabinet members certainly argued with each other, these arguments, once resolved, were not repeated again at the weekly 'stock taking' report to the full cabinet. Nevertheless, special cabinet meetings were summoned to endorse the crucial decisions, thus emphasising the collective nature of cabinet government and offering ministers an opportunity at least to question what was being done in their name.[89]

The composition of the 'war cabinet' meant that in the nature of things the members of the full cabinet would be unlikely to want to overturn something the 'war cabinet' had agreed, provided they were not in open disagreement. Where there were disagreements, the full cabinet backed the majority 'war cabinet' view. It is therefore somewhat academic to speculate on the nature of the relationship between the two bodies: the 'war cabinet' acted on behalf of the full cabinet but required, and received, its endorsement. The prime minister was thus able to implement the policy of her government through the smaller group with reasonable assurance of political support from all her cabinet colleagues and her parliamentary party. And, unlike Suez, she also received support from the Opposition and from Britain's American allies.

When the Falklands crisis came, it presented Thatcher with enormous dangers as well as rewards. That she, unlike Eden over Suez, met that challenge successfully brought her substantial political rewards within the government as well as outside. Her leadership was vindicated and her personal position made secure. The recovery of her party's position in the opinion polls followed by a landslide election victory further increased her political dominance, which was expressed first in the radical content of the Conservative election manifesto and then in a post-election reshuffle in which she sacked Pym as foreign secretary.

The two cases, a quarter of a century apart, show a remarkable similarity in the relationship between prime minister and cabinet. In both the prime minister gave a vigorous personal lead in response to an international crisis. The prime ministers' policies had the support of the full cabinet, even if some ministers were more reluctant about the use of force (Monckton, Pym). The conduct of the crisis, and of the military campaign, was in both cases entrusted to a small cabinet committee. The lapse of time which divides these crises illustrates the greater formalisation of cabinet committees in the later period. The Egypt Committee had a variable membership; the Falklands Committee did not. It is unthinkable that Howe would have simply come along in 1982 as Butler did in 1956. In both cases the key decisions of the small committee were successfully taken to full cabinet for endorsement.

89   Ibid., p. 193.

The prime ministers' personal prestige was deeply involved in both cases; for Eden, the failure of policy, in conjunction with his ill-health, led to resignation; for Thatcher, her role in the successful re-capture of the Falklands was a significant factor in the landslide Conservative general election victory of 1983.

Cutting public expenditure. Economic management issues and the control of public expenditure have been central to political and governmental debate in postwar Britain. 'Getting the economy right' has been seen as a prerequisite of electoral success as well as desirable in itself. It is a well established convention (still intact at the time of writing in spite of the introduction of a unified budget) that the cabinet receives only advance notification of the chancellor's budget proposals (usually on the morning of budget day) but is not consulted about them; whereas decisions about public expenditure levels are made collectively and involve extensive consultation and negotiation between ministers. To the extent that expenditure decisions play an important part in a government's economic management strategy (and how important a part they should play is highly controversial among economists as well as politicians) such decisions have a high political significance. Moreover, the expenditure share-out has a significance within Whitehall as an indicator of relative priorities – administrative, personal and political – and thus of status. And, because it is a share-out, there is a significant element of competition between ministers in pursuit of their own departmental programmes.

In the political and economic circumstances of the Callaghan and Thatcher administrations, public expenditure decisions had an even greater importance than usual. The Callaghan government did not command a secure parliamentary majority, but it was committed by the party manifesto to extensive increases in expenditure despite severe inflationary forces at home and abroad and the possible collapse of the pound. The spectre of the party split caused by the economic crisis of 1931 was ever present.[90] The Thatcher government had made the reduction of public expenditure, and control of the money supply, the principal means of cutting inflation, its primary political objective. This was to be combined with reductions in direct taxation, notwithstanding the considerable expenditure commitment inherited from the previous government. Thus both prime ministers had the task of steering their cabinets to a collective decision on public expenditure levels in particularly difficult circumstances. The methods used, and the outcomes, were markedly different, reflecting not only the different styles of the

90   See, e.g., Tony Benn, *Against the Tide – Diaries: 1973-1976*, Arrow Books, 1990, pp. 649 and 677–8; Callaghan, *Time and Chance*, p. 439.

two prime ministers but also differences in the political circumstances in which they had to work.

At the end of the summer of 1976 the Callaghan government was faced with a collapse of confidence in sterling in the international money markets, despite expenditure-cutting measures taken in July that were intended to keep the Public Sector Borrowing Requirement (PSBR) within a limit of £9bn. The July measures had been taken explicitly to avoid an application to the International Monetary Fund (IMF) and had been agreed only after what the Chancellor described as 'an appallingly difficult series of meetings with my cabinet colleagues'.[91] The measures failed and the government had after all to seek a loan from the IMF, a loan for which there were conditions, including further substantial cuts in public spending to reduce the PSBR.

The prospect of 'IMF conditionality' was deeply worrying to Labour ministers and particularly to Callaghan, who had previous experience of dealing with the IMF as Wilson's first Chancellor. It was clear that the effective price of an IMF loan would be the adoption of a more monetarist economic policy with continuing cuts in public expenditure, by implication abandoning much of the 1974 manifesto and substituting for it an economic policy very like that being advocated by the Conservatives. In July Callaghan had insisted that the economic options should be fully and openly discussed in cabinet and not 'bounced through by the Treasury'. The cabinet was divided into four camps: those supporting the Treasury's proposed cuts; the 'Keynesian dissenters' who opposed cuts when unemployment was already too high; a left-wing group that wanted an alternative economic strategy based on import controls and higher not lower public expenditure; and the remainder who waited to see what line the prime minister would take.[92]

The task facing Callaghan in the autumn was to enable the cabinet, which he knew to be deeply divided on economic strategy, to agree on how to respond to the collapse of international confidence in sterling. If that response were to take an IMF loan, it had to decide what conditions were acceptable, including the level of further expenditure cuts, and then actually make those cuts in departmental programmes. Moreover, this had to be done against a political background of a very weak parliamentary position and growing dissension within the Labour movement, manifested at the Party Conference in October.

It is instructive to read how Callaghan himself viewed this task:

My aim was to keep the Government intact by preventing any Ministerial resignations; second, to keep the Party together by making clear that as we had no Parliamentary majority, failure to support the conclusions the cabinet would

91   Healey, *The Time of My Life*, p. 428.
92   Bernard Donoughue in King, *The British Prime Minister*, p. 63.

eventually reach would mean defeat in the House and a General Election; and third, to avoid a break with the TUC which would have destroyed the Social Contract ... The cabinet was divided and deeply suspicious of the IMF ... It would have been best if we could have reached a quick decision, but I knew this would not be possible if we were to remain together, so by instinct more than by rational judgement I decided not to bring matters to a head but to allow time to work and Ministers to become familiar with the arguments and with the possible solutions ... There were many occasions in the lifetime of the Government when on particular issues I did not hesitate to express my views clearly and, some of my colleagues might think, too bluntly. But throughout the IMF negotiations I was determined to carry all my colleagues with me and so, although I knew how far I was ready to go to secure agreement with the IMF, I saw no advantage in making my position clear at an early stage. The best way to guide the cabinet towards a united conclusion in the face of their deeply held opposing views was not suppress Ministers' unhappiness or to attempt to bludgeon them but to bring everything out into the open.[93]

Thus the prime minister again insisted that the cabinet review all the policy options available. He also made clear (by making the IMF team wait a fortnight in London before authorising Treasury officials to open negotiations with them) that the government would not have terms dictated to it but would make its own decisions on what package was politically acceptable and could be recommended to parliament. There followed an even longer series of cabinet meetings than had been needed in July in which the alternatives were fully explored.[94] Callaghan said that no agreement would be made by the chancellor with the IMF without the approval of his colleagues, that he would report regularly on the progress of the negotiations, and that he encouraged other ministers to put forward any alternative strategy.

Callaghan carefully watched the development of opinion. Early on he invited Benn to present the Left's preferred alternative and ensured that other ministers had their questions and criticisms ready.[95] Callaghan was aware that two groups (the Left and the Keynesian dissenters) were intending to hold meetings to co-ordinate their views and he recognised the danger that if those two groups acted together they would deny the Chancellor a majority for his position, which might lead him to resign, and thus be fatal to the government's continuance in office. So Callaghan insisted that any alternative strategy should be submitted to, and openly debated by, the full cabinet. The Chancellor too was subjected to close questioning about the Treasury's analysis (not least because the IMF's analysis showed the Treasury's figures to be wrong) and on his regular reports on the progress of the negotiations. As the

93 Callaghan, *Time and Chance*, pp. 433–44.
94 Hennessy (*Cabinet*, p. 91) says there were twenty six in November; Donoghue (*Prime Minister*, p. 63) mentions seven in July.
95 William Rodgers, cited in Hennessy, *Cabinet*, p., 92.

cabinet debate proceeded, Callaghan continued to hold his hand, but noticed how 'under the force of prolonged questioning and argument, ministers gradually began to adjust their positions'.[96]

Independently Callaghan focussed his attention on two key colleagues who carried particular weight in cabinet: Anthony Crosland, the intellectual heavyweight among the Keynesian dissenters, and Foot, the deputy leader, who was in close touch with the Left. He had several private discussions with Crosland, seeking to convince him that the real issue was market confidence for which an IMF loan was essential, and eventually persuaded him, albeit reluctantly, to support a package of cuts. Similarly, Callaghan stressed privately to Foot the overriding importance of avoiding a party split such as had occurred in 1931.[97]

After securing Crosland's support for a package of cuts. Callaghan felt able to reveal his own position to the cabinet on 2 December in support of the chancellor's recommendation that borrowing be reduced by £1bn worth of expenditure cuts and a £500 million sale of British Petroleum shares. He stressed that, while the time had come to make a decision, ministers should only support the package if they were prepared individually to carry through the necessary reductions in their own spending programmes. He then 'went round the table one by one, inviting the opinion of every member of the cabinet', from which it was clear that there was a substantial majority in favour of the chancellor's proposed package.[98] With the cabinet thus united, the issue became how to get agreement with the IMF and then how to deliver the further spending cuts, a process achieved without the resignation of any member of the cabinet.

Callaghan's skill in achieving united cabinet support for an IMF loan and further expenditure cuts has justly received tribute from all sides. Healey has commended his 'consummate skill' and Benn and William Rodgers have commented similarly from their very different positions.[99] It was an unusual cabinet style, but the political and economic conditions of 1976 could hardly be described as typical. Nevertheless, it is clear that Callaghan's success required both the exercise of his considerable political talents and a very full process of collective discussion. To that outcome the adherence of Healey, Crosland and Foot was essential: that was what the prime minister had to secure if he were to achieve what he wanted – the IMF loan and a united cabinet.

The circumstances of 1979–81 were very different. So were the prime minister's objectives. Thatcher's overwhelming objective was to deliver

---

96   Callaghan, *Time and Chance*, p. 436.
97   Callaghan, *Time and Chance*, pp. 436, 438; see also Donoughue in King, *The British Prime Minister*, p. 68.
98   Callaghan, *Time and Chance*, p. 440; see also Benn, *Against the Tide*, pp. 678–9.
99   Healey, *The Time of My Life*, p. 431; Hennessy, *Cabinet*, p. 91.

her monetarist economic strategy and reduce inflation. Precisely what that meant, and even more how it could be achieved, were matters of considerable controversy both inside and outside the government. In her first few years in office Thatcher led a cabinet in which only a minority of ministers were wholly in support of her economic policies. She remarks in her memoirs: 'I had said at the beginning of the government "Give me six strong men and true, and I will get through." Very rarely did I have as many as six.'[100] The cabinet divisions of this period are not easy to characterise, as the allusive use of the terms 'wet' and 'dry' indicates. Ministers were in general agreement on the central objective of controlling inflation, cutting public expenditure and reducing the role of the state. What was at issue was how far and how quickly these objectives should be pursued and what account should be taken of the difficulties created by such circumstances as the world recession, the price of North Sea oil or the party's standing in the opinion polls. To some extent the divisions reflected the ideological differences between economic liberals and Tory pragmatists, but it was hard to make an adjustment in the level of the PSBR or of interest rates – an issue of fundamental principle, as the 'wets' were to discover. In particular the fatal weakness of Thatcher's critics was their inability to offer a plausible alternative policy.

In the period preceding the 1981 Budget the government's economic strategy seemed not to be working. The key figures – inflation, unemployment, public spending – were moving in the wrong direction. In part this reflected spending commitments inherited from the previous government, like the Clegg awards on public sector pay, but more significantly it reflected the consequences of key decisions in the first Thatcher/Howe budget. VAT was increased to 15 per cent, interest rates were raised to record levels, and public expenditure cuts affected nationalised industry prices adversely; all had acted to increase both inflation and unemployment, at least in the short term. And they had also led to a rapid increase in the exchange rate, which further intensified the severe pressures on competitiveness.[101]

Faced with such a dismal picture, the government was urged to ease the severity of the squeeze by relaxing its fiscal stance and reducing the cuts in public expenditure. But Thatcher and her economic ministers had clearly signalled their determination to stick to their chosen course with the announcement of the Medium Term Financial Strategy (MTFS) in the March 1980 budget; targets were set, and announced, for 'a steady deceleration in the rate of monetary growth over a four year period, buttressed by a gradual reduction in the underlying budget deficit,

100 Thatcher, *The Downing Street Years*, p. 149.
101 Riddell, *The Thatcher Government*, pp. 60–3, 86–7.

which in turn is to be achieved by a steady reduction in the real level of total government expenditure'.[102] Cabinet critics launched a counter-attack against the policy in the summer of 1980, which Thatcher viewed as an attempt to frustrate the strategy upon which the party had been elected. To change course would be to abandon that clear public commitment in which so much political prestige – especially the prime minister's – had been invested. Hence in a speech delivered to the Conservative Party conference, but really aimed at her cabinet critics (in which she memorably said 'The lady's not for turning'), she vigorously re-stated her commitment to her chosen course, deriding the infamous U-turn of the Heath government, when several major tenets of the 1970 election platform had been reversed, a process which to Thatcher was as abhorrent as Ramsay MacDonald's 1931 apostasy was represented in the minds of post-war Labour leaders.

Translating a policy of public expenditure cuts into practice is always difficult. In the autumn of 1980, much stronger cabinet opposition surfaced when decisions were required to give effect to the agreed strategy. The final resolution of the public spending round that autumn required three cabinet meetings in early November and in the end the chancellor had to settle for an overall reduction of only half the figure the cabinet had agreed in July.[103] This was one of the reasons behind the reshuffle of January 1981 when Thatcher dismissed St John Stevas and moved Nott to Defence in place of Pym. This, she hoped, would enable the cabinet 'to face our economic difficulties with greater unity and determination'.[104] But the struggle was far from over. Battles over public expenditure never end; the results are always provisional, in the sense that there are further rounds of decisions to be taken: no sooner is one year's programme settled than consideration of next year's is under way.

The March 1981 budget itself illustrated this. Its fiscal severity came as a considerable shock even to senior ministers. Some of the 'wets' – Prior, Gilmour, Walker – considered resignation. But the severity of that budget was in part a consequence of the 'wets' victory the previous November when the cabinet decided to accept only half of the expenditure cuts then sought by the chancellor. The spring budget caused a major row within the cabinet. The dissenting ministers were 'stunned' when they learnt its contents.[105] Although they could do little other than protest about the budgetary *fait accompli* once they had decided not to resign, they did succeed in ensuring that in future the full cabinet would be able to debate economic strategy – although in Lawson's view no real

102 Ibid., p. 64.
103 Lawson, *The View from No. 11*, p. 89.
104 Ibid., p. 131.
105 Thatcher, *The Downing Street Years*, p. 138; Prior, *A Balance of Power*, pp. 140–1.

derogation of the Chancellor's 'sovereignty' over the budget resulted.[106] Thatcher, however, recognised the danger of cabinet dissent and sought to outflank it by mobilising the party in the country in support of her policy with a vigorous speech to the Conservative Central Council in Bournemouth.[107]

The policy continued to agitate the cabinet, especially when unemployment was predicted to exceed three million. Battle was joined in a two-hour general discussion of the economy by the cabinet in mid-June, after which at least six ministers made it known that they would resist any further curbs on government spending.[108] The arguments came to head on 23 July when, in continuation of the MTFS, the chancellor, backed by the prime minister, presented to cabinet proposals for a further £5bn expenditure cuts. This produced 'one of the bitterest arguments on the economy, or any subject' during Thatcher's premiership.[109] The known 'wets' such as Prior and Walker were now joined in their criticisms not only by traditionalists like Pym and Lord Hailsham but even by Biffen and Nott who had previously been considered Thatcherites. The prime minister and her chancellor were supported only by Joseph and Brittan.[110] The outcome was that the cabinet adopted a public expenditure total a full £5bn higher than that proposed.

This was without question also a defeat for the prime minister as well as the chancellor, for she was unambiguously committed to the proposed expenditure reductions. Unlike Callaghan, Thatcher had not held her hand in anticipation of divisions amongst her colleagues, but had made no secret of what she wanted and of her contempt for the dissenters.[111] She was not, however, able to force through the further public expenditure cuts as she and Howe had succeeded in forcing through the budget a few months earlier. The cabinet's decision, with the prime minister in a minority, had to be lived with. It was a reversal for Thatcher, but not a total defeat.

Fundamentally, Thatcher's political position within the cabinet remained secure, particularly while her opponents had no alternative strategy or alternative prime minister and she retained the support of Whitelaw and Carrington, who voluntarily abstained from involvement in domestic policy issues. For her the implications were clear:

'When I closed the meeting I knew that there were too many in cabinet who did not share [my] view. Moreover, after what had been said it would be difficult for this group of ministers to act as a team again ... If the goals I had set out in

106 Lawson, *The View from No. 11*, p. 96.
107 Thatcher, *The Downing Street Years*, pp. 138–9.
108 Lawson, *The View from No. 11*, p. 108.
109 Ibid., p. 148.
110 Ibid., p. 108; Riddell, *The Thatcher Government*, p. 46; Young, *One of Us*, pp. 218–19.
111 Young, *One of Us*, p. 219.

opposition were to be achieved they must be reaffirmed and fought for by a new cabinet. So it was quite clear to me that a major reshuffle was needed if our economic policy were to continue, and perhaps if I were to remain prime minister'.[112]

Her response to the July reversal came in a September cabinet reshuffle. She dismissed Gilmour, Carlisle and Soames, three of the wets, and replaced them by Tebbit, Parkinson and Lawson, then her close supporters. None of the dismissed ministers was a potential leader of a rebellion in the Commons. Pym, Heseltine and Walker remained, although Pym was to go after the 1983 election.

The prime minister, having suffered a policy defeat in cabinet, could use her power of patronage to reconstruct its membership more in sympathy with her policy preferences.[113] Reinforced by the reshuffle, the chancellor announced in December measures to increase charges and national insurance contributions which recouped about half the extra £5bn in dispute in July. And in his 1982 budget Howe announced a further cut in the PSBR.

The subsequent course of economic policy, including public expenditure, was heavily influenced by the Falklands war and the 1983 general election. While the MTFS remained in place, the emphasis on monetary targets became more catholic. And, as inflation reduced, interest rates and unemployment fell and public expenditure pressures eased, although each year press reports of cabinet battles over spending continued to appear. And the later experiences of 1989 and 1990 showed that cabinet unanimity was no easier to attain then than it had been in 1980 and 1981, notwithstanding the prime minister's exercise of her patronage powers.

Battles over public expenditure show the complex realities of the decision-making process in Whitehall, with its many centres of power, bureaucratic and political. The prime minister may well be the most powerful player in most circumstances and can control most of the game; but all prime ministers are keenly aware that other players can influence the outcome too and that therefore the game has to be played with skill and foresight and no little good fortune if the right result (in the prime minister's eyes) is to occur. The events of 1980–1 certainly show that a prime minister does not win every round and may have to endure major defeats, like that of July 1981. The public expenditure game, like elections, is one in which there is no final result, only an unending series of replays, as the Major cabinet experienced in 1993.

112 Thatcher, *The Downing Street Years*, pp. 149–50.
113 See ibid., p. 152: 'The whole nature of the cabinet changed as a result of these changes. After the new cabinet's first meeting I remarked ...what a difference it made to have most of the people in it on my side ... It would be a number of years before there arose an issue which fundamentally divided me from the majority of my cabinet.'

Problem ministers: Benn and Heseltine. Prime ministers have to deal with ministers individually as well as collectively. Some individual ministers find themselves out of sympathy with major aspects of cabinet policy; the personality and vitality of others can make them difficult colleagues. Even if they cannot gather much support from their fellow cabinet members, they cannot necessarily be discounted; for they may have support, actual or potential, in the parliamentary party or in the country. Prime ministers as party leaders are always conscious of the risk of providing their party critics with a focus for potential rebellion, an alternative standard (-bearer) around which they might gather, a Cave of Adullam to which the discontented may repair. Tony Benn presented such a problem to Wilson (and later to Callaghan too) and Michael Heseltine did so to Thatcher. How do prime ministers respond?

The 1970–4 period in opposition saw a substantial shift to the left in the Labour movement, reflected in the more overtly socialist emphasis of the 1974 manifestos. From his base on the Party's National Executive Committee Benn had played a significant part in this shift and his appointment as Industry Secretary after the February 1974 election seemed to give him the opportunity to push ahead with more extensive proposals for public ownership and regulation of private industry. Such an interventionist approach did not find favour either with Wilson[114] or with a majority of the cabinet, even though it had a powerful appeal to the left wing of the parliamentary Labour Party and the Labour movement generally. The prime minister was also keenly aware of the threat which such radical policies could present to the government's precarious parliamentary position, not to mention international confidence in the pound. Thus Wilson saw the need to contain Benn in two senses. It was necessary to restrain his policies, yet also to keep him within the cabinet.

To achieve this Wilson initially used two techniques. A member of the Number 10 Policy Unit was specifically charged with monitoring the activities of Benn's department, and a cabinet committee took over the drafting of a White Paper on the government's industrial policy. The latter move in particular signalled clearly to Whitehall that Benn's radical policies did not have the support of either the prime minister or the cabinet. Wilson had reacted acidly to Benn's own draft policy paper, describing it as 'a sloppy and half-baked document, polemical, indeed menacing in tone' and determined to ensure that the 'marauding' role proposed for the National Enterprise Board (NEB) was removed. Significantly, Foot, known to be a standard-bearer of the Labour Left,

---

114 Harold Wilson, *The Governance of Britain*, Weidenfeld and Nicolson, 1976, p. 66, and *Final Term*, pp. 30–1, 33–6.

played a major part in re-writing the policy, demonstrating Benn's isolation.[115]

After the October 1974 election, the way was open for Labour's industrial policy to be given legislative effect. Benn continued to pursue an activist policy but was frequently reined back by his cabinet colleagues. At this point Wilson was using the Treasury as a source of information about Benn's activities, which caused considerable difficulties for the industry department's officials. While Benn's initiatives on co-operatives – one at Meriden making motor-cycles, another at Kirkby making electrical goods – were allowed to proceed, Wilson was careful to ensure that he himself chose the chairman (Lord Ryder) for the National Enterprise Board and that, during the interim period before the legislation took effect, he was based in the cabinet office, not the industry department, and reported direct to Number 10.[116]

In 1975 the referendum on Britain's continued membership of the European Communities took place. This itself was the fruit of an initiative of Benn's while in opposition and it proved a useful device for keeping some semblance of unity within the Labour Party despite its deep divisions over Europe. In the cabinet discussions leading up to a decision on what the government should recommend, Benn was an active and persistent critic of the line taken by the prime minister and the foreign secretary during the negotiations.[117] Not surprisingly, he was one of the seven ministers who, having voted against acceptance of the terms in cabinet, were exceptionally given permission to campaign against them in the referendum.

The referendum's result in favour of continued membership visibly enhanced Wilson's position. In the cabinet reshuffle which followed, Benn was moved from Industry to Energy, a clear demotion, but one postponed to limit public comment during the debate over membership of the EC. Benn's demotion was a blow to him and to his left-wing supporters.[118] For a time he hesitated over whether to resign from the government and return to the backbenches. Eric Varley, industry minister designate, warned the prime minister that he would not be prepared to take over in such circumstances and Foot intervened on Benn's behalf, but unsuccessfully. Thus, with this transfer, Wilson ensured that the government's industry policy would be administered by a minister whose views were more closely in accord with his own and those of a majority of the cabinet (although this did not prevent a great deal of argument

115 Wilson, *Final Term*, p. 33; Hennessy, *Cabinet*, pp. 86–7.
116 Wilson, *Final Term*, p. 136; Anthony Part, *The Making of a Mandarin*, André Deutsch, 1990, pp. 167–75.
117 Benn, *Against the Tide*, pp. 163, 177–8, 283.
118 Castle, *The Castle Diaries*, p. 410; Benn, *Against the Tide*, pp. 388–99; Wilson, *Final Term*, p. 144.

about Chrysler later in the year, with the Cabinet eventually agreeing a multi-million support package for the British-based factories of this ailing American car giant).

In this instance the prime minister used three techniques to deal with a difficult minister: monitoring by officials in the Policy Unit and the Treasury; supervision by a cabinet committee; and, ultimately, when political circumstances made it possible, a reshuffle. And the industrial policy which the government ultimately followed was that favoured by Wilson rather than that advocated by Benn.

Thatcher's difficulties with Heseltine culminated in his dramatic resignation from her government in the middle of a cabinet meeting early in January 1986. In his subsequent comment Heseltine made it clear that his differences with the prime minister were as much about her method of conducting government business as about the substance of policy.[119] Notwithstanding his comments, there had been substantial differences over a range of policies, and not just over the future of the Westland helicopter company which had occasioned his dramatic resignation. Thatcher's preference for a link with the American Sikorsky company ran directly counter to Heseltine's concern to retain Westland, which he saw as a strategic matter, within European ownership.

Heseltine was not a typical 'wet'. He believed that in some ways the economic policy of the Thatcher government had not been 'dry' enough in its early years. He differed fundamentally from the prime minister and her economic liberals, however, on his willingness to use the power of the state. Lord Young describes him as 'an unrepentant Heathite, in that he believed passionately in an interventionist government exercising strategic industrial leadership'.[120] Such an attitude, combined with his previous close links with Heath, made him the object of considerable suspicion in the Thatcher circle. However, he was not only independent and unpredictable but also an extremely popular performer with the party, as the rapturous reception for him at annual conferences showed.

The tension between Heseltine and Thatcher thus pre-dated the Westland affair. Indeed, Thatcher traces it back as far as her election as leader of the party in 1975.[121] It was probably at its most intense in 1981 when Heseltine was among the first to criticise the Chancellor's proposed expenditure cuts in the July cabinet revolt and even suggested a pay freeze instead. Put in charge of the government's response to the riots in Liverpool, he produced a paper proposing an ambitious programme of investment and the designation of cabinet colleagues

119 Text of Resignation Statement, *The Times*, 10 January 1986; see also Hennessy, *Cabinet*, p. 106.
120 Young, *One of Us*, p. 200.
121 Thatcher, *The Downing Street Years*, p. 423.

for various decaying areas, and 'evangelised Whitehall on behalf of his cause.'[122]

Thatcher used her control of cabinet machinery to thwart this initiative. In September 1981 she convened an *ad hoc* ministerial group on the inner cities to consider Heseltine's paper, but stacked its membership against him.[123] He was effectively isolated and had to succumb to the verdict of a loaded ministerial group, knowing that appeal to the full cabinet in such circumstances would be fruitless. In contrast to January 1986, he did not at this stage wish to suffer a defeat in full cabinet which might lead to resignation. Battle was joined again after the 1983 election when Heseltine, now transferred from Environment to Defence, persisted in criticising the plan to abolish the Greater London Council and received what Prior has described as 'one of the most violent rebukes I have witnessed in cabinet'.[124] Again, the prime minister got her way. Early in 1985 there was further conflict, this time over the placing of an order for a Type 22 frigate. Heseltine wanted it to go to Cammell Laird of Merseyside, whereas the prime minister and the majority of the cabinet committee considering the issue were in favour of Swan Hunter of Tyneside. Heseltine felt so strongly that he threatened to resign and on this occasion Thatcher arranged for a reversal of the decision to accommodate his wishes.[125]

The Westland affair brought the conflict to a head.[126] Heseltine was determined to establish a European alternative to the Sikorsky rescue plan (Sikorsky being a US company) favoured by Brittan at the Department of Trade and Industry, backed by the prime minister. Initially, Thatcher sought to hold the ring between the two options, using the formula that the choice was one for Westland's board (and its shareholders) and that the government should remain neutral. This neutrality became increasingly hollow as Brittan and Heseltine strove to promote their competing solutions. The Westland board was enraged by Heseltine's attempts to thwart its preferred option and lobbied Thatcher and Brittan to prevent him. The issue was dealt with at three ministerial meetings in early December, the first two *ad hoc* groups of ministers, and the third the full economic committee of the cabinet.[127]

Exactly what transpired at these meetings is the subject of dispute.

122 Hennessy, *Cabinet*, p. 102.
123 Ibid.,
124 Prior, *A Balance of Power*, p. 150.
125 Lawson, *The View from No. 11*, p. 674.
126 For a short account, see Young, *One of Us*, pp. 431–57. For the 'inside story', see M. Linklater and D. Leigh, *Not With Honour*, Sphere Books, 1986; for Mrs Thatcher's version, see *The Downing Street Years*, pp. 423–37. Compare House of Commons Defence Committee, *Westland PLC: the Government's Decision-Making*, HC 519, 1985–6.
127 Hennessy, *Cabinet*, pp. 106–8; Young, *One of Us*, p. 437.

Heseltine believes a majority initially favoured his proposals and that a further meeting would have confirmed this, which is why the prime minister cancelled it. Thatcher's supporters deny that Heseltine's proposals had majority support and argue that no further meeting was actually planned.[128] Lawson's recollection is that the understanding was that another meeting *might* be needed, not that it would.[129] The relationship between Heseltine and Thatcher deteriorated further when he raised the issue of Westland without warning in cabinet on 12 December. Thatcher cut short an ill-tempered discussion on the grounds that the issue was not on the agenda and could not be discussed without papers. Heseltine's annoyance was intensified when the cabinet secretariat initially failed to circulate a proper record of the discussion.[130]

The non-meeting of the committee, the abbreviated and ill-tempered discussion at cabinet, and the subsequent attempt to gag him by insisting that all ministerial statements on Westland should be cleared through the cabinet office provoked Heseltine's walk-out from the cabinet on 9 January 1986 and his resignation from the government. He had actually previously discussed resigning with Whitelaw and the chief whip but had rejected it,[131] which may explain how his very full and carefully drafted resignation statement could have been issued so quickly, causing the prime minister and her supporters to wonder whether the Westland saga was merely an excuse for a much more highly calculated political act.[132] Equally, the speed with which Thatcher conducted the reshuffle after Heseltine's walk-out (she made all the appointments during a break in the cabinet meeting) indicates that she was not exactly taken unawares by the turn of events. She had concluded that 'unless he were checked, there were no limits to what he [Heseltine] would do to secure his objectives at Westland. Cabinet collective responsibility was being ignored and my own authority as prime minister was being publicly flouted. This had to stop.'[133] Lawson concludes that she 'set out to humiliate Michael, in the full knowledge that this would almost certainly lead to his resignation'.[134] She had certainly correctly calculated that Heseltine would be isolated in cabinet.

After his resignation Heseltine was widely seen as an alternative leader of the Conservative Party. There was repeated speculation that he might at some stage stand for the leadership against Thatcher, although he constantly denied it – until the moment come more than four years

128   Young, *One of Us*, p. 437; Thatcher, *The Downing Street Years*, p. 430.
129   Lawson, *The View from No. 11*, p. 677.
130   Thatcher, *The Downing Street Years*, p. 430.
131   Young, *One of Us*, p. 446.
132   Thatcher, *The Downing Street Years*, p. 433.
133   Ibid., p. 431.
134   Lawson, *The View from No. 11*, p. 678.

later after Howe's resignation speech in the House of Commons. One might say that the Westland affair was the end of a battle, but not the end of the war. At the time the outcome, Heseltine's resignation, looked like a total victory for the prime minister. The rescue of Westland by Sikorsky went through and Thatcher had rid herself of an awkward critic within the government.

Heseltine chose to resign. That he was not dismissed reflected anxiety in the prime minister's circle about the threat he would present to her leadership if he were sent to the backbenches to join Pym, Gilmour and other critics.[135] It demonstrated the political limits to the exercise of a prime minister's power of patronage. Although Thatcher attained her apparent policy objective and did rid herself of a cabinet critic, this double outcome can hardly have been a calculated objective; it was more an indication of a prime minister's inherent weakness in dealing with a popular colleague who takes a critical and independent line. To gain her objectives, a price had to be paid.

The full extent of that price became apparent at the end of 1990. Howe was another minister with whom Thatcher had had serious differences and he was finally goaded into resignation from her government on 1 November 1990 over her policy towards the European Community. His resignation statement to the House of Commons, with its critical allusions to Thatcher's style of leadership and relationship with cabinet colleagues, echoed the explanation Lawson had given a year earlier when he had resigned as chancellor.[136] Howe's speech concluded with a guarded invitation to 'others to consider their own response to the tragic conflict of loyalty with which I have myself wrestled for too long'. There could hardly have been a more explicit invitation to Heseltine to challenge Thatcher for the leadership of the Conservative Party. And in the first ballot of the leadership contest, when it came, he achieved substantial support (152 votes), sufficient to deprive Thatcher of victory. The ensuing discussions with cabinet colleagues convinced Thatcher, against her original inclination to fight on, that her authority as leader of the parliamentary party had been fatally wounded and that she must resign,[137] the first instance in more than fifty years of a British prime minister in good health being forced out of office other than by defeat in a general election.

135 Her reasons for not dismissing him are revealing: 'Michael was at that time a popular and powerful figure in the party. No one survives for long as prime minister without a shrewd recognition of political realities and risks'; Thatcher, *The Downing Street Years*, p. 436.
136 *The Independent*, 14 November 1990; HC Deb, 13 November 1990, cols 461–5.
137 Thatcher, *The Downing Street Years*, pp. 846–55. Compare Baker, *The Turbulent Years*, chapter 18. For fuller accounts of the leadership contest see *The Economist*, 9 March 1991; and R.K. Alderman and N. Carter, 'The ousting of Mrs Thatcher', *Parliamentary Affairs*, April 1991, vol. 44, no. 2, pp. 125–9.

It was a sudden and dramatic fall. In addition to the continuing weakness of her party's position in the opinion polls which led many Conservative backbenchers to fear they could not win another general election under her leadership, a major factor was Thatcher's fragile relationship with her senior cabinet colleagues. Heseltine had resigned over Westland in 1986; Lawson in 1989 over Thatcher's apparent preference for her economic adviser Alan Walters rather than her chancellor; Howe in November 1990 over Britain's future in the EC. And when, after her failure to win sufficient support in the first ballot for the leadership, the cabinet were consulted individually, it became clear that the basis of Thatcher's support had been eroded beyond repair. Even as prime minister she was not able to sustain the support of sufficient members of her parliamentary party and her cabinet. She may have achieved a succession of victories on specific policies, as in the Westland affair; but the long-term price of such victories was the fatal erosion of support for her as leader of the party. And without that support she could not remain as prime minister, even though, on the day she announced her intention to resign, her government had no difficulty in defeating an opposition 'no confidence' motion in the House of Commons.

Politics, it has been often said, is the art of the possible. For a prime minister the cabinet is part of the context which defines the limits of possibility. It is the collective expression of the 'core executive' which can be circumvented on particular issues by informal groups, cliques or bilateral dealings but ultimately is a political reality which all ministers, including the occupants of 10 Downing Street, have to take into account.

It would be naïve to suggest that there have been any clear trends in the development of prime minister-cabinet relationships in the postwar period. That relationship is a function of three distinct factors: the flexibility of the constitutional structure and powers; the current political context; and the personalities of the key actors. The interplay of those factors has produced significant variations in the degree to which the style of government has been personal or collegial, and the degree to which prime ministers have been able to dominate their cabinets or been constrained by them.

Some developments (such as the increased media personalisation of politics, the growth of cabinet committees, the expansion of the prime minister's private office, international summitry) have added to a prime minister's potential for domination. But those very opportunities have intensified the danger that prime ministers will overreach themselves and find their personal political position slipping away, as happened with Macmillan in 1963, Wilson in 1969 and Thatcher in 1989–90. Prime ministerial power is elastic and can be stretched a long way, as it clearly was by Margaret Thatcher. But it does eventually snap if it is stretched too far. How far is too far depends as much upon the tolerance and ambition of cabinet colleagues (Callaghan and Jenkins in 1969; Lawson, Howe, Hurd and Major in 1989–90) as upon the prime minister. The limits are not fixed, and prime ministers can influence their extent by exercising the powers of patronage, the techniques of chairmanship and the skills of political leadership. But they must ensure that the cabinet will at the very least acquiesce, in their policies and even better support them and that it maintains at least the appearance, and better the substance, of unity in parliament, party and country. In that context, prime ministers must ensure, above all, that their own position of leadership remains secure. The price of that security is the limit to their power.

3

PRIME MINISTER AND PARLIAMENT

R.L. Borthwick

Anyone inclined to doubt that the relationship between prime ministers and Parliament has changed since 1945 need only try to imagine Clement Attlee or Winston Churchill coping with some of the demands placed upon a modern prime minister. Equally instructive is a comparison of the reactions to the resignation of Harold Macmillan's entire Treasury team in 1958 and the reactions to the resignations of Nigel Lawson or Norman Lamont as chancellor of the exchequer more than thirty years later.

However, crude such comparisons may be, they serve nevertheless to show that there *have* been changes; more difficult is the task of defining their nature. In part they reflect wider changes in the political system, such as the impact that the mass media, and particularly television and a more intrusive style of tabloid journalism, have had on the way we perceive and treat political leaders. One has only to see the deference displayed in early television interviews to Attlee or Eden to recognise that later prime ministers had to inhabit a wholly different world. This change in the way political leaders are treated by the media outside Parliament has also had an impact on the way prime ministers are now treated inside the institution.

A second aspect of the change is simply that Parliament has had a much more obvious rival for the attention of the public. Radio and television, especially when Parliament allowed its proceedings to be featured directly, provided a focus for national debate that reached the public in a more direct way than newspapers in an earlier period ever could. Journalistic mediation was reduced in importance as people could hear and see exactly what was occurring in those parts of Parliament's work which were directly recorded. And it was those selected parts which created the public image of Parliament.

At the same time as these changes were taking place, there was a significant change in the composition and behaviour of the House of Commons which made it less amenable to executive leadership. Basically, prime ministers are now less able to rely on the willingness of backbenchers to support them in the division lobbies than they once were. The sanctions which prime ministers had over their followers turned out to be limited and it is difficult, for example,. to imagine Margaret Thatcher or John Major making the 'dog licences' speech warning backbenchers about the limits of their freedom as Harold Wilson did in 1967.[1]

Other changes were more strictly internal to Parliament. Most notable has been the growth in attention paid to prime minister's question time after it became a fixed fifteen-minute slot twice a week in the early 1960s. As a result prime ministers gradually came to be seen as answerable for any aspect of their government and would find their standing being increasingly judged on their ability to joust with all comers in the twice-weekly skirmishes.

Not all of these changes happened at the same speed or took hold at the same time. In many ways 1960 is a turning-point. The change in question time and the growing confidence of television in relation to politicians can be dated from this period. Programmes like 'That Was the Week That Was' and the publication of *Private Eye* epitomised the end of a deferential age and brought criticism of politicians into a more public arena. Certainly by the 1980s the treatment accorded to prime ministers was quite different from what it had been thirty years earlier. This is not to say that earlier prime ministers were necessarily gently handled in every way; the treatment Anthony Eden received in the Suez crisis clearly indicates otherwise. However, once prime ministers regularly entered the nation's living rooms they lost much of their protective armour. Furthermore, their standing in Parliament was partly a reflection of their success outside. However, the relationship went both ways; perceptions outside continued to be based to some extent on performance inside Parliament. Ability to command the House is still seen by fellow-MPs as one of the most important qualities that prime ministers should have, and their perceptions feed through to the general public through newspapers and radio comment.

The importance of performance inside Parliament illustrates one of the continuities that must be set against the changes that have taken place. Another is even more basic. It remains as true for Major as it was for Attlee that his hold on 10 Downing Street depends on support in the House of Commons, whose confidence prime ministers still need in order to remain in office. The willingness of the House to provide this has only occasionally been in doubt since the end of the Second World War but the nature of the relationship underwent significant, if subtle, changes in the early 1970s, a decade later than some of the

1   See pp. 86 and 156 for details.

other changes in the relationship between Parliament and the prime minister had begun to show themselves.

In seeking to understand the nature of the relationship between prime ministers and Parliament in the post-war period, it is tempting to search for consistent patterns of change. It may be that here, as in other aspects of the prime ministership, the metaphor should be that of 'the snakes and ladders board'.[2] Individual prime ministers at different stages of their time in office have varied enormously in their hold on the House of Commons. The rise and fall of individual prime ministers as different as Macmillan, Wilson and Thatcher show how much that relationship can vary within the tenure of a single individual.

The House of Commons as a Source of Power

Parliament is likely to appear in any list of the sources of a prime minister's power. At the same time, Parliament is also a constraint on that power, which in the last resort depends on retaining the confidence of the House of Commons. The House of Lords has the capacity to be an irritant to prime ministers but it does not determine their fate. Parliament is important also in that prime ministers must belong to it and in practice be members of the Commons, the body which will also contain their senior colleagues, among whom is likely to be any prime minister's eventual successor. Parliament has an effective monopoly on providing the personnel of government. Only occasionally will a minister be appointed who is not a member of one or other House. In that event he or she is quickly found a place, usually in the Lords.[3]

Parliamentary government as understood in Britain presumes that prime minister and cabinet have the confidence of the House of Commons. The notion of cabinet government explicit in this makes it more difficult to disentangle the connection between a prime minister and Parliament; there is inevitably a danger of confusing the individual with the group. In so far as the notion of parliamentary government described here implies control by Parliament over prime minister and cabinet, it is misleading; normally the control is very much in the other direction. Prime minister and cabinet have it within their power most of the time to direct the work of Parliament and especially of the House of Commons.

Central to the day-to-day business of governing, now as in 1945, is that prime ministers are accountable to the House of Commons for the activities of their governments. This means that governments operate on the basis of collective responsibility; all ministers share in the responsibility, at least in theory, for government actions. Only twice in the

2   A. Brown, 'Prime ministerial power'. *Public Law*, 1968, p. 33.
3   D. Shell, *The House of Lords*, Harvester Wheatsheaf, 1992, pp. 80-81.

post-war period has this presumption been publicly abandoned, and then only temporarily. In 1975 the Wilson government allowed its members to speak on opposite sides in the referendum campaign over the renegotiated terms for British membership of the European Community. On the second occasion, in 1977, members of the Callaghan government were allowed to disagree publicly over the method of election to be used for members of the European Parliament.

Accountability may mean no more than that governments must answer in Parliament for their actions and individual ministers must answer for the work of their departments. There has been much debate about whether that implies also that ministers must resign when errors have been committed by their staff. There are few examples to support the idea that this aspect of the doctrine survives. More common is the practice of surrounding ministers in difficulty with a blanket of collective responsibility – although sacrifices may occasionally be made, as with the resignation of Lord Carrington following the Argentine invasion of the Falkland Islands.

These are the most dramatic moments. Failure to defend the government's position in the House effectively, the sense that a job is too much for its holder, errors of judgement in the parliamentary fray – all these are noted, by the whips as much as by the backbenchers and the parliamentary journalists. It is not long, once weaknesses have been identified and noted, before the individual is moved sideways or out of office altogether. Thus the way in which accountability works is usually more subtle than the sanction of resignation.

Throughout the postwar period the prime minister has been the person who is the leader of the largest party in the House of Commons. For most of that time, that party has also had a majority in the House, although this was not the case between March and October 1974 and again between April 1976 and May 1979. In those periods minority government operated. Obviously in such situations the possibility of defeat is greater, but if the prime minister leads the largest party (as was the case in both instances) there is a degree of security if the other parties fail to combine effectively or lack the incentive to bring about the defeat of the government of the day.

Normally, however, prime ministers since 1945, and usually before then too, have been able to rely on party support in the House of Commons. While the possibility of the withdrawal of that support always exists, and therefore life is never wholly predictable, in practice defeat on an issue of confidence is unthinkable and unprecedented unless a government is already a minority one, as the Callaghan government was in 1979. In the post-war period the types of Commons defeat that might prove fatal to a government have been narrowed down until it is clear that only defeat on a vote of confidence will have the effect of bringing the government down or precipitating a dissolution of Parliament.[4] To that point we return later.

Support in the division lobbies is important: it says something about the grasp which a leader has over the party. Backbenchers can calculate with care precisely how far they can go without actually threatening the government's majority, and a leader's authority within the parliamentary party is reduced, and thus his or her position made more vulnerable, if the expected majorities are regularly reduced by defections. The relationship between size of majority and degree of prime ministerial confidence is not a direct one. Since the early 1970s MPs have become less amenable and the weakness of the sanctions over them more obvious. When things begin to go wrong, the mystical hold over the House which a confident prime minister might once have had can mysteriously disappear. Once again, the importance of the House lies less in its formal powers than in its informal influence, in the way it reduces the authority of a prime minister, and implicitly places on the public agenda the possibility of an alternative. In the spring of 1994 John Major must have been acutely aware of the fickleness of parliamentary support.

For most of the post-war period, prime ministers have been able to secure passage of their (or perhaps more accurately their governments') legislative programme through Parliament. The struggles in 1993 to secure passage of the Maastricht legislation indicate how tortuous that can be on occasion but also how, when the very survival of a government is at issue, the loyalty of parties to their leaders protects the prime minister of the day in the short term.

Gaining and Losing Office

After most general elections since 1945 it has been obvious who would be prime minister. Twice only was there any uncertainly. The first occasion was in 1945 when Labour won its first majority in the House of Commons. On the face of things, and as it turned out in the event, there was no doubt. At the time, however, there were moves to insist that Clement Attlee should not accept the King's invitation to form a government until he had been confirmed as leader of the Labour Party by the newly-elected parliamentary party. This argument, associated with the wiles of Professor Laski, was supported by those who hoped for a different leader, notably Herbert Morrison. In the event Attlee ignored the reservations of such constitutionalists and accepted the King's invitation with alacrity.

4   P. Norton, *The Commons in Perspective*, Martin Robertson, 1981, p. 153.

A much more real case of doubt occurred in February 1974. Following the election called by Heath in an effort to win national support against the striking National Union of Mineworkers, there was a confused situation. Labour emerged from the February 1974 election as the largest party in the House of Commons, but without an overall majority; the Conservatives had gained more popular votes than their opponents but they had won fewer seats. Heath did not immediately leave Downing Street but instead entered negotiations with the Liberals to see whether some formula could be found to enable a Conservative-dominated government to continue in office. When no such deal proved possible, Heath was obliged after a few days to advise the Queen to send for Harold Wilson. Wilson then formed a minority government which stayed in office till another election in October, when a small Labour majority was forthcoming. That majority was eventually eroded by by-election losses and defections so that by April 1976 Labour were once again in a minority. They stayed in office, partly with the help of an agreement with the Liberal Party, the so-called 'Lib-Lab pact', which lasted from March 1977 till July 1978. Thereafter their hold on office was increasingly tenuous. The critical decisions, however, depended essentially on what the individual *parties*, rather than the House of Commons as a collective body, really wanted.

On two other occasions there was uncertainty about who would become prime minister following the resignation of the incumbent. These uncertainties, however, had to do with internal party politics rather than the balance of forces in the Commons. Following the resignations of Eden in 1957 and Macmillan in 1963, the most obvious candidate (in both cases R.A. Butler) was not in fact chosen. On the second of these occasions, when Sir Alec Douglas-Home (as he eventually became) was the choice from the Byzantine process then used by the Conservative Party, there was still an element of doubt as to whether he would be able to form a government. In the event there was sufficient support for him among Conservative MPs to enable him to do so. Since the change in the Conservative Party rules in 1965, the process for choosing a new leader has been made much clearer (though, as the events surrounding Thatcher's fall in 1990 show, still with the capacity to provoke controversy).

The other transitions were achieved either quite peacefully by internal party decision – as when Eden succeeded Churchill and Callaghan succeeded Wilson – or at least by a clear party process – as when Major was chosen following the ousting of Thatcher.

It is extremely rare for the House directly to determine the fate of a prime minister; it did so in 1940 by its judgement on the Chamberlain administration, although even then it did not actually defeat the government of the day. Its real significance and power is less direct, for it contributes to impressions about the standing of prime ministers and about the need for change. This contribution can be explicit when criticism is voiced on the floor of the House, which is then usually transmitted outside and magnified by the media (witness the difficulties of Macmillan and Thatcher towards the end of their periods in office). Less directly still, criticisms voiced in Parliament may have an impact outside over a longer period as they come to form part of the background to the electorate's judgement at the next general election. The most immediate influence is exercised when the House of Commons performs its electoral college function and the majority party chooses not to support the existing prime minister in sufficient strength or, which is much more common, by seriously criticising government policy in party meetings, e.g. of the 1922 Committee or the Parliamentary Labour party.

Since 1945 only one prime minister, Callaghan, has suffered the ultimate sanction of having his period in office brought to an end by a vote of the House of Commons – in a vote of confidence in March 1979. The motion of confidence was precipitated by the failure of the plan for Scottish devolution to secure sufficient support in the referendum earlier that month. Callaghan had no alternative but to seek a dissolution and face a general election.

With Thatcher in 1990 it could be argued that proceedings in the House of Commons had contributed to her downfall, notably some intemperate observations by her on European matters and a dramatic resignation speech from Sir Geoffrey Howe. These events strengthened a growing view within her party that she would have to go. Her basic unpopularity with the electorate, particularly over the poll tax, meant that enough Conservative backbenchers feared for their own seats at the next election. In part this reflects a prime minister who stayed in office for an abnormally long time (perhaps with hindsight too long) and who was beginning to seem accident-prone, as with the resignations of Lawson and Howe. The preconditions for a challenge to her leadership were present in the political events outside Parliament. Howe's resignation speech helped to propel the candidacy of Heseltine, and this in turn led inexorably to the demonstration that her support within the Conservative Party in the Commons was insufficient. The critical point is that the *formal* decision about her premiership was taken by her own party and not by the House of Commons as a whole.

Four other prime ministers lost office as a result of the verdict of the electorate: Attlee in 1951, Home in 1964, Wilson in 1970 and Heath four years later. Of the other departures from the premiership, three are ascribable to ill-health in varying degrees: Churchill in 1955, Eden in 1957 and Macmillan in 1963. Of these it could be said that

Churchill's was overdue on grounds of age and that Eden's position had become untenable following the Suez adventure. Macmillan's popularity was also at a low ebb in 1963 following such events as the Profumo affair. In all these cases the House of Commons played no direct role, except in so far as its recomposition following a general election affected the balance of *parties* and hence the prime minister.

The only truly voluntary departure among postwar prime ministers is Harold Wilson's retirement in 1976. In four of the other cases impairment of the ability to lead the government effectively in Parliament played some part in the decision, while in one other (Callaghan) the voice of the Commons was tantamount to dismissal.

Prime ministers can strengthen their own hold on office by their timing of the dissolution of Parliament, which is an important aspect of their power. The convention has developed that the choice is theirs alone to make. Used well, as it was by Wilson in 1966 and by Thatcher in 1983 and 1987, it guarantees a further period of office; used badly it will be held against the prime minister responsible, as was Heath's dissolution of February 1974. Thus the fate of most prime ministers rests ultimately with the electorate rather than with Parliament.

Parliamentary Management

Parliamentary management is a major part of a prime minister's job, but it is an imprecise term and affected by a variety of influences. In essence it involves the ability of prime ministers to use the resources of the office to achieve their aims or avoid unpleasant outcomes. It covers such things as the work of the whips, the use of patronage and the maintenance of good relationships with backbenchers. It is affected by party culture, by the party balance in the Commons and by the prevailing patterns of behaviour among backbenchers.

The most important source of prime ministerial power is patronage in the form of posts in government. Since 1945 there has been a growth in the number of those whose careers are directly linked to office-holding. As Table 3.1 shows, the growth has been substantial, less at the top level of Cabinet posts than in the middle and the very bottom with the growth in the number of parliamentary private secretaries (PPSs) who, since the 1960s, have been treated increasingly as though they were unpaid members of the government. The result is that something like a third of the governing party's MPs are likely to have to demonstrate loyalty to the government since their career development depends greatly on such 'good behaviour'.[5]

5   P. Norton, *Does Parliament Matter?*, Harvester Wheatsheaf, 1993, p. 46.

Table 3.1. SIZE OF GOVERNMENTS, 1940–1989

	1940	1950	1960	1970	1980	1985	1989
Cabinet Ministers	9	18	19	21	22	22	22
Non-Cabinet Ministers	25	20	20	33	38	32	37
Junior Ministers	40	43	43	48	47	49	46
No. of MPs in paid government posts	58	68	65	85	86	83	83
No. of peers in paid government posts	16	13	17	17	21	20	21
Total paid government posts	74	81	82	102	107	103	105*
PPSs in Commons	25	27	36	30	28	21†	49
Total MPs involved in government	83	95	101	115	114	104	132

* Includes one minister not a member of either House.
† This figure is almost certainly an underestimate.
Source : D. Butler and G. Butler, *British Political Facts, 1900-1985*, Macmillan, 1986, p. 82; P. Norton, *The British Polity* (2nd edn), Longman, 1990, p. 210; P. Norton, *Does Parliament Matter?*, p. 46.

There are some differences between the parties in the degree of freedom which prime ministers initially possess in this area. Whereas Conservative prime ministers have no formal restriction on their appointments, Labour prime ministers in the past have had to pay some attention to the fact that in opposition the shadow cabinet is based on elections in the parliamentary party. While this constraint will be even stronger on future Labour prime ministers, the longer an individual, of whichever party, remains prime minister, the smaller are the constraints of past decisions imposed by others.

While the expansion of government posts as well as other types of patronage, such as political honours, may have enhanced the power of prime ministers, other changes have made the job of prime minister more difficult. Especially important has been the considerable change in the background and behaviour of MPs. The decline in numbers of the most obvious loyalists, elderly trade unionists on the Labour side and country squires and retired military officers among Conservatives, has made the job of the whips more difficult. This is partly because their replacements have been from backgrounds which make them much less likely to be blindly loyal, and more likely to question the wisdom of party policy and to believe that they should be in ministerial posts or at least participating in decisions, whether it be over the content of legislation or the choice of the Speaker. In short, MPs have become more professional and therefore less deferential.

Notwithstanding such changes, the major task of the whips in essence remains unchanged, being still to try to secure, through a mixture of sticks and carrots, support for prime ministers and their governments.

But they have also become the essential ears and eyes of prime ministers, advising them on the lower appointments. There remain differences between the parties, with the Conservatives retaining a great instinct of loyalty to the idea of leadership and the Labour Party conspicuously less deferential to its leaders. While this distinction between parties remains important (a difference unrelated to the passage of time) the Conservative instinct for loyalty, as Major has recognised, is not as strong as it once was. At the same time that MPs have become less amenable to appeals to loyalty, the perceived sanction of a possible government defeat and its consequences have been made less credible. The threat of dissolution, like that of a nuclear weapon, is as likely to destroy everyone's political ambitions as it is to punish only the critical. Thus the task of the government whips has become more difficult. Governments have to listen more to their followers, as the 1992-3 row over the pit closure programme indicates. What has become clear since 1972 is a new convention: that many defeats for governments need not threaten their existence. It is now generally accepted that a government need resign only if defeated on an issue of confidence. One of the consequences of this recognition has been to increase the freedom of government backbenchers to rebel without adverse consequences for their government. In that way the task of parliamentary management has been made more difficult.[6]

One of the most basic facts of life for prime ministers is the size of their majority in the House of Commons. Table 3.2, setting out the size of the government majority after each general election since 1945, shows the very obvious fact that there have been enormous variations in the apparent strength of a government's position in the Commons.

On five occasions prime ministers have been granted by the electorate majorities of a size that made them virtually immune from defeat in the Commons: Attlee in 1945, Macmillan in 1959, Wilson in 1966, and Thatcher in 1983 and 1987. However, their position proved to be less comfortable than those figures might suggest. Short of a massive rebellion by government backbenchers, it is inherently more likely that prime ministers enjoying a substantial majority will be able to enact their legislative programme. Certainly major legislative programmes were enacted, most obviously by the Attlee government after 1945 and by the Thatcher government after 1979. Yet, with the exception of Thatcher's 1983 majority, all were followed by either defeat at the next election or a much reduced majority and in several cases with the position of the prime minister having been much weakened in the mean time, as with Macmillan, Wilson and Thatcher after 1987.

---

6   Norton, *The Commons in Perspective*, p. 153.

Table 3.2. GOVERNMENT MAJORITIES IN THE
HOUSE OF COMMONS SINCE 1945

Election	Prime minister	Overall majority	Majority over next largest party
1945	Attlee	146	180
1950	Attlee	5	17
1951	Churchill/Eden	17	26
1955	Eden/Macmillan	58	67
1959	Macmillan/Douglas-Home	100	107
1964	Wilson	4	13
1966	Wilson	96	110
1970	Heath	30	47
1974 (Feb.)	Wilson	-33	4
1974 (Oct.)	Wilson/Callaghan	3	42
1979	Thatcher	43	70
1983	Thatcher	144	188
1987	Thatcher/Major	100	146
1992	Major	21	65

Source: Derived from D. Butler and G. Butler, *British Political Facts, 1900-1985.*

Furthermore, large majorities are no guarantee that prime ministers will be able to legislate as they please. The defeat in 1986 of the Shops (Sunday Trading) Bill, which would have liberalised the law on Sunday trading is the most extreme example of this, but the Wilson government was unable to enact its trade union reform plans in 1969, partly because of backbench opposition, while its legislation to reform the House of Lords also had to be abandoned. Large majorities mean, by definition, that defections cannot threaten the government; hence the constraint on criticism and defection is reduced. Once criticism then becomes explicit, it is difficult for a critic to recant and rejoin the government position without seriously offending individual credibility.

Nevertheless, any prime minister would prefer a large majority, whatever problems it brings, to a small one or none at all. Small majorities were given to Attlee in 1950 and Wilson in 1964 and October 1974. Of these the happiest experience was probably Wilson's after 1964. He was able to govern effectively, although some plans – like the renationalisation of steel – had to be delayed until a more secure majority was obtained. For backbenchers the cost of defaulting – possible defeat in a subsequent election – was greater than the benefit of holding stead-fastly to a position at variance with that of the leadership.

Before 1970 the only postwar prime ministers to suffer actual defeats in the House of Commons were those with tiny majorities: Attlee in

1950-1 and Wilson in 1964-6. The Attlee government was defeated on an adjournment motion at the end of a debate on fuel and power in March 1950, while Wilson suffered a reverse on an amendment to the Finance Bill in July 1965. Neither defeat was regarded as life-threatening. Of course there were numerous examples between 1945 and 1970 of prime ministers being *embarrassed* by their backbenchers; but that, important though it is in the medium term, is a different matter. The Attlee government had difficulties in 1947 over the National Service Bill, the Eden government over Suez in 1956 and Macmillan over the Profumo affair. Douglas-Home struggled to maintain his majority during the debates on the bill abolishing resale price maintenance, on one occasion winning by only a single vote. Apart from its problems over House of Lords and trade union reform, the Wilson government faced a considerable rebellion by its own supporters over the reintroduction of prescription charges in 1968.

The major change came after 1970. Although on paper Heath had a comfortable majority, he secured the second reading of the European Communities Bill in 1972 by only eight votes – admittedly it was a somewhat exceptional piece of legislation. Later the same year he was defeated on immigration rules and in 1973 on details of the Maplin Development Bill. Indeed, he suffered several defeats but held that they were not serious enough to require resignation.

The Wilson government of March 1974 was in a minority from the outset and during the short Parliament of that year suffered seventeen defeats.[7] However, in that Parliament, as Philip Norton has pointed out, 'Opposition parties ... avoided defeating the Government in the first three months of its life for fear of precipitating an early general election which they did not want.'[8] Between 1974 and 1979 the Wilson and Callaghan governments suffered a series of defeats. Initially Wilson had a very small overall majority, but what Table 3.2 does not show is that by 1977 this had evaporated. In March 1976 one of Wilson's last battles as prime minister was to secure reversal of a defeat on the government's expenditure plans by winning a vote of confidence.

The Callaghan period was more difficult. His government suffered a string of defeats on issues such as the Dock Work Regulation Bill, the guillotine resolution for the Scotland and Wales Bill, important clauses in the separate devolution legislation for Scotland and Wales, and the need for an enquiry into the Crown Agents. In 1977 he technically avoided defeat on his public expenditure proposals by the device of not contesting the division at the end of the debate. When this was

7   P. Norton, *Dissension in the House of Commons, 1974-1979*, Clarendon Press, 1980,
     p. 469.
8   P. Norton, 'Government defeats in the House of Commons: Myth and reality', *Public
     Law*, 1978, p. 377.

followed by a motion of censure from the Opposition, he was able to survive by devising a pact with the Liberals which lasted until the summer of 1978.

Thatcher always enjoyed considerable majorities in the Commons, especially after 1983. Even so, her majority on paper of 140 or more was not enough to avoid defeat on Sunday trading legislation in 1986. Less dramatic but still significant was the defeat on immigration rules in 1982. On many other matters the Thatcher government had an uncomfortable time: local government issues were a source of much discontent, including the ill-fated Community Charge. Proposals for changing the basis of support for students in higher education produced a rapid retreat, while the government came close to actual defeat over its acceptance of proposals for salary increases for senior public servants and over the introduction of charges for eye and dental checks.

In addition, all governments since the mid-1960s in particular have had to contend with a more activist House of Lords. Although defeat there cannot affect the life of a government, it can make for considerable difficulties. In the late 1960s the Wilson government found itself defeated in the Lords over Rhodesian sanctions, while in the 1970s the Labour government had to cope with sustained opposition from the Lords on bills dealing with the rights of trade unions and the nationalising of the aircraft and shipbuilding industries. At times, too, the Lords proved to be a thorn in Thatcher's side. In all, her governments were defeated in the Lords 156 times.[9] Many of these defeats were on minor matters but others were important; for example, on right-to-buy legislation, local government reform and, most remarkable of all, on the War Crimes Bill, which became the first piece of legislation to be forced through under the Parliament Acts since the 1949 Parliament Act itself and the first bill under a Conservative government ever to be so treated.[10]

A prime minister needs to keep an eye on the House of Lords. Twenty front bench spokesmen must be found from among its members to oversee the government's programme there and this has become a more demanding task as the chamber has increased in professionalism. Parliament *is* bicameral and prime ministers must manage the total institution. An effective performer in the House of Lords may be provided by an elevation from the lower House, but this has increasingly become something of a gamble, since by-elections have become so hazardous for governments. Following the 1983 general election Thatcher risked an immediate by-election in order to elevate Whitelaw, but the Con-

9   D. Shell, 'The House of Lords in context' in D. Shell and D. Beamish (eds), *The House of Lords at Work*, Clarendon Press, 1993, p. 13.
10   Shell, *The House of Lords at Work*, p. 6.

servative majority in Whitelaw's constituency fell from 15,000 to under 600. No prime minister since has felt free to take such a risk.

In seeking to secure their position in Parliament, prime ministers rely a great deal on their team of whips. It is important to see the whips as part of a two-way process of communication and not just as persuaders or dispensers of discipline. An important part of successful management is the ability to alert a prime minister to backbench feeling before it becomes a public embarrassment. To varying degrees, all prime ministers have to be capable of what Benemy calls the 'judicious retreat'.[11] Even Thatcher, who perhaps made more of a virtue of her unwillingness to compromise than most of her predecessors, knew that there were some situations where concessions were called for. Over such issues as the speed of trade union reform, the phasing-out of mortgage tax relief, grants for university students and her first clash with the National Union of Mineworkers over pit closures, she chose to back down. Earlier examples of the discreet adjustment of direction are Attlee's change of mind on the length of the conscription period in 1947 following party criticism and the Macmillan government's change of heart about amendments to the Rent Act in 1957.[12]

The extent to which backbenchers feel loyalty to their prime minister varies with their perception of the electoral popularity of that prime minister. It is significant that several prime ministers had much greater difficulty maintaining support once they became regarded as electoral liabilities rather than assets. To appreciate this one has only to compare the treatment of Macmillan in 1958–9 with that in 1962–3, Wilson in 1965–6 with 1968–9 or Thatcher in, say, 1983 or 1987 and her position in 1990.

Macmillan moved from being perceived as 'Supermac', who could brush off the resignation of his entire Treasury team as 'a little local difficulty', to the bedraggled figure who seemed unable to cope with economic problems or a series of scandals culminating in the Profumo affair and who suffered the humiliation of seeing his application to join the EEC rejected by de Gaulle. Wilson suffered a loss of reputation that was equally sudden. The apparently invincible leader of the 1964 and 1966 election campaigns was never held in such awe after the devaluation of November 1967. Before long he was suspecting plots to remove him from office and having to accept humiliation in the rejection of his plans for trade union reform. Thatcher took longer to suffer serious decline, but by 1990 she was widely perceived in her own party as a vote-loser. In the past even those in her party who did not like her personally had respected her ability to win elections

11　F.W.G. Benemy, *The Elected Monarch*, Harrap, 1965, p. 106.
12　P. Gordon Walker, *The Cabinet*, Cape, 1970, p. 64.

for them. She had survived earlier temporary unpopularity: over her economic policies in 1981 and, more dangerously, over Westland in 1986, when she herself had recognised the possibility of defeat.[13] Major too would recognise the fickleness of political popularity. In April 1992 he was praised for bringing off an unexpected election victory, but within a few months he was the embattled defender of policies perceived to be electorally unpopular and his competence as prime minister was being widely questioned.[14]

Electoral calculations are ever-present in politicians' minds. But the relationship between prime ministers and backbenchers is not always so crudely instrumental. Some prime ministers have simply been better at keeping in touch with their backbenchers than others. All the first four postwar Conservative prime ministers were to varying degrees what Kavanagh calls 'grandees'. Not only were they socially superior but all had emerged as prime ministers by a process that owed little to formal democracy. By the time he returned to office in 1951, Churchill was inevitably somewhat distant from most of his backbenchers. Of Macmillan it has been said that 'he was not aloof or completely remote from the rank and file, little though he had in common in tastes or life-style with the rising generation of middle-class Conservatives'.[15] He made the effort to mix occasionally with backbenchers in the smoking room or tea room of the Commons. The link between leaders and followers was carefully cultivated.

A major change came with the premiership of Heath. He was, by background and method of accession, very different from his predecessors and he lacked the social skills that might have helped him to cement relations with his backbenchers. Kavanagh puts it bluntly: 'Mr Heath was notorious for his remoteness from his backbenchers.'[16] Anthony King describes him as 'an aloof man, with little small talk and, so far as anyone could tell, no interest whatever in his fellow Tory MPs, let alone their wives and family. ... More important, Heath apparently did not realise that, in addition to being friendly with his supporters, it was in his interest to listen to what they had to say.'[17] The consequence of the distance was that, at times of crisis, he could not call upon a personal well of affection or respect. It reduced his political capital.

Part of Thatcher's initial success and popularity was because she

---

13   J. Barber, *The Prime Minister since 1945*, Blackwell, 1991, p. 57.
14   See, for example, W. Rees-Mogg, 'Major fails the leadership test', *The Times*, 10 May 1993.
15   K. Sainsbury, 'Harold Macmillan' in J.P. Mackintosh (ed.), *British Prime Ministers in the Twentieth Century*, vol. II, Weidenfeld and Nicolson, 1978, p. 121.
16   D. Kavanagh, *Thatcherism and British Politics* (2nd edn), Oxford University Press, 1990, p. 266.
17   A. King, *The British Prime Minister* (2nd edn), Macmillan, 1985, p. 100.

had observed her predecessor's style and was determined not to make the same mistakes. Of her fellow Conservative MPs she is recorded as saying: 'They elected you. They can un-elect you. Never lose touch with them.'[18] For a time she was conspicuously successful at maintaining contact with her backbenchers and being accessible to them. According to King, one of her boasts was that she had never refused a private meeting with a Conservative backbencher, in addition to being accessible in various places in the Commons.[19] Being accessible does not necessarily mean that the access is used. Indeed, the pressures on modern prime ministers make it almost impossible for them to mix casually and informally with their backbenchers and leave time for one-to-one meetings with them. James Barber notes: 'Although in her early days Thatcher had been seen regularly in the Commons tea room she lost the habit and it was an unusual event when she reappeared in November 1990, as she sought support in her campaign against Heseltine.'[20] In the end she was not sufficiently in touch with her backbenchers to survive. Partly this was due to the burdens of the office – so much greater than when Attlee was prime minister – and partly to the passage of time, which tends to distance chief executives from their more humble parliamentary colleagues.

On the Labour side there has always been a considerable understanding of the need to listen to the parliamentary party. Attlee, while not a grandee, was from an upper-middle-class background and less obviously gregarious than either Wilson or Callaghan. Although he was not exactly aloof, his efforts to mix with backbenchers informally were handicapped by his 'formidable taciturnity'.[21] Wilson's relations with his backbenchers underwent some considerable changes; initially he was very good although, as one observer points out, he had little feeling for the life of a backbencher because he had never been one.[22] His ability to keep in touch with backbenchers diminished after his re-election in 1966 as the government's troubles grew; and his 'dog licences' speech was hardly an exercise in backbench diplomacy. According to one well-placed observer, 'Wilson regarded the Parliamentary party as a body to be managed and sometimes he let his impatience, bordering on contempt, show very clearly.'[23] By his own confession, Wilson found less time for mixing with backbenchers after his return in 1974. By contrast

---

18 Ibid.
19 Ibid., p. 129.
20 Barber, *The Prime Minister since 1945*, p. 62.
21 Sainsbury in Mackintosh, *British Prime Ministers in the Twentieth Century*, vol. II, p. 121.
22 J.P. Mackintosh, 'Harold Wilson' in Mackintosh, *British Prime Ministers in the Twentieth Century*, vol. II, p. 202.
23 Ibid.

Callaghan, who had been a backbencher and retained his trade union links, was a much more relaxed figure and understood a great deal about how Labour backbenchers felt and operated. The personality and the experience of each prime minister colours relationships with parliamentary colleagues, but the need to keep in touch, and in favour, has remained unchanged for fifty years.

Prime ministers have to cope with a degree of organised factionalism among their parliamentary supporters. Labour prime ministers have suffered more over the years from this internal argumentation. From the Keep Left group of the 1940s through the Tribune group to the various campaign groups of the 1970s and 1980s. Labour leaders have been assailed by those who believed their leadership was insufficiently socialist. Although such groups could be an irritant to Labour premiers, they usually took care not to wound too seriously within the ambit of Parliament. However, it could be argued that the activities of the Campaign for Labour Party Democracy in the late 1970s and early 1980s, by their effect of driving out those who formed and joined the SDP and affecting the popular image of the Labour Party itself, contributed massively to the party's exclusion from office for the rest of the 1980s.

By contrast, for much of the postwar period Conservative prime ministers had less trouble with organised groups: in Rose's phrase, theirs was a party of tendencies rather than factions. Those groups that organised, like the Suez group of the mid-1950s, have had limited impact, although some, like the Monday Club, became influential at constituency level. Instead there have been sudden eruptions of opposition for Conservative prime ministers on individual issues – for example over the abolition of resale price maintenance in 1964, over Sunday trading in 1986 and over Europe from the 1960s onwards. Since the early 1980s, such a contrast stands up to scrutiny less well. Factionalism, while diminished within the Labour Party has been more conspicuous within the Conservative Party. Under both Thatcher and Major organised groups were more active. The Bruges group and the No Turning Back group made Major's life extremely difficult at times, and those opposing the Maastricht legislation represented perhaps the most serious internal challenge faced by any Conservative prime minister since 1945.

Backbench Conservative MPs have been more willing than their Labour counterparts to act on the biggest issue of all: the leadership of the party. This occurred both when the party was in opposition, as with the replacement of Douglas-Home and Heath, and when it was in government, as the departure of Thatcher showed. By contrast, the Labour Party, though often boisterous, has been much more reluctant to dispose of its leaders.

In both parties leaders, whether in government or not, will try to balance the pressures on intra-party views and avoid exacerbating whatever divisions exist among their backbenchers.[24] To help them do this, at least in government, leaders can use a combination of hope and fear. There will be hope for office and equally fear of doing anything that might bring serious disapproval, or be used to benefit political opponents. Once backbenchers lose a substantial measure of that hope and fear then a prime minister may be in trouble. Patronage is thus something of a two-edged sword. When used over parliamentary colleagues, it is of course an important part of the power of all post-war prime ministers; it has been rightly said that 'patronage is the most immediate and tangible resource that a prime minister can use to ensure loyalty within the governing party.'[25] As Table 3.1 shows, for prime ministers of both parties there has been an increase in the number of posts available to be filled. But used too extensively, especially when removing colleagues from office, a prime minister can so reduce the realistic opportunities that backbenchers, former ministers and convinced no-hopers alike have little to fear in seeking out an alternative. Electoral calculations and personal ambition then coincide to make revolt a realistic possibility.

Parliamentary Questions

Backbench revolt is exceptional. Prime ministers are kept accountable to the House of Commons most regularly and continuously in other ways. From the vantage point of the 1990s nothing better typifies this relationship between prime minister and the House of Commons than prime minister's question time. To be able to perform adequately there, and preferably to out-point the leader of the Opposition, is one of the major requirements of the contemporary prime minister. Increasingly since the early 1960s it has represented an opportunity for prime ministers to put their stamp on the news. At the same time it is a threat to them because it cannot be avoided and repeated failure to 'win' will have a demoralising effect on supporters inside and outside Parliament.

The intensity of the attention focused on the twice-weekly gladiatorial contests is one of the most dramatic changes in the prime ministership in the post-war period. The decisive change came in 1961, when questions to the prime minister were given a guaranteed slot in the House of Commons rota at 3.15 p.m. on Tuesdays and Thursdays. Before that

24   R. Rose, *The Problem of Party Government*, Penguin, 1976, p. 324.
25   R. Rose, 'British government: The job at the top' in R. Rose and E.N. Suleiman (eds), *Presidents and Prime Ministers*, American Enterprise Institute, Washington, DC, 1980, p. 4.

date, questions to the prime minister were not taken at a fixed time but at question No. 45 and then, for a brief period, at question No. 40. Questions could be put down to the prime minister for answer on any day except Friday. The change to regarding Tuesdays and Thursdays as the days on which the prime minister answered came quite accidentally in 1953: 'In deference to Mr Churchill after his illness in June 1953 the House accepted the arrangement that normally he would attend to answer questions only on Tuesdays and Thursdays, an arrangement continued by Mr Eden and Mr Macmillan without the same reason.'[26]

The change to a fixed slot in the timetable rather than relying on the uncertainty of whether Question No. 45 (or for a brief period in 1960–1, No. 40) would be reached has had a profound effect. From the premiership of Macmillan onwards prime minister's question time has become a centrepiece of parliamentary and public attention. The change was also partly a matter of personality. Macmillan appeared to revel in the occasion, although this may have been something of an illusion since he was in reality extremely anxious, appearances not-withstanding. Subsequent prime ministers have had no choice but to make the best of it. The clashes of Macmillan with Hugh Gaitskell and Wilson, Wilson with Heath, and Thatcher with Callaghan, Foot and Neil Kinnock have formed an important part of perceptions of political success since the early 1960s. Ability to compete in this form of political arm-wrestling is important for the morale, not just of the individuals concerned or their supporters in Parliament, but also for the party outside.

One result of the increase in attention given to prime minister's question time is the growth in the volume of questions tabled to the prime minister for oral answer. Despite gradually tightening restrictions surrounding the tabling of questions, there has nevertheless been a marked increase in their number. Immediately after 1945 relatively few questions were put down to the prime minister.

Until Mr Macmillan the prime minister had not been a major target at question time. Few saw much point in eliciting monosyllabic replies from Mr Attlee. A few eccentrics might regularly question Sir Winston Churchill, but most of his questions related to the narrow range of clear prime ministerial duties. Questions to Mr Macmillan grew in number and scope, and question time was the occasion for many verbal jousts between Mr Macmillan and Mr Gaitskell ...[27]

According to Chester and Bowring, writing in 1962, 476 questions

---

26   D.N. Chester and N. Bowring, *Questions in Parliament*, Clarendon Press, 1962, p. 163.

27   G.W. Jones, 'The prime minister and parliamentary questions', *Parliamentary Affairs*, vol. 26, 1973, pp. 262-3.

were addressed to the prime minister in the first post-war session (a
rather longer than average one): 'Since that session the number ... has
fluctuated from as low as about three per week in 1953-1954 to about
fifteen per week in 1958-1959.'[28] Obviously sessional totals of questions
are affected by variations in the length of sessions. However, for sessions
of normal length in the 1960s the total tabled to the prime minister
was around 1,200 each session (more than to any other minister); by
the early 1970s it was approaching 2,000. By the time the Procedure
Committee looked at the problem in the 1989-90 session, more than
13,000 questions for oral answer were being tabled to the prime minister
in each session. By then it was not simply that more were tabled to
the prime minister than to any other minister but, as the House of
Commons officer responsible pointed out in a memorandum to the Committee, the figure of over 13,000 represented 'well over 50 per cent
of the total of oral questions'.[29] He went on to note that on average
about 200 questions were on the Order Paper each Tuesday and Thursday.
He was able to look back to a previous Commons enquiry in 1971-2
when one of his predecessors had commented on 'the "startling" increase
from an average of 12.8 questions on the Order Paper in early 1970
to an average of 16.5 in early 1971'.[30] Contrasts with earlier years
were even more dramatic. In 1951 every question tabled to the prime
minister had been answered, while in 1961 the most that were tabled
for any one day to Macmillan was ten and they had all been answered.
The response by the Procedure Committee in 1990 was to recommend
that only a limited number of questions tabled to the prime minister
(and other ministers) should be printed. This was accepted by the Commons in October 1990.

The explosion in the volume of questions to the prime minister in
the course of the 1970s and especially the 1980s reflected a number
of factors, among them a change in the style of question, the greater
willingness of prime ministers to answer on any topic without seeking
to transfer questions to other ministers, and the growth of syndication
(the practice of MPs organising multiple entries of identical questions
to increase the chances of one of them drawing a high number on
the order paper).

For many years after 1945 the questions faced by prime ministers
were quite specific in their wording and prime ministers had a relatively
clear idea about topics on which they would answer, but since the
early or mid-1970s there has been a dramatic change in form of questions
to the prime minister. By the end of the 1980s the specific question

28   Chester and Bowring, *Questions in Parliament*, p. 162.
29   First Report from the Select Committee on Procedure, 1989-90, *Oral Questions*, HC
       379, Appendix 1, p. xiv.
30   Ibid.

had become the exception and nearly all were of a standard type. Three types became popular: these related to visits (for example, to a MP's constituency), meetings (for example, with bodies like the TUC or the CBI) and finally engagements.[31] By the end of the 1980s the clear winner as the standard question was asking the prime minister to list his or her engagements for the day in question. The first engagements question was asked in 1964-5 (although that related to the prime minister's future engagements) and the current style was first used in 1974-5.[32]

The advantages of this style were that it was immune to transfer to other ministers – although Thatcher in particular took pride in not transferring questions anyway – and it gave the questioner the widest possible freedom to ask whatever supplementary might be topical on the day it was asked if the MP had the good luck to be drawn high in the raffle. The fact that being able to ask a question inevitably became a lottery was both a reflection of, and a spur to, syndication.

With the growth of less specific questions to the prime minister there has been a much greater effort required by prime ministerial staff to try to discern what a questioner's supplementary might be about. Harold Wilson has given us a picture of the preparations that were involved in his period of office. This involved working through a substantial amount of material the night before each question time and a period of last-minute discussions at 2.30 p.m. on the day itself. These preparations involved 'the members of the Private Office, the Press Office and the ... PPS'.[33] Efforts were made to find out from government backbenchers the likely area of their supplementaries. The attempt to secure as many slots as possible for government backbenchers and feeding them with helpful topics is a logical extension of the process of trying to find out what backbenchers are likely to ask. According to one former Conservative MP writing in the late 1980s;

Government whips find out which Tory MPs are well placed on the list of questioners, enquire of Number 10 what Mrs Thatcher would like to be asked, and then give the backbencher the appropriate question. This excellent procedure ensures that nothing unexpected or embarrassing comes up, that the PM is able to give a series of mini-statements on subjects of her choice, and that she is always copiously briefed with just the facts and quotations she needs to fit the enquiry.[34]

In a sense the process described in that quotation is the logical conclusion of post-war developments. As far back as Churchill, elaborate

31   H. Irwin, A. Kennon, D. Natzler and R. Rogers, 'Evolving rules' in M. Franklin and P. Norton (eds), *Parliamentary Questions*, Clarendon Press, 1993, p. 54.
32   Ibid., p. 56.
33   H. Wilson, *The Governance of Britain*, Weidenfeld and Nicolson/Michael Joseph, 1976, p. 140.
34   M. Parris, 'Primed minister's question time', *The Times*, 28 April 1989.

care has been taken over prime ministerial replies to questions. Many of Churchill's replies were carefully prepared.[35] Macmillan understood the theatrical nature of question time; while of Wilson it has been said that at question time 'virtually all his key phrases and many of his apparently casual ones were carefully composed'.[36] His press secretary has described how 'off-the-cuff witticisms were invariably rehearsed at a gathering of private secretaries' and other close advisers.[37]

Questions to the prime minister in the course of the 1970s and 1980s became a much more organised and formalised part of the party battle. The degree of participation by the leader of the Opposition also increased. For example, the average of 1.6 supplementaries in 1967-8 had increased to 3.0 by 1987-8.[38] For the parties there was inevitably a desire to try to get as many as possible of the high-numbered slots. For Opposition MPs these represented a chance to put the prime minister on the defensive; for government backbenchers they were a chance to bowl slow full-tosses to the prime minister or to denigrate the ideas of the Opposition. The new convention, with its stylised adversarial format, in fact gave prime ministers an advantage since they always had the last word. Poor performances naturally negated such an advantage, but the balance of advantage clearly lay withe the prime minister.[39]

The process of preparation for question time is now an important part óf the work of the Downing Street staff. It provides an opportunity for the prime minister to discover what is happening in departments and, to that extent, it has played a part in strengthening the prime minister's influence in relation to departmental ministers.

With the increased emphasis on prime minister's question time has come greater physical and psychological stress. Macmillan has been described as formidable at question time;[40] yet we know that he was at times almost sick before it. Wilson suggests that 'no prime minister looks forward to "PQs" with anything but apprehension'.[41] One of his closest advisers has said: 'Even after thirty years in the House, Harold Wilson was still tense and nervous every time he waited to go on stage.'[42] Callaghan is recorded as having said that he hated question time as prime minister.[43] Thatcher, it is said, 'prepared

35   Chester and Bowring, *Questions in Parliament*, p. 242.
36   N. Shrapnel, *The Performers*, Constable, 1978, p. 47.
37   J. Haines, *The Politics of Power*, Cape, 1977, p. 11.
38   First Report from the Select Committee on Procedure, 1989-90, Appendix 5, p. xxii.
39   R.K. Alderman, 'The Leader of the Opposition and Prime Minister's Question Time', *Parliamentary Affairs*, vol. 45, 1992, pp. 66-76.
40   Shrapnel, *The Performers*, p. 31.
41   Wilson, *The Governance of Britain*, p. 132.
42   Haines, *The Politics of Power*, p. 11.
43   B. Redhead, 'James Callaghan' in J.P. Mackintosh, *British Prime Ministers in the Twentieth Century*, vol. II, p. 231.

meticulously and ate little before the ordeal' of prime minister's questions.[44]

Prime minister's question time has now become perceived very much as a test of individual ability; it is a highly personalised scrutiny of the performance of the prime minister and the Leader of the Opposition. In part these performances are understood as part of a parliamentary game. Normally, as Shrapnel has suggested, the hostility is merely acted, but in some cases it has seemed personal: 'When Heath and Wilson got up each Tuesday and Thursday for their question time bout, the parliamentary spectators were excited but also rather disconcerted to find that they meant it...'[45]

Along with the greater emphasis on that personal scrutiny has gone an increase in the level of organised barracking. This is part of a wider pattern of changing parliamentary behaviour with organised campaigns of heckling and other forms of interruption more prevalent. The arrival of radio broadcasting drew attention to this; however, fears that televising the House would lead to a further deterioration in behaviour have not been realised. The direct access to the public which these media offered thus affected behaviour as parliamentarians used every opportunity to create the impression of unity and virtue on their side and disunity and wrongheadedness on that of their opponents.

As with other aspects of prime ministerial behaviour, not only are there differences between postwar prime ministers in their success at question time but also differences in the perceived competence of the same individual at different times. One other obvious variable is that the test has changed: for Attlee, for instance question time, was very different from what it was for Thatcher. That said, some prime ministers were better at coping than others; there was little in his previous parliamentary experience that had prepared Douglas-Home for his jousting with Wilson. Yet even he, Barber argues, was more effective as prime minister than he was later in opposition.[46] The office itself, of course, conveys a certain authority at question time, but some prime ministers – notably at their peak Macmillan, Wilson and Thatcher – stand out as individuals who could dominate the House and their principal opponent in this style of play.

Precisely what is the major factor is more difficult to say. It has something to do with the advantages of office: 'Prime ministers have the advantages of being clothed in the robes of authority and backed by both the machinery of government and the majority party.'[47] Unless and until they are judged to be on the downward slide or as not being

44   Barber, *The Prime Minister since 1945*, p. 60.
45   Shrapnel, *The Performers*, p. 65.
46   Barber, *The Prime Minister since 1945*, pp. 56-7.
47   Ibid., p. 56.

up to the job they are likely to be perceived as powerful. This perception
is largely a self-fulfilling prophecy. Once the bubble has burst, however,
failure also feeds on itself. That simple but indefinable characteristic
of prime ministerial power has not changed in fifty years, nor does
it differ as between parties.

Debates and Statements

Although by the 1990s performance at question time had come to be
seen as the most important test of a prime minister's parliamentary
skill, other types of Commons activity had enjoyed greater emphasis
earlier. Chief among these are major speeches in debates, other interventions in debates and statements. Up until the Second World War,
it was usual for the prime minister also to be the leader of the House
of Commons, but throughout the period since then the job of leading
the Commons has been in the hands of a separate leader of the House.[47]
But, as Rose points out, 'The sacrifice by the prime minister of this
role because of exigencies of time has not reduced concern with parliamentary business.'[48] One consequence of the separation is that prime
ministers now spend less time in the House of Commons. Margach suggests:

Whereas Baldwin spent many hours each week listening to backbench MPs in
order to get a feel of what Parliament was thinking ... latter day premiers perform
their question time spots twice a week and then quickly disappear behind the
Speaker's chair, with few contacts with the mass of MPs.[49]

Compared with the twice-weekly participation in question time, other
prime ministerial participation in proceedings is relatively infrequent.
Writing at the end of the 1970s, Rose suggested that prime ministers
confined themselves to international affairs, economic affairs and the
business of government and were likely to participate less frequently
in formal debates than their senior colleagues or the leader of the Opposition. His assessment pointed to participation in an average of about
six debates a year and the making of a similar number of statements.[50]
The most systematic study of prime ministerial participation in Commons proceedings measured the level of such activity by all prime
ministers since 1868, and drew the general conclusion that prime ministers
have been less active in the House of Commons since 1940 than they
were before that date. Within the post-1940 period the conclusion is
that answering parliamentary questions is an 'activity more than four

---

47   Although both Attlee and Eden served as Leader of the House during the Second
     World War.
48   Rose, *Presidents and Prime Ministers*, p. 11.
49   J. Margach, *The Anatomy of Power*, W.H. Allen, 1979, p. 79.
50   Rose, *Presidents and Prime Ministers*, p. 16.

times as common as any other mode of parliamentary intervention by PMs'.[51]

According to this study, statements by prime ministers have been more common since than before 1940. Statements are also more significant. Whether that is *because* prime ministers make them or because the issue *requires* the prime minister to speak is a moot point. Before 1940 the average rate of statement-making was only once every eighty-two parliamentary sitting days, whereas since 1940 the average has been once every 13.5 sitting days. In the period covered in the study only Thatcher among postwar prime ministers made a statement less often than once every sixteen sitting days.[52] Up to the end of 1987-8 the rate for Thatcher was a statement on average every twenty-four sitting days. Of the other post-war premiers Eden and Wilson seem to have made statements most frequently, with Heath next to Thatcher at the other end of the scale.[53]

The average rate for making speeches since 1940 has been once every twenty-six sitting days, and only two post-war prime ministers depart substantially from this: Eden, who on average made a speech in the Commons once every fifteen days and, in the other direction, Thatcher who, at least up to the end of the 1987-8 session, was making a speech only once every forty-five sitting days.[54] This pattern became even more pronounced later: she made only one speech in the House in the 1988-9 session (in the debate on the Address in reply to the Queen's Speech at the start of the session). This change reflects a decline in the importance of the Commons as a centre of public debate – and an increase in the pressures of the prime minister's job, together with a growing reluctance to avoid unscripted situations. Possibly it also reflected an unease with the predominantly male atmosphere of the House of Commons and a sense that the level of bitterness had risen during her time in office.[55]

Apart from making speeches, prime ministers intervene in debates in smaller ways; they may interrupt other speakers or respond to points made by them. Here Dunleavy *et al.* find evidence that the most recent prime ministers in their study (Callaghan and Thatcher) were least likely to participate in this way. Whereas Hansard records interventions in debate on average once every eight to nine days for Churchill, Eden, Home and Heath, and for Attlee, Wilson and Macmillan between once every thirteen to seventeen days, the figure for Callaghan was once

51 P. Dunleavy, G.W. Jones and B. O'Leary, 'Prime ministers and the Commons: Patterns of behaviour, 1868 to 1987', *Public Administration*, vol. 68, 1990, p. 130.

52 Ibid. p. 131.

53 Ibid.

54 Ibid., p. 132.

55 Barber, *The Prime Minister since 1945*, p. 59.

every 34.5 days and for Thatcher (again up to the end of 1987-8) once
every 99.2 days.[56]

One of the conclusions reached by the authors of the study is:

> Before 1940 prime ministers were often multi-faceted parliamentary performers
> who would, for example, both make a speech in a debate and then intervene
> subsequently. But in the modern period PMs have tended to attend the Commons
> only for a set and specific purpose, especially the effectively mandatory prime
> minister's question time.[57]

The increased attention paid to prime minister's question time has had
the effect of making prime ministers less willing to expose themselves
at other times to Commons proceedings, a development enhanced by
other factors such as temperament and the sheer pressure of other business.

Statistical surveys have their limits. For example, in the study
described above, Thatcher emerges as the least active participant in
three out of the four categories of business among postwar prime ministers. There is clearly a discrepancy between the quantitative data and
the widespread perception of observers that she dominated the House
of Commons for much of the time that she was prime minister. There
is no necessary contradiction between these two pieces of evidence,
but they do suggest that the impact a prime minister has is a more
complex phenomenon. It is likely that possession of the confidence
of the Commons arises from external factors in addition to parliamentary
performance itself; thus an ability to handle the media, especially
television, success in the arts of news management and a perceived
dominance over cabinet colleagues all play their part.

One other aspect of debating and other skills that is not measured
by a quantitative approach is the extent to which these skills may be
crucial for survival. In a general way, as has already been remarked,
a good parliamentary performance by the prime minister is important
for the morale of backbenchers as well as for the standing of the party
outside Parliament. Sometimes it is the prime minister as an individual
whose judgement and character are being exposed to scrutiny. One
of the best examples of this is the debate on Westland in 1986, when
only a fighting performance by Thatcher, aided by what was perceived
as a poor speech by the leader of the Opposition, enabled her to dispel
any doubts about her ability to survive. Less successful was Macmillan's
response to the debate on Profumo in 1963 when, although he survived
the debate, he was wounded by it. The weakness of his performance
is reckoned by some observers to have been partly because the Opposition

56   Dunleavy, Jones and O'Leary, 'Prime ministers and the Commons: Patterns of
     behaviour, 1868 to 1987', p. 134.
57   Ibid., pp. 136-7.

decided to give him no opportunity to respond to interruptions by hearing him in complete silence.[58]

What has changed more than anything in this area in the postwar period is the personalisation of the office. Prime ministers have come to be seen as embodying all the virtues and vices of their party. The degree of attention – and in particular what might be called the 'tabloid' style of attention – has oversimplified praise and blame. Like England soccer managers and cricket captains, prime ministers have in 1990s the 1990s to endure a level of scrutiny largely unknown to their predecessors in the 1950s.

Parliamentary Style

It is commonly held that the effectiveness of a prime minister partly depends on ability to handle the House of Commons. This, as we have seen involves, the ability to cope particularly with the demands of prime minister's question time and to perform competently in debates. One observer speaks of the obligation on a prime minister to participate in debate and therefore for him or her to be an effective speaker.[59] Another suggests: 'A successful prime minister must firstly, since our system is a parliamentary one, be an able parliamentarian.'[60] This writer goes on to mention Macmillan's ability to dominate the House, arguing that he did so by aggressiveness in debate: 'He was not, like his predecessor Eden and his successor Home, one of those debaters who gains acceptance by a conscious courtesy towards the Opposition.'[61]

A further problem is that prime ministerial effectiveness varies with time and circumstance. Rose contrasts Attlee in 1951 and in 1945, and Churchill in his second administration and his first.[62] King makes a similar point: 'The badly battered Harold Wilson of 1967-1969 was a very different prime minister from the triumphal Wilson of 1964-1966, just as Eden post-Suez bore little resemblance to Eden pre-Suez.'[63] Others have noted that Wilson returned to office in 1974 with a much more experienced team of colleagues than he had begun with ten years earlier. In some degree this may explain the rather different parliamentary style he adopted after 1974, but a critical observer suggests: 'By the 1974-1976 government, Wilson had lost many of his skills in the House, his capacity to rally and comfort his supporters and to score off the

58   Shrapnel, *The Performers*, pp. 30-1.
59   B.E. Carter, *The Office of Prime Minister*, Faber and Faber, 1956, p. 267.
60   Sainsbury in Mackintosh, *British Prime Ministers in the Twentieth Century*, vol. II, p. 120.
61   Ibid.
62   Rose, *Presidents and Prime Ministers*, p. 44.
63   King, *The British Prime Minister*, pp. 6-7.

Opposition.'[64] It is suggested by the same observer that in this period his speeches became longer and were often boring.

These examples make the point that it is difficult to encapsulate with any accuracy the essential features of each postwar prime minister's style in handling the Commons. Attlee is of course legendary for his terseness in speech. A man of whom it was said that he would never use one syllable when none would do is unlikely to emerge as a great parliamentary performer. Moreover, his essential modesty enabled him to see himself as a cricket captain leading his team in the field rather than as a star player.[65]

No greater contrast could be imagined than that between Attlee and his successor. Opinions vary about the competence Churchill showed in his period of office after 1951. One view is that it was an anti-climax after the war years: 'His second premiership was an honour bestowed on him at the end of his career in recognition of his first, by which he will always be judged.'[66] Certainly he had the reputation and style to dominate the Commons; words like 'Olympian' tend to be used to describe his performances there. On the other hand, his increasing physical ailments were to cause problems. Not only was he becoming deaf, but in the judgement of one observer 'after October 1954 he lacked the physical and mental energy to do the job'.[67] Yet because of who he was, it was difficult to persuade him to give it up.

When Churchill did eventually retire, his long-designated successor, Eden, was immediately able to strengthen his position by calling an election and increasing his party's majority. However, despite this and his long political apprenticeship for the job, Eden proved less successful than might have been expected. He never mastered the House. This was partly because his experience had been almost entirely in overseas matters, and partly because of ill-health and ultimately policy misjudgements which caused his downfall. Margach speaks of the savagery with which the House of Commons treated Eden towards the end of his period in office. Once down, it is hard for a prime minister to regain that ascendancy which depends upon intangible qualities.

An important part of Macmillan's success was his ability to rally his party in the Commons after the disarray of the Suez fiasco. His combination of wit and style, his apparent unflappability and his capacity

---

64 Mackintosh, *British Prime Ministers in the Twentieth Century*, vol. II, p. 204.
65 Quoted in Margach, *The Anatomy of Power*, p. 4. For an analysis of Attlee's speaking style, see J.V. Jensen, 'Clement Attlee and twentieth century parliamentary speaking', *Parliamentary Affairs*, vol. 23, 1970, pp. 277-85.
66 P. Addison, 'Winston Churchill' in Mackintosh, *British Prime Ministers in the Twentieth Century*, vol. II, p. 34.
67 A. Seldon, 'The Churchill administration, 1951-1955' in P. Hennessy and A. Seldon (eds), *Ruling Performance*, Blackwell, 1987, p. 74.

for handling his political opponents all enabled him, for a time, to appear the dominant figure on the parliamentary scene. That image was reinforced by a large election victory in 1959. Yet within four years his reputation had been severely damaged. A combination of economic problems, failure in initiatives like seeking membership of the EEC, the evidence of prime ministerial panic and a series of security and other problems combined to make him vulnerable to attack in Parliament.

His successor, Douglas-Home, had not been a member of the House of Commons since 1951 and thus was unique among postwar premiers in that his immediate prior experience was in the Lords. Not only did this mean that he was unaccustomed to the rougher ways of the Commons, but the controversy surrounding his selection for the job meant that sections of his own party in Parliament were less than enthusiastic about him. He was chosen as prime minister for his ability to hold the party together rather than for his parliamentary skills; in this he compared unfavourably with his principal opponent, Wilson, who was at the height of his ability as a parliamentary performer.

In the event Home had the briefest tenure of all postwar prime ministers. Although Wilson won the 1964 election, the margin was small, but despite this, in the next eighteen months he was perhaps at his strongest as a prime minister. Not only could he dominate the House of Commons, but his experience was much greater than that of his parliamentary colleagues and his parliamentary skills were such that neither Home nor Heath was a match for him on the floor of the House. That dominance, however, became less pronounced as problems grew in the late 1960s. Moreover, when Wilson returned to office in 1974, he consciously embraced a different parliamentary style. In part this may have been due to exhaustion, something which affects nearly all prime ministers (although Thatcher seemed virtually immune from it); and in part it was related to the increased stature and confidence of his colleagues.

On the whole, Heath has not enjoyed a high reputation as a parliamentary performer. Some attribute this to his having spent his formative years in the House as a whip: 'After his promising maiden speech of 1950 he virtually never spoke again in the House for nine long years.'[68] In the view of one observer, he missed part of the training for being a successful parliamentary leader. His style as prime minister has been described as 'calm, cold, peremptory, unWilsonlike'.[69]

In contrast to Heath, no prime minister has had wider preparation for the office than Callaghan. His style as prime minister was relaxed and avuncular. Yet his personal skills were not enough to overcome

68   Shrapnel, *The Performers*, p. 57.
69   Ibid., p. 64.

the weakness of his party's parliamentary position. His period of office was dominated by economic problems and by his being in a minority in the Commons for the greater part of it. Ultimately success is measured by tangible achievements and failure follows basic policy weaknesses. Style can help accelerate the one and slow down the other; but it is no alternative to a good majority, a booming economy, and a healthy lead in the opinion polls.

The problems of the Callaghan government provided the opportunity for Thatcher's arrival in Downing Street. She had absorbed some of the lessons of Heath's shortcomings as a party leader and was determined to succeed in an office that had hitherto been a male preserve. Her rise to dominance in the Commons was aided by the weaknesses in her opponents. Despite his reputation as an orator, Foot was no match for her at question time, and for a while Kinnock lacked the experience to match her – oratory and missionary zeal being insufficient compensations.[70] Despite events like Westland and despite what some have seen as an increasingly bad-tempered Commons (reflecting the frustrations of the Opposition in their weak numerical position), she was able to demonstrate effective parliamentary ability.

Prime ministers have varied in the amount of interest they have shown in parliament as an institution. Clearly they have all been concerned about the outputs of parliament; getting their legislation through and ensuring their own survival have obviously been top priorities. To expect prime ministers to bend their minds to deep thought about parliamentary procedure might seem rather like expecting gamekeepers to devise tools and tactics for poachers. Such changes as have been made have usually been part of a tacit deal, with both government and backbenchers gaining benefits. Generally too the Opposition frontbench has displayed a greater affinity of interest with the government than with backbenchers.

Churchill loved the great parliamentary occasions. Nothing that detracted from the floor of the House found favour in his eyes. When the Commons chamber had to be rebuilt after wartime bombing, he spoke of the importance of there being 'on great occasions a sense of crowd and urgency'. Hence seats for only just over half the number of members were provided, 'lest nine-tenths of the Debates be conducted in the depressing atmosphere of an almost empty or half-empty chamber'.[71] Attlee too was a traditionalist, although he also recognised the need to reform certain aspects of the way the House worked to ensure the efficient despatch of business; hence the wider use of standing com-

70   P. Riddell, 'Cabinet and parliament' in D. Kavanagh and A. Seldon (eds), *The Thatcher Effect*, Oxford University Press, 1989, p. 113.
71   Churchill, House of Commons Debates, 1943, quoted in Robert Rhodes James, *An Introduction to the House of Commons*, Collins, 1961, p. 34.

mittees. Attempts at reform of the House of Lords foundered because insufficient agreement could be secured between the parties, but in its absence Attlee did curtail the powers of the upper House. Macmillan showed little interest in parliamentary reform. But when the House of Lords looked like withering away into total obscurity he introduced life peers, a simple and rather obvious reform, but one which conjured up no enthusiasm in either party. Significantly Macmillan himself never even mentions the subject in his own voluminous memoirs. Later, in 1963, it was the Macmillan government that brought in the Peerage Act, allowing hereditary peers to disclaim their peerages and thus be available to become – or remain – members of the Commons. Again this was more a matter of minimal change in order to conserve than the product of any prime ministerial aspiration for real reform.

Wilson stands out for his interest in parliament as an institution, but this was part of his wider obsession with institutional reform, mistakenly seen as a painless way to modernise the country. His appointment of Richard Crossman as leader of the House in 1966 heralded a period of reform. From the government's point of view, allowing the establishment of a couple of specialist select committees was a reasonable price to pay for getting most of the Finance Bill off the floor of the House (where it had hitherto been considered in its entirety). Furthermore, with a large Labour majority having brought into the House a whole new generation of younger, more professionally – minded MPs, creating a few more select committee places could be seen as one way to keep some of them occupied and out of mischief. Wilson and Crossman did initiate the most thorough attempt in the postwar period at reform of the House of Lords, securing the agreement of the Conservative frontbench to proposals embodied in legislation brought to parliament in 1969. But this ran aground in the House of Commons because of backbench opposition from both sides. Subsequently for most of the 1970s and 1980s the very idea that the two main parties might agree on a comprehensive scheme for Lords reform was laughably remote.

Heath, like Wilson, was a moderniser. He encouraged further reform of the Commons select committee system, replacing the Estimates Committee with the Expenditure committee, and extending the range of other select committees. Callaghan's preoccupations lay elsewhere, understandably given his government's parlous parliamentary condition. Thatcher claimed that she wanted to change everything, but parliament as an institution largely escaped 'handbagging'. Having sought to present the Conservatives as the party believing in the importance of parliamentary government in the 1970s, when Labour in office stood accused of abusing parliament, she was in a sense hoist on her own petard when the Conservatives gained power in 1979. Once Thatcher had put the party in opposition behind proposals for the introduction of a comprehensive new system of departmental select committees, it fell to Norman St John Stevas, her leader of the House, to hold her and a sceptical cabinet to this commitment. But other possible reforms were definitely relegated to the back-burner. Special standing committees, affording select committee-type consideration of government bills, were tried but quickly abandoned by a government either embarrassed at their effectiveness or at least worried by their potential to delay legislation which ministers always wanted to see enacted as speedily as possible. In the early 1980s some Conservatives pressed for reform of the House of Lords on the grounds that, if their party did not carry this through in a form that at least safeguarded bicameralism, then Labour when next returned to office would abolish the place altogether. But Thatcher had other priorities.

Her surprising opposition to televising the Commons in 1985 almost certainly delayed the entry of the cameras for four years. Perhaps it was the near-unanimity of Labour support for television that alerted her to its potential disadvantage for a party enjoying such a near-monopoly of support from the printed media. Her continued opposition proved unavailing in the next parliament, and regular coverage of the House began in late 1989. In other ways too Thatcher found herself overruled by the House, in particular over MPs' pay and allowances.

It is not easy to summarise the changing nature of the relationship between prime ministers and Parliament since 1945. One can point to significant variables: for example, the size of a prime minister's majority, the mood and degree of malleability of backbenchers. One can record the growing emphasis on prime minister's question time and the somewhat reduced role of other forms of parliamentary scrutiny. One can trace the vicissitudes of prime ministerial popularity which are likely both to reflect and be reflected in the prime minister's relationship with the House of Commons. We have seen, too, something of the variety of prime ministerial speaking styles: some unadorned and direct, others more high-flown. But do these elements add up to any kind of overall picture? How are we to summarise the changes that took place in the forty-five years between 1945 and 1990?

Certainly the patterns are not very clear. For example, all prime ministers have experience of the House of Commons before becoming prime minister, but the extent of that varies considerably. That period of training serves in principle to help prepare them for office. Of post-war prime ministers Home stands out in that his Commons experience was somewhat distant by the time he became prime minister. As we have seen, Heath's prior experience did not, in the view of some, entirely equip him for the role, while Eden's focus had been largely in overseas matters, although this proved no protection when the major crisis of his short administration arose.

Whatever the degree of their prior experience, prime ministers once in post have to cope with the Commons as best they can. It is important to their reputation to be able to 'handle' the House, and the consequence of failing to do so is likely to be the demoralisation of supporters inside and outside Parliament. That reputation may be slowly built up and is obviously assisted by the resources of office in the battles across the floor of the House. But, however carefully it is gained, such a reputation can also be lost; and it can be lost with remarkable speed. The fall in the reputation of such skilled performers as Macmillan and Wilson towards the end of their time in office was rapid. Others in Parliament may play their part in denting a prime ministerial image. The resignation speech of Howe in the autumn of 1990 played an important part in weakening Thatcher's position in the eyes of her party. Debate in Parliament can have an impact on opinion inside and outside Parliament, although it often does not.

The nature of these perceptions outside Parliament has been much changed by the rise since the late 1950s of the part played by television. From the time of Macmillan onwards, Parliament has had a rival for the attention of the nation. For much of this period it could be argued that television and, to a degree, radio have been more immediate as a source of political impressions than has Parliament. Colin Seymour-Ure's chapter examines this fundamental development in much more detail. Macmillan was the first prime minister to understand the importance of television and it is inconceivable that any prime minister could now be as indifferent to it as Attlee. Television has arguably had another effect on Parliament: that of bringing about a less deferential attitude to politicians on the part of interviewers and of thus contributing to a different way of looking at prime ministers.

Over the period since 1945 Parliament has suffered somewhat in the competition for attention. What is said there receives less attention than it once did – certainly it receives less coverage in the press. Television itself has become a rival, while interest groups for much of the postwar period often seemed to receive more attention than Parliament from ministers. Yet, for all the predictions about the decline of Parliament, it still has a potentially crucial role to play. No prime minister can avoid dealing with it, or being subject to critical examination in it. At the very least, prime ministers need support there to survive, and more than bare support if their tenure of office is to be either long or happy.

4

PRIME MINISTER AND WHITEHALL

Martin Burch

This chapter investigates the role of the prime minister as top government manager and co-ordinator. Its area of enquiry covers Whitehall, which can be broadly defined as consisting of those agencies at the central government level: namely, the departments of state and the staff (both ministers and civil servants) employed within them. In theory prime ministers are in a strong position in relation to Whitehall, but in practice their powers are limited by the scope and specialised nature of business, accepted procedures, political constraints and counter-balancing sources of power.

Underlying the analysis is a general problem concerning the exercise of policy influence by lay people in the modern state. Government today is both complex and specialised so that, to operate effectively, personnel require wide knowledge and a range of managerial skills. Given their general, non-specialist backgrounds, few party politicians in government are likely fully to possess such skills. This consideration is especially telling in the case of the prime minister who, by implication, is expected to show a measure of competence in a wide range of fields. This problem of competence is one that affects all chief executives, and on this point the prime minister is no exception.

In addition to this universal problem, prime ministers have to be able to overcome other difficulties in order to be effective, such as those involved in controlling their own ministers and allocating their limited time. Arguably the relations with Whitehall constitute one of the most constrained areas for the exercise of influence by the prime minister because the problems of competence and the sheer magnitude of business are compounded by the relative independence of departments, and the codes governing and traditions surrounding the work of the civil service. By contrast, the prime minister's relationship with other sets of institutions, such as party and cabinet, tend to be closer, more immediate and more easily mastered.

In dealing with Whitehall the general picture since 1945, nevertheless, is one in which the powers and resources of the prime minister have been extended. All the same, many with direct experience in government consider that these powers and resources still remain insufficient. They diagnose a weakness at the very centre of the state, the solution to which lies in enhancing the position of the prime minister by creating a fully fledged prime minister's department.[1] Certainly the powers that the prime minister holds in relation to Whitehall are limited. To put this point in some sort of perspective, it is helpful to begin by outlining the kinds of powers that a chief executive in a large organisation such as a business corporation might be expected to have. The contrast between such a person and a prime minister is marked.

There are at least five major sets of powers and resources that are usually invested in the chief executive of a large company. Taken together these provide considerable opportunities to exercise control. First, there is the power to hire and fire personnel through appointment and dismissal. This is an essential power. It means that the chief executive can shape the work of the organisation by placing the right people in the right posts and by removing those not performing adequately. Secondly, there is the power to require and receive full information about what is going on within the organisation. Knowledge is a key component of power, lack of it a major constraint. Thirdly, there is the power to monitor and examine the work of others. This is partly a function of information, but it extends beyond that to cover intervention and oversight. Fourthly, there is the power to shape the purpose of the organisation by setting objectives and priorities. Establishing the framework within which others are obliged to operate is an important ingredient of effective influence. Finally, there is the ultimate control over finance and its distribution between sub-sections of the organisation and those subordinates who manage them. Saying who can have what in terms of money, salaries and bonuses is an essential tool for the management of personnel. In order to make effective use of these powers, apart from personal qualities, a chief executive needs an efficient, loyal and effective personal staff.[2]

The British prime minister has powers in each of the first three areas – appointment, information and monitoring – but only to a limited extent. The power to set objectives must at some point be shared with others, while the prime minister has very little personal, direct control over the distribution of finance. Moreover, the prime minister has a relatively small personal staff and, while they are undoubtedly loyal and reliable, the sheer weight of business raises questions about their efficiency and effectiveness. In essence, the powers of the prime minister,

1　Kenneth Berrill, 'Strength at the centre: The case for a prime minister's department' in Anthony King (ed.), *The British Prime Minister* (2nd edn), Macmillan 1985; Lord Hunt of Tanworth, 'Contribution' in William Plowden (ed.), *Advising the Rulers*, Blackwell, Oxford, 1987, pp. 66-70.
2　Jeffrey Pfeffer, *Power in Organisations*, Pitman, 1981, chapter 4.

compared to those of a chief executive in industry, are limited in principle
and constrained in practice. Some of these constraints are built in to
the organisation of British central government and the ethos of administrative practice which pervades it. These impose four major sets
of limitations.

The first stems from the convention of collective responsibility. this
holds that ministers may disagree when discussing policy, but once
a decision is reached they must support it or resign.[3] This convention,
despite some breaches, has remained a constant factor throughout the
postwar period. It implies that in the British political system executive
power resides, at least partly, in a collective body, the cabinet, rather
than in a single individual, the prime minister. For how, feasibly, can
ministers be expected to concur in a decision if they do not feel themselves
a party to it? This both creates some uncertainty about the exact and
proper location of power in the British executive and highlights the
need to consult and involve others. Clearly this limits the freedom of
manoeuvre available to any prime minister.

Secondly, British central government is departmentalised. In theory
a 'prime minister's authority reaches into every department of state',[4]
yet in practice departments have a high degree of autonomy. This is
a tradition of British government, which is bolstered by the convention
that individual ministers are responsible to Parliament for the work
of their departments.[5] This tradition of autonomy helps to restrain the
extent to which any prime minister can justifiably and persistently intervene in the work of a particular department.

Thirdly, it is difficult for a prime minister to intervene in a department's
affairs for administrative reasons. Central government operates through
long-established routines which ensure that most of the information
and expertise concerning policy is either channelled through the departments or departmentally organised.[6] When specialist information and
expertise are brought into the collective system of the cabinet and its
committees, they are brought in from departments and are not usually
reconstructed at the central, core level. Moreover it is departments which
usually liaise with external interests and are the major repositories of
specialised knowledge. This means that the prime minister is still largely
dependent on departments for information and advice. Moreover this
reinforces the principle of departmental autonomy. When information
and advice are gathered together collectively, they not only have a

3   *Questions of Procedure for Ministers*, Cabinet Office, London, 1992, paragraphs 17
     and 18.
4   Rodney Brazier, *Constitutional Practice*, Clarendon Press, 1988, p. 84.
5   Sir Ivor Jennings, *Cabinet Government* (3rd edn), Cambridge University Press, 1959,
     pp. 177-99, 224.
6   Bernard Donoughue, *Prime Minister*, Cape, 1987, pp. 5-6.

departmental source but usually, outside a small range of policy issues that may be taken up by the prime minister, the particular department concerned will take the lead in the development of policy. Drafting a manifesto or developing a general theme within which departmental activities have to be placed may give party leaders greater influence. Certainly prime minister have long been conscious of this problem. The establishment of the Central Policy Review Staff was originally designed precisely to limit such departmentalism; Major's call to go 'back to basics' clearly originated from Number 10, although it is not clear whether that can accurately be described as a policy.

Finally, British central government has continuity in staffing. The overwhelming proportion of personnel are permanent, non-partisan, career civil servants; there are hardly any changes among these personnel when a new government or prime minister comes in. It is the ministers who may change, and it is in these positions that the prime minister's main power of appointment is vested.

So the main thrust of the argument pursued in the following pages is that Whitehall is a difficult and challenging area for prime ministerial influence. Simply because of the size, complexity and specialised nature of the tasks undertaken by the central administration, there are bound to be problems about any one single person significantly shaping such a large organisation. Moreover the effective powers vested in the office of the prime minister are not substantial compared to those of other types of chief executives in, say, business corporations. Indeed the more telling analogy would be with a chief executive running a group of companies, all enjoying a reasonable measure of autonomy. As a consequence, the powers of the prime minister have to be exercised with caution. And, while it is true that since 1945 the prime minister's resources have been enhanced, the complexity and difficulty of overseeing Whitehall have also increased. The effect is that although the position of the prime minister in a general sense *has* been enhanced, it still remains constrained *vis-à-vis* the departments. Moving from the general to the particular, there are significant sources of variation to be taken into account. Much depends on the style of the prime minister and the way he or she chooses to use the powers vested in the office and the opportunities which arise for exercising influence. The public perception is that the prime minister *is* the chief executive and chairman of the company, but the public's perception is inaccurate. For some prime ministers the analogy is more apposite than for others, but for all of them the problem of managing the departments has presented difficulties.

Certain powers concerning departments are usually accepted as being vested in the prime ministerial office. As is common in Britain, few powers are laid down in statute law; what the prime minister can or cannot do is a matter of accepted practice and convention. It is generally accepted that, as far as the immediate relations with departments are concerned, the prime minister can attempt to operate in two areas: through the appointment and dismissal of ministers and junior ministers, and through a measure of general oversight over the work carried out within them. The latter power is the less certain.

There are, however, limits on both of these areas of operation. Astute prime ministers who are determined to fulfil a leading role will attempt to overcome these limits, but much depends on circumstance. Prime ministers can only channel the exercise of their formal powers through the means available to them, notably through their ministers and the handling of these relationships by the prime minister's office and the Cabinet Office.

Exercising Influence through Ministers

In theory prime ministers can directly affect the work of departments through the appointment and dismissal of ministers. As with a company's chief executive, the power to hire and fire ministers is presumed to ensure that the right people are in place, i.e. those who share the same values and opinions as prime ministers or are dependent on their patronage. This power to place personnel is underpinned by the threat that, if ministers fail to keep in line, they might lose their jobs.

In practice all prime ministers attempt to shape their administrations in keeping with their personal and policy preferences. However, the extent to which they can do this is limited by the need to maintain a balance between different ideological strands within the party, the competence of ministers and powerful personalities within the cabinet. Some individuals with strong bases of support within the party will have to be accommodated with important ministries. These people may not be of the prime minister's persuasion or share the same outlook. Often they may be people who were themselves contenders for the leadership, such as Heseltine in Major's cabinet, Whitelaw in Thatcher's and George Brown in Wilson's first two administrations. Or they may have to be included because they represent an important section in the parliamentary party or were already well established figures in the party leadership by the time the prime minister first gained office. In fact, the appointment of ministers is best seen as a form of coalition building, reflecting in a more concentrated form the complex of forces that makes up the governing party.[7]

It matters also when the power of appointment is used. A prime

7   Michael Laver and N. Schofield, *Multiparty Government: The politics of coalition in Europe*, Oxford University Press, 1991.

minister has far more discretion in choosing ministers after being in office for some time or immediately after an election victory following a period in power than when taking office from a previous incumbent from the same party after a bruising leadership contest. When appointing her first cabinet in 1979, Thatcher was careful to include those, such as Ian Gilmour and James Prior, who were not of her policy persuasion. Only after a couple of years in power – and in particular after the 1983 General Election, when she became more secure in her position – did she begin a thorough re-casting of her ministry. And even then she was careful to maintain some balance between the various strands of party opinion. Her successor, Major, felt able to make only two changes in the membership of the cabinet when he formed his government in November 1990.[8] Later, following the general election victory in April 1992, he made no more than three dismissals from the cabinet, despite his enhanced status after a success which few had anticipated.

The effective prime minister has to work within these limits and exploit whatever advantage is available. The best way of doing this, given that a completely free choice is not to hand, is to ensure that people of a like mind hold the key portfolios in the policy areas with which the prime minister is most concerned. Thatcher did this in relation to the major economic ministries such as the Treasury and the Departments of Trade and Industry and, later, Employment. This allowed economic policy to be more easily shaped in keeping with her preferences by devolving work to the sub-cabinet level of committees and informal groups.[9] With the sole exception of Eden in foreign and defence policy, no other postwar prime minister hived off areas of policy from the oversight of cabinet as much as did Thatcher. Admittedly this was attempted from time to time by Attlee, Macmillan, Wilson, Heath and Callaghan, but never to the same extent.

Moreover, all prime ministers develop a variant of this technique at least with one or both of the two major offices of state, the Treasury and the Foreign Office. Here appointment is sometimes used as a means of influencing and intervening in the operation of these key departments. Yet such a strategy is not always effective. For it cannot be assumed that, once appointed, a minister will remain loyal to the viewpoint of the prime minister. Ministers can be colonised by their departments and, as it were, 'go native'. Or they may simply change their minds when faced with facts presented from a departmental perspective. There is nothing new in this; it is in the nature of cabinet government and the principle of collective responsibility.

8   D. McKie (ed.), *The Election: A voter's guide*, Fourth Estate, 1992, pp. 216-18.
9   Martin Burch, 'Mrs. Thatcher's approach to leadership in government', *Parliamentary Affairs*, vol. 36, 1983, pp. 399-416; Hugo Young, *One of Us* (2nd edn), Macmillan, 1991.

However, loyalty is assisted by the prime minister's power of dismissal. This, too, can be a blunt instrument and can only be exercised with prudence and if the circumstances are right. Too substantial a change of personnel suggests panic or an administration in difficulty. The classic case of over-reaction was Macmillan's dismissal of one-third of his cabinet in July 1962, which brought eleven backbenchers into his government. As Jones notes, his action 'did not enhance his position, rather it damaged an already fading reputation'.[10] Equally the dismissal or loss of ministers can have an indirect consequence by limiting the freedom of manoeuvre for removing ministers at a later date, and as a consequence strengthening the independence of the ministers remaining in the administration. The resignation of Lawson as chancellor of the exchequer in November 1989 after a badly executed ministerial re-shuffle in July and the subsequent resignations, for personal reasons, of Norman Fowler and Peter Walker in December 1989 and March 1990 respectively greatly restricted Thatcher's freedom to re-cast her cabinet thereafter and served to strengthen the positions of Douglas Hurd, the foreign secretary, and of Major, Lawson's successor as chancellor of the exchequer.

There is also the matter of the appointment of junior ministers. Again in theory these are in the gift of the prime minister, who in practice needs to take into account the same sort of considerations about party position and competence already mentioned in the case of cabinet ministers. There are, however, additional problems in appointing junior ministers, all of which are a restriction on the prime minister's discretion. A major difficulty is knowing who is available for appointment. Since the war the governing party has provided a pool of between 301 and 397 MPs from which most ministers have to be appointed. About fifteen are usually appointed from among government supporters in the Lords. The prime minister cannot know the strengths and weaknesses of all of these and will consequently take advice from cabinet colleagues and party managers, especially the chief whip and the deputy chief whip. This particularly applies to MPs being brought into the administration for the first time. Some MPs are automatically excluded on the grounds of either political position or personal behaviour or competence, but advancement is much helped if the whips' office views an aspiring MP positively. Unless a new party is coming into office after a general election victory, the room for choice will be constrained since about 100 MPs will already be in the administration. Even a prime minister coming into office straight from opposition will be bound to transform many of the members of the shadow administration into fully-fledged ministers. All of these factors serve to limit the pool of possible recruits.

10   George Jones, 'The prime minister's power' in Anthony King (ed.), *The British Prime Minister* (2nd edn), Macmillan, 1985, p. 210.

It is from among these serious contenders that prime ministers must attempt to select ministers compatible with their viewpoint, while ensuring that, in the interests of party management, the balance of forces within the party is also represented in the administration, both in senior and junior positions.

Two specific changes have taken place in the postwar period which are relevant to the prime minister's powers of appointment. First, the number of junior ministerial posts has doubled from thirty-two in 1945 to sixty-three at the time of writing. There has therefore been an increase in the government posts that are within the patronage of the prime minister. And secondly, there has been some change in the function of the most junior ministers in departments, the parliamentary under-secretaries, so that they fulfil a more independent administrative role with particular responsibilities delegated down to them. This emerged as an established pattern in the late 1960s and was very much developed by certain key secretaries of state during the Heath administration; notably Walker at the Department of the Environment and, later, at Trade and Industry.[11] The consequence of this for the exercise of prime ministerial influence has been to complicate further the line of potential command from the prime minister to departmental ministers through to the junior ministers. In some ways this change has tended to strengthen top departmental ministers in relation to prime ministers since they have a larger say in how responsibilities in their department are to be organised and how junior ministers are to relate to each other and to the work of the department.

Moving beyond hiring and firing, there are two further sets of factors relevant to the relationship between the departments and the prime minister. These concern the nature of the links between the prime minister and the departmental ministerial head after appointment – specifically, the prime minister's approach and that of the minister.

There is a wide variation in the extent to which particular prime ministers have attempted to intervene and oversee the work of departments. There is no set pattern or trend here; it very much depends on each person's style. Prime ministers can roughly be distinguished by whether they are delegators (allowing ministers to get on with the work of their departments), intervenors (getting involved in departmental business) or overseers (keeping a general check on departments). The third category may move into the intervention mode if things go wrong in the area covered by the department or if they become particularly interested in some aspect of the department's work. Attlee was a delegator, as is Major; and Thatcher was in the mould of the intervenor. Callaghan

11   Michael Heseltine, *Where There's a Will*, Hutchinson, 1987, p. 12; Kevin Theakston, *Junior Ministers in British Government*, Blackwell, 1987, pp. 86-7.

provides a good example of the overseer, and he in particular developed the practice of meeting each of his ministers individually about once a year specifically so that they could inform him of what was happening in their departments, what was planned for the the future, and whether they had any particular problems or difficulties.[12]

All prime ministers intervene to some extent, and there are variations in the policy areas in which they do so. Some intervene in a wide range of policy areas, others concentrate on one or two departments. Nearly all prime ministers, by the nature of their job (being, as it were, the *de facto* representative of the state abroad), have inevitably been drawn into Foreign Office matters and increasingly so through the development of European Community and international summitry.[13] Another clear trend over the postwar period has been greater prime ministerial involvement in economic policy questions. In his peacetime administration Churchill showed little interest in the economy. He was mainly concerned with defence and foreign relations, and in his lucid and active moments dominated his foreign secretary, Eden. When Eden succeeded as prime minister he in effect took over as foreign secretary, with disastrous results in the Suez adventure. While Attlee took some interest in economic policy, Macmillan was the first postwar prime minister to be actively and personally concerned with it.

The increasingly central importance of general economic policy to the success of a government has meant that the relationship between the prime minister and the chancellor of the exchequer is the key one in any government. Ideally it should be an agreeable partnership; when it is not, there are liable to be problems for either the government or the chancellor or for both. This was demonstrated in the awkward relations which developed between Major and his chancellor, Lamont, following the withdrawal of sterling from the European Exchange Rate Mechanism in September 1992. After some friction Lamont was sacked in May 1993 and the reverberations haunted Major for a long time thereafter. Likewise Thatcher and her chancellor, Lawson, became estranged. The result was a breakdown in co-ordinated economic policy-making and ultimately Lawson's resignation.[14] Macmillan suffered similar difficulties in his relations with his chancellor, Peter Thorneycroft. A difference of opinion on monetary policy and reflation resulted in the resignation of the entire team of Treasury ministers in January 1958. Thatcher, Heath and Macmillan were particularly prone to trying to direct their Treasury ministers, and the results were usually inharmonious

12   James Callaghan, *Time and Chance*, Collins, 1987, p. 408.
13   Hans Daalder, *Cabinet Reform in Britain*, Stanford University Press, 1963, p. 247; S. James, *British Cabinet Government*, Routledge, 1992, pp. 136-45. See also the chapter in this volume by J.M. Lee.
14   Nigel Lawson, *The View from No. 11*, Bantam, 1992, pp. 949-68.

since politicians who reach the position of chancellor of the exchequer are persons of confidence, ability and views of their own.

The extent of intervention is not a matter simply of prime ministerial style, but also of circumstances. Certain situations tend to encourage prime ministerial involvement. This happens especially when a policy area becomes a matter of great political and media interest, so that the prime minister will inevitably be drawn in if only to defend the reputation of the government. For example, the National Health Service became a major focus of media and public concern in the period following the 1987 general election. An ineffectual secretary of state for health, John Moore, failed to deal with the problem and a review was launched under the direct control of the prime minister. This resulted in the 1989 White Paper, *Working for Patients*, and the beginning of a comprehensive reform of health care.[15] Additionally, and for much the same reasons, if there are mistakes or policy errors by a department the prime minister may be inclined to get involved. Indeed, oversight of the work of a department is usually most easily achieved when something has gone badly wrong, for it is evidently departmental weakness which provides the most acceptable justification for the prime minister to act. Equally the prime minister is likely to be drawn in when a policy area becomes central to government strategy. This happened in 1969 when Wilson decided to seize hold of the reform of industrial relations, an intervention which led to the production of the ill-fated White Paper, *In Place of Strife*, and the defeat of the prime minister by other members of the cabinet.[16] Alternatively a prime minister may take a special interest in a particular policy area, as Callaghan did in 1976 when he launched a 'Great Debate' on education standards and curricula.[17] apart from these types of opportunity, prime ministers mostly tend to seek to balance forces and personnel so that their power is exercised at a distance, through negotiation rather than direct command.

Prime ministerial intervention involves a two-sided relationship, for while the prime minister's approach matters, so does that of the minister. Some ministers are more able and willing than others to resist the whims of their ostensible boss and maintain a measure of independence. Similar factors concerning the power-bases of particular ministers are at work here as they are when the prime minister's power of appointment is being exercised. There is the additional question of which issues will tend to be taken beyond the department and how much liaison is likely with the prime minister's office. The minister will not want to overburden Number 10, and in any case will be discouraged from

15   E. Griggs, 'The politics of health reform', *Political Quarterly*, vol. 62, no. 4, 1991, pp. 419-430.
16   Peter Jenkins, *The Battle of Downing Street*, Charles Knight, 1970.
17   Donoughue, *Prime Minister*, p. 111.

doing so by his own private office and by that of the prime minister. But much depends on the particular issue, especially if it is a matter of high saliency, has significant cross-departmental implications or is likely to have political repercussions.[18] There is a continual flow of gossip between the prime minister's private office and the ministers' private offices and the permanent secretaries who head each ministry on the official side. Through this Whitehall grapevine the areas of policy in which the prime minister is especially interested, soon become known and thus automatically attain a high priority in departments. The ability to set agendas is a significant power, much overlooked if the focus is merely on distant intervention or oversight.

Exercising Influence through the Prime Minister's Office

The development of a prime ministerial staff is one of the major changes which has taken place in the postwar period. The change is important but should not be exaggerated since the number of non-clerical staff in the prime minister's office is still in absolute terms small – twenty-four in 1993 as compared to seven in 1945.[19] In this period the prime minister's office has been consolidated, with the functions of its various parts becoming more clearly defined, and it has been recognised as a formal organisation within the structure of the central executive, and hence for the first time in 1977 given a separate entry in the *Civil Service Yearbook*.

At the time of writing, the prime minister's staff divides into four sections, each with a distinct task. Every section lies at the centre of a web of personnel fulfilling similar functions in the Whitehall departments. This network of informal contacts ensures that the prime minister's office is informed about what is happening and what is being discussed in departments. Moreover, the prime minister's office is one of the few organisations in central government which receives information from right across the government machine. The others are the top levels of the cabinet secretariat and the cabinet secretary's private office and, to a lesser extent, the Treasury, while a further channel of cross-departmental information is provided through the weekly meeting of all the civil service heads of department (the senior permanent secretaries) under the chairmanship of the secretary of the cabinet.[20] Thus some members of the prime minister's staff are able to gain a perspective on how

18   Martin Burch, 'Who organises what? The management of business in the British cabinet system', *Manchester Papers in Politics*, 3/90, Department of Government, University of Manchester, 1990, pp. 10-11.
19   George Jones, 'The United Kingdom' in William Plowden (ed.), *Advising the Rulers*, Blackwell, 1987, p. 45.
20   Burch, 'Who organises what?', p. 16.

the various parts of the Whitehall 'village' interconnect. They may not be particularly well informed about each and every part of it, but they do have a broad understanding of what is going on within their policy areas. In this sense the small size of the office is a clear advantage. It is the essence of Number 10 that it works in an informal and friendly way;[21] gossip is best communicated through face-to-face contacts, and therefore a small, well-integrated group is far more effective than a large-scale, formally organised bureau. These contacts not only assist the receipt of information but also provide the staff with opportunities to influence the flow of information around Whitehall and, by conditioning their perception of the world, to influence the work of the departments. It is also the source from which nearly all prime ministerial messages are sent out into Whitehall. As the number of issues addressed by government has increased beyond what any prime minister could hope to be aware of personally, the growth in staff has enabled Number 10 to keep in touch with departmental thinking to much the same extent as in 1945.

Of the four sections of the prime minister's office the two dealing with party and media relations are the least central to relationships with Whitehall. Indeed the political office, which deals with the prime minister's relations with the party in the country, has few formal, or frequent, contacts through into Whitehall. However, it does have connections with the whips' office. This is located next door in No. 12 Downing Street and it enjoys close and frequent contact with the prime minister, especially through the chief whip. The whips liaise with departmental ministers about the business coming up in departments. It has been an accepted procedure in Conservative governments, at least since 1970, that most members of the whips' office (ten out of fourteen at the time of writing) will be concerned with the business of one or more departments, and some secretaries of state (e.g. Walker and Heseltine) developed the practice of bringing them into departmental ministerial meetings so that they should be fully informed and aware of what was going on.[22] This information is often fed back to the prime minister's office. It also means that matters of concern to MPs of the governing party are channelled into the department at the highest level.

The prime minister's press office deals with media relations and has a staff of ten. Its links into Whitehall are maintained through the network of departmental information and press officers. Formal co-ordination is through a weekly meeting of all departmental heads of information, which meets on a Monday evening in the Cabinet Office. During Thatcher's tenure her chief press officer, Bernard Ingham, or

21   Douglas Hurd, *An End to Promises*, Collins, 1979, pp. 32-9.
22   Heseltine, *Where There's a Will*, p. 13.

his deputy usually presided over this meeting.[23] The presentation of business to the wider world is of course a major concern of government in the modern media age. The press section was first established on a substantial basis in 1945, although its roots go back to 1929, and it has slowly evolved to its present staffing level.[24] For Whitehall the major development was an effort throughout the Thatcher period to centralise the co-ordination of government information services either in the hands of one minister or later, from February 1989 onwards, under the control of Ingham. This constituted a considerable extension of influence by those close to the prime minister over the way in which departments presented themselves to the media.[25] Attempts to co-ordinate and control the government's media relations from the centre were tried under previous prime ministers, most notably Wilson. Thatcher's initiatives were more successful and marked a shift from established operating principles in that they involved the use of the information service in a more cross-departmental and, it must be said, party political way. The fall of Thatcher has meant a reversion to the practice whereby the head of the Government Information Service is no longer in the prime minister's office,[26] although effectively the centralising of day-to-day responsibility for press and media relations has remained.

The bulk of the relations between departments and the prime minister's office is conducted through the remaining two sections, the private office and the policy advisers. The private office is made up of career civil servants. They serve as the main formal channel through which the prime minister communicates with the departments. The office is nowadays staffed by five private secretaries headed by the prime minister's principal private secretary. These key personnel usually serve for a term of between two and three years before moving on to senior posts in the departments. The number of private secretaries has hardly changed since 1945 when it stood at four, but the work of the office has become more structured so that, apart from the principal private secretary, each secretary covers a particular area of prime ministerial business such as economic, home, overseas and parliamentary matters. These divisions closely mirror the organisation of the cabinet secretariat. One of the secretaries keeps the prime minister's diary and a further secretary, not located in the private office, deals with appointments. The principal private secretary oversees the Number 10 office and organises the submissions which go to the prime minister, thus fulfilling the important

23   Bernard Ingham, *Kill the Messenger*, Collins, London, 1991, pp. 184-5.
24   Colin Seymour-Ure, 'Prime minister's press secretary', *Contemporary Record*, vol. 3, no. 1, 1989, pp. 33-5. See also his chapter in this volume.
25   R. Harris, *Good and Faithful Servant*, Faber and Faber, 1991, p. 170.
26   M. Devereau, 'Do we need government information services?', *RIPA Report*, vol. 13, no. 1, 1992, pp. 1-2.

function of gatekeeper. According to Jones, the private office is the 'operations room of Number 10'. Its staff undertake a number of tasks on behalf of prime ministers, including organising their time and the flow of business and people who come before them, as well as briefing them on issues and developments and keeping notes about their meetings and conversations.[27]

In its role as the main channel of communication with Whitehall the private office performs two major functions. First, it selects and provides comments on the materials from the departments which go through to the prime minister. Secondly, it sends back to the departments the prime minister's views on issues. Where the first function is concerned, there are basically two sources from which material arises: from the Cabinet Office and directly from the ministers and departments. The private secretaries tend to select and comment on material which has come directly from the departments more than they do with material coming from the Cabinet Office. This is because the latter has already been filtered and commented upon. The prime minister's views are usually communicated back to departments, through a memo to the minister from the private office, but this is also done less formally through the grapevine connecting Number 10 with the private offices of ministers.

Heath saw himself as a manager and felt that he needed more independent advice than was provided by the traditional system of civil service networks. Therefore he set up in 1970 the Central Policy Review Staff (CPRS), which was designed to serve the cabinet as much as the prime minister. Wilson felt that he wanted something more immediately responsive to his needs and in 1974 set up the Policy Unit, although its antecedents can be traced back further. In the post-war period it had been common for prime ministers to bring into their office one or two advisers or confidants to provide policy opinions of a more personal or partisan nature than could be provided by the civil servants in the private office. For instance, Attlee brought in Douglas Jay, Churchill relied on Lord Cherwell, and Macmillan brought in John Wyndham. But this involved just particular individuals, whose functions varied enormously. They had little obvious impact on the work of the departments. The Policy Unit was more institutionalised and larger than these personal arrangements, and it was more sensitive to a prime minister's need than the Cabinet Office and its links.

The Policy Unit has developed close relations with Whitehall. The unit has always remained relatively small, with 8-9 full and part-time members under Wilson and Callaghan (1974-9). Initially, under Thatcher, it was cut back to a staff of about four, including one or two civil

---

27   Jones, *The United Kingdom*, p. 51.

servants. Following the abolition of the Central Policy Review Staff in 1983,[28] the Unit was expanded back to a complement of eight or nine staff, and under Major has grown to an establishment of thirteen. The role of the Unit in the broadest sense is to provide the prime minister with policy advice on papers as they are received in the prime minister's office. Under Wilson and Callaghan it concentrated on forward policy analysis over the medium to long term by commenting on the advice coming from departments.[29] It concentrated then on economic policy advice, since this tended to dominate the agenda of the Labour government.[30]

Under Thatcher the Policy Unit developed a far more interventionist role in relation to the work of the departments, especially after the Central Policy Review Staff, which was thought to have become too independent, was abolished. It attempted to monitor the government's main economic strategy and to 'pinpoint the implications for overall economic performance of departmental policy decisions'.[31] More significantly, it became proactive and served to originate new policy ideas and, if these were approved by the prime minister, to liaise with the departments to see if these ideas could be developed. This required working closely with departments, an essential characteristic of the Unit's approach after 1983.[32] It even attempted a general oversight of the work of departments, giving particular attention to those proposals which crossed departmental boundaries.

Policy Unit members gather information on what is going on in Whitehall by having access to the prime minister's papers in the private office and to information passed on through the Whitehall grapevine, especially through the network of special advisers attached to individual ministers.[33] These were another innovation brought in by Wilson in 1974, once again with the intention of providing a counterweight to civil service analysis and advice and, as in the American model, appointing officials whose loyalties lay with the minister rather than the department. Under Thatcher the number rose to about twenty, and they increased under Major to a total of thirty-two.[34]

During his first two administrations from 1964 to 1970 Wilson attached to his office two special advisers on economic matters, Thomas Balogh and Nicholas Kaldor, while George Wigg was involved as an adviser on security. These arrangements were initially very informal, and the

28   Tessa Blackstone and William Plowden, *Inside the Think Tank*, Heinemann, 1988, chapter 9.
29   Donoughue, *Prime Minister*, pp. 20 ff.
30   David Willetts, 'The role of the prime minister's Policy Unit', *Public Administration*, vol. 65, no. 4, 1987, p. 444.
31   Burch, 'Mrs Thatcher's approach to leadership in government', p. 407.
32   Willetts, 'The role of the prime minister's Policy Unit', p. 450.
33   Donoughue, *Prime Minister*.
34   PMS, *Parliamentary Companion*, no. 16, PMS Publications, London, 1993.

press dubbed these individuals, along with others in his political office, as the 'kitchen cabinet'. What Wilson did in 1974 was to formalise these arrangements to some extent by introducing the Policy Unit. Later Thatcher followed in the footsteps of Wilson Mark I by appointing a number of special advisers, especially on overseas and defence and economic policy. These had a free-standing position within the office and were drawn into the work of the Policy Unit on some issues, while on others they reported directly to the prime minister. Major continued this practice with advisers on foreign affairs and the efficiency of government operations.

Overall the size of the prime ministerial staff has grown over the postwar period, especially since 1974, and its relationship to the prime minister has grown closer. This represents an important change in the scale and disposition of the resources available to a prime minister, even though the numbers involved remain small. The main link of communication has remained the private office, which is marginally more structured in fulfilling its primary task of organising the flow of business into and out of Number 10. But the most notable change has been in the number and functions of advisory personnel. The significance of this change for the departments is that prime ministers are now more capable of knowing what is going on in Whitehall and of initiating policy from the centre. The input from the Policy Unit in particular has extended the ability of the prime minister to set an agenda and develop policy ideas, to oversee the general strategy of the government and, though to a lesser extent, to monitor the work of the departments.

Exercising Influence through the Cabinet Office

Since April 1992 the Cabinet Office has been divided into two main sections. One is the Office of Public Service and Science (OPSS). This is responsible for the Citizen's Charter, Major's first substantial policy initiative which sought to specify standards of service people could expect from a wide range of public authorities, and for the subsequent Charters dealing with specific public services. It is also responsible for civil service reform (including the 'Next Steps' programme) and science and technology policy. It is headed at the ministerial level by the Chancellor of the Duchy of Lancaster, who is a member of the cabinet and directly responsible to the prime minister. The other section is the cabinet secretariat, which consists of a series of sub-secretariats and is responsible for servicing the cabinet and its committees. In performing this function, it plays an important role in the relations between the departments and the central core of government.

The secretariat is under the direct management of the secretary of the cabinet – as, ostensibly, is the rest of the Cabinet Office – and about 100 of the 900 staff employed in the Cabinet Office are engaged in its work. There are five secretariats dealing with economic, home affairs and legislation, overseas and defence matters, European affairs and telecommunications. There is also a separate section dealing with intelligence and security matters. The first four secretariats are the most important, and these handle the substantial flow of papers coming into the cabinet and its committees from the individual departments and other sources. They are responsible for timetabling the business to be handled, setting agendas for discussion, organising committee meetings and recording the decisions of committees and cabinet. In order to fulfil these tasks the top officials in each section maintain a close connection with the relevant departments.

In theory the cabinet secretariats serve the cabinet as such and not the prime minister. However, since prime ministers appoint and chair the cabinet and some of its main committees, the secretariats are bound to work closely with and for them. Moreover, because of the close proximity of the Cabinet Office to that of the prime minister (they occupy the same group of buildings), there is a constant interchange between the two. Secretaries of the cabinet are often referred to as being the nearest approach to the prime minister's permanent secretary. They act as close advisers to prime ministers, briefing them on policy matters as well as the management of business. Under Thatcher it became the practice that the top officials heading some of the secretariats would liaise directly with the prime minister, rather than through the cabinet secretary, and so provide her with briefing on those policy areas for which they were responsible.[35] This practice has continued under Major, so that now the prime minister in effect has first call on the assistance of all the top members of the secretariat.

In the prime minister's relations with the departments, these senior secretariat officials fulfil three main tasks: they watch, they inform and they brief. They provide information about what business is being considered in the departments and is likely to come up to the cabinet system level, and they brief the prime minister on policy matters, especially those coming before cabinet and its committees. They will ensure that, if a matter is being raised in the departments about which they feel the prime minister should be aware, the information is passed on. The secretariats form the centre of yet another network of contacts with the departments. The need to have and maintain good relations is the very essence of the job, and this is one reason why nearly all

35 Anthony Seldon, 'The Cabinet Office and co-ordination', *Public Administration*, vol. 68, no. 1, 1990, pp. 105-6.

senior secretariat officials, other than the secretary of the cabinet, are on secondment from departments for two to three years.[36] No other minister, not even the chancellor of the exchequer, has such inside knowledge of what is happening in departments and no other minister can feed ideas and requests into the system as a prime minister can. It is through these secretariat officials that the pulse of departments can be measured and at times significantly affected.

Since the 1945–51 period of Labour government, the cabinet secretary has taken on the major role of providing handling briefs for prime ministers on the business coming before cabinet and the cabinet committees which they chair. In recent years this briefing function has also been carried out by the top personnel in charge of the secretariats. Such handling briefs are also provided for other committee chairmen. These aim to provide the prime minister and committee chairmen with an indication of what business needs to be covered in the meeting and on what items decisions need to be reached. The importance of these in the prime minister's relations with departments is that they give a summary of the various positions currently being advocated, the points at issue between different departments and any options that lie concealed in the papers submitted. This is one of the ways in which they provide the prime minister and other committee chairmen with detailed information about what is happening within the wider system of central government.

In addition to watching and informing on the work of departments, the secretariats also organise and manage the flow of business through the cabinet and its committees. Most important departmental matters that involve other departments, or are likely to require legislation, or relate to the central policies and strategy of the government will need to be taken beyond the department. These usually go into the cabinet system, although if they are essentially minor matters, they may be settled between the departments or through correspondence centred on one of the secretariats. When and how cross-departmental business is actually addressed is greatly influenced by the secretariats, especially those dealing with economic, home affairs and overseas and defence matters. They plan and schedule the order of business and control the distribution of information. The prime minister's office is centrally involved in this process and in theory this gives the prime minister influence over the flow and outcome of departmentally-inspired business once it enters the cabinet system.[37] Richard Crossman was a participant who argued that this was one of the main instruments of prime ministerial

---

36   J. Burnham and George Jones, 'Advising Margaret Thatcher: The prime minister's office and the Cabinet Office compared', *Political Studies*, vol. 41, no. 2, 1993, p. 307.

37   Donoughue, *Prime Minister*, p. 27.

power.[38] According to this view, prime ministers, through the secretariats, have an opportunity to slow down or hold back departmental initiatives by keeping them away from a point of formal decision such as the cabinet or one of its committees. This is a negative power and it is by no means always easy to exercise. The *potential* to manipulate the flow of business is certainly there, but the *opportunities* to alter this flow once it has gathered momentum and reached a relatively late stage in its development are limited. Power is closely related to skill. Thus, if prime ministers wish to intervene they must do so at an early stage in the process and probably ensure that the business goes to a committee which is chaired by them or is stacked with those likely to support them.

Finally, these secretariats record the decisions reached by the cabinet and its committees. These are based on the summing up of the chairman (the prime minister or another senior minister) and are regarded as binding on the departments. This is a position clearly laid down by Attlee in response to an independently minded minister; cabinet does not advise, it commands. In this nothing has changed since that first postwar government. The same principle applies to matters decided in cabinet committees. So the summing-up of the findings of a committee and the expression of these in the minutes is an important way in which prime ministers are able to exert a measure of control. Prime ministers will try to follow the views expressed at the meeting (there will be trouble if they do not), but their summing-up can shift the decision in favour of one faction or another at the margin.

The secretariat dealing with European affairs is also situated in the Cabinet Office, and as European affairs have become more important, the effect has been to enhance the significance of the central machinery of government. It is involved in the co-ordination of the sort of policy and information which by its very nature spans a number of departments. This enhancement has been mirrored in other areas as other aspects of cross-departmental policy have from time to time been brought within the confines of the Cabinet Office in the form of special units such as those dealing with devolution policy between 1974 and 1979 and inner cities and urban policy in the 1980s. The trend from the late 1950s on has been to draw more functions into the Cabinet Office, some temporarily but others on a more established footing. An early development was the transfer of the Joint Intelligence Committee in 1957 from the Chiefs of Staff. This was followed by the establishment of the Cabinet's Overseas and Defence Committee in 1963 after the creation of a federal Ministry of Defence.[39] In the early years of the

38   Richard Crossman, *Inside View*, Cape, 1972, pp. 55-75.
39   J.M. Lee, 'The ethos of the Cabinet Office', *Public Administration*, vol. 68, no. 2, 1990, p. 236.

1964-70 Labour governments the economic secretariat was created, and by 1968 the Cabinet Office had emerged as an institution clearly separate from the Treasury in its establishment and financing.[40]

This expansion in function and organisation was further extended in the 1970s and 1980s. The European secretariat was established in 1973, while the bringing together of security and intelligence information continued apace as further responsibilities were transferred from the Ministry of Defence and the Foreign and Home Offices. At much the same time, the lead responsibility for emergency planning in relation to internal unrest and war was shifted from the Home Office. The advisory and co-ordinating machinery to cover science and technology questions began to emerge on a significant scale in the early 1970s in the form of a Science and Technology group, and from 1982 this was expanded into a science and technology secretariat.[41] From 1982, responsibility for the oversight of the government's internal efficiency programme (the Financial Management Initiative), which covers each department, was placed in the Cabinet Office – as from 1988, was responsibility for the hiving-off of departmental functions into executive agencies according to the 'Next Steps' initiative, so called after the title of the 1988 Report prepared by Sir Robin Ibbs, Thatcher's adviser on efficiency, which had recommended this major change. In 1992 these responsibilities for efficiency and civil service reform were reorganised within the Cabinet Office and placed in the Office of Public Service and Science, which also absorbed the science and technology secretariat.

From these changes, it is clear that the cross-departmental nature of government business and those functions involving departmental oversight have expanded. Overall the trend has clearly been towards strengthening the position of the Cabinet Office *vis-à-vis* the departments and consequently enhancing the position of those players at the very centre of government – prime ministers and the officials and aides who serve them. Small though each individual change may be, the cumulative effect over time has been centralisation. The managing director of the group has restructured the lines of responsibility so that many more important matters must pass through the central office.

The development of the functions of the Cabinet Office has been accompanied by two further major changes affecting the relationship between the prime minister and departments. First, there has been a gradual extension and more thorough organisation of the management of the flow of business.

40   J.M. Lee, 'Central capability and established practice: The changing character of the "centre of the machine" in British cabinet government' in Brian Chapman and Alan Potter (eds), *WJMM: Political Questions*, Manchester University Press, 1974, p. 165.

41   P. Gummett, 'History, development and organisation of UK science and technology up to 1982' in R. Nicholson, C. Cunningham and P. Gummett (eds), *Science and Technology in the United Kingdom*, Longmans, 1991, pp. 23-5.

This took place particularly when Sir John Hunt was cabinet secretary and involved the much more extensive planning and organisation of business over a three-to six-month timescale. In order to achieve this, secretariat officials have become more organised in discovering what departments are doing and encouraging the flow of business according to timetables set at the centre.[42] Secondly, the secretariat has extended its information net by establishing the practice of seconding top officials from departments. All this has meant a strengthening of the Cabinet Office facilities on which the prime minister is able to draw.

As with the prime minister's office, the crucial staff involved in the Cabinet Office are small in number, but they are at the very centre of one of the main information networks in Whitehall. This facility to gather information – together with the ability to fulfil cross-departmental functions, the opportunity to influence departmental agendas, and the provision of advice on policy and departmental matters – has been greatly developed since 1945. All this leaves modern prime ministers, in their dealings with the departments, with much more extended sources of information and advice than they had in the immediate postwar period.

Departmental Structure and Administration

Two sets of powers concerning the management of departments and the civil service are now accepted as being vested in the office of prime minister. First, the prime minister can alter the structure and function of departments, through either the creation of new departments or the amalgamation or winding-up of old ones. The prime minister can transfer functions from one department to another, although this change sometimes requires legislation; the Lord Chancellor's Department is a case in point.[43] Secondly, as first lord of the Treasury and, since 1968, minister for the civil service, the prime minister has broad responsibility for civil service affairs. This includes the general administration and organisation of the civil service, including the approval of the appointment of the permanent official heads of departments. These formal powers are not absolute. They depend most obviously on the approach of the prime minister but they depend also on the precise circumstances of the moment. The overall postwar trend, however, has been towards strengthening these powers.

The power to restructure departments has not been extensively used

---

42   Burch, 'Who organises what?', p. 16.
43   H. Street and R. Brazier, *Constitutional and Administrative Law*, Penguin Books, 1986, p. 178.

by prime ministers of their own volition. Most changes in departmental structures and functions have been more determined by the requirements of government or an incoming administration's policy programme than by the whims of particular prime ministers. As King has pointed out, changes by an incoming government are usually a product of party pressure.[44] For instance, on entering office in 1964 the Labour government created the Department of Economic Affairs in fulfilment of a party commitment. Likewise in 1970 the Heath government abolished some of the ministries established under the previous Labour administration and created a number of large, amalgamated 'super ministries'. Although Heath was personally interested in the structure of government, these changes were in keeping with the party's programme.[45] This move towards larger, combined departments has been a trend throughout the period since the 1960s, beginning with the amalgamation in 1964 of the Admiralty, the War Office and the Air Ministry into the Ministry of Defence. These 'super ministries' have included the Foreign and Commonwealth Office (created in 1968), the Department of Health and Social Security (created in 1968 and split in 1988), the Department of the Environment (1970) and the Department of Trade and Industry (1970). The last-named was split in 1974 and re-merged in 1983, the Department of Energy having been created from it in 1974. In turn, the Department of Energy was abolished in 1992 and the Department of Trade and Industry expanded. While such changes may usually reflect the requirements of government, here again party positions can play a part. Wilson's creation of the DEA was occasioned in part by the need to give George Brown a major role, while Thatcher's treatment of the Department of Health and Social Security owed much to the failure of John Moore.

Prime ministers have tended to take the lead in restructuring departments and redistributing functions when it suited their tactical requirements in cabinet or cabinet committee to recruit an extra minister of a particular persuasion. This was the case with Callaghan's creation of a separate Department of Transport with a seat in the cabinet in 1976. So in general the prime minister's power to restructure departments is usually only applied to a limited extent. This is an area where change is always expensive, complex and time-consuming and is not undertaken lightly.

There is, however, one aspect of the management of departments in which the position of the prime minister has been considerably strengthened in recent years, namely internal efficiency. This matter was raised in the report of the Fulton Committee on the civil service

44 Anthony King, 'Margaret Thatcher as political leader' in Robert Skidelsky (ed.), *Thatcherism*, Chatto and Windus, 1987, p. 53.
45 David Howell, *A New Style of Government*, Conservative Political Centre, London, 1970.

in 1968 which proposed 'in the interests of efficiency' that accountable units with defined objectives be established in each department.[46] It also led Wilson to create the Civil Service Department under the prime minister's control. This was an important accretion to prime ministerial functions and had consequences for both the operation of the civil service and the internal management of departments.

The drive for efficiency was taken up by the Heath government under a system called Programme Analysis and Review (PAR). This had little effect on the internal operation of departments, partly because the programme was colonised by their civil servants and partly because throughout the 1970s it was not given a strong enough lead from the centre.[47] The major alteration in relationships came during the Thatcher administrations and in particular with the introduction of an efficiency policy run from the centre, in the form initially of one-off investigations into departmental activity (the so-called 'Rayner Scrutinies') and later of an integrated programme involving all departments under the general heading of the Financial Management Initiative (FMI). These are important developments from the point of view of prime ministerial influence over Whitehall and constitute one of the changes in the balance of power between the prime minister and the departments that Thatcher institutionalised and bequeathed to her successor.

The Rayner Scrutinies involved the creation of an Efficiency Unit connected to the prime minister's office. At first this was under the control of Sir Derek Rayner who, with a small team, had the task of examining particular areas of departmental administration and investigating whether the work being undertaken was necessary and, if it were found to be so, whether it was being done effectively at a reasonable cost. These one-off evaluations were limited in scope and intermittent in terms of their application; they did not amount to a comprehensive programme. In 1982 the Financial Management Initiative (FMI) was launched: this was centred upon the Efficiency Unit and required all departments to develop some means of measuring and evaluating performance in relation to aims and costs with the expectation that performance would in time be related to staff remuneration and career development. In effect the FMI works not only as a system to encourage efficient practices in departments but also as a means of gathering information at the centre – in the cabinet and the prime minister's offices. The involvement of these central institutions in the process of managing and evaluating departmental performance served to extend the opportunities available to the prime minister for influencing

---

46   Lord Fulton, *The Civil Service,* vol. 1: *Report,* Cmnd, 3638, HMSO, London, 1968, p. 105.

47   A. Gray and W. Jenkins, *Administrative Politics in British Government,* Wheatsheaf, 1985, pp. 104-14.

management practices in Whitehall. The result has been to strengthen the core elements of government in relation to the departments, especially in management and information gathering.

Organisation and Operation of the Civil Service

The prime minister's responsibility for the overall management and operation of the civil service is potentially the most important of the functions that provide an opportunity to influence the work of Whitehall. Yet none of the prime ministers in the period up to the mid-1960s actively exploited this power in practice. All delegated the responsibility directly to others and the effective administration of the civil service was left largely to the top civil servants. However, the trend since then has been for prime ministers and other ministers to be drawn more closely into the way the service works. This growing concern with civil service matters has been accompanied by shifts in the distribution of responsibility for the civil service so as to bring it closer to the central core of the executive and closer to the potential surveillance of the prime minister. At the same time prime ministers have become more interventionist in these matters – most evidently under Thatcher, although the shift in disposition began before her time and the opportunities which she exploited were at least partly the result of changes made by her predecessors. The upshot has been a centralising of the function of administering the civil service and a reassertion of a measure of political and ministerial control over bureaucrats. The development of this position can be examined in relation to three areas of prime ministerial involvement in civil service matters: the general management of the civil service, the appointment of top officials and the scope and operation of the service itself.

Formal responsibility for the civil service was brought closer to the core of government and the prime minister following the proposals of the Fulton Committee in 1968. Since 1920, overall responsibility for the civil service had rested with the Treasury, but in 1968 the management of the civil service was transferred to a newly-created Civil Service Department. At the same time the prime minister was designated as the minister for the civil service, although this position was actually delegated to a junior minister.

In 1981 the Civil Service Department was wound up and the responsibility for personnel and pay were returned to the Treasury. However, responsibility for the organisation, management, recruitment, training and overall efficiency of the civil service went to the Cabinet Office in the form of a Management and Personnel Office. At the same time the cabinet secretary became joint head of the Home Civil Service along with the permanent secretary to the Treasury.[48] Later, in 1983, the cabinet secretary became sole head of the Home Civil Service, a position that had also been held by the cabinet secretaries between 1956 and 1962, although at that time the office and the functions were maintained within the Treasury. In 1987 the Management and Personnel Office itself was disbanded. Its responsibility for civil service pay and conditions of service were restored to the Treasury, but the rest of its functions were transferred to a new Office of Minister for the Civil Service attached to the Cabinet Office. In 1992 these functions were placed in the Office of Public Service and Science (OPSS) within the Cabinet Office. Despite a return of some functions to the Treasury, all this has resulted in a strengthening of control over the civil service in the core executive, especially within the Cabinet Office and in the person of the secretary of the cabinet and the cabinet minister responsible for OPSS. The effect has been to bring the lines of control and administration much closer to the prime minister than previously.

Of more immediate policy relevance is the opportunity to appoint top officials in the departments. The practices for prime ministerial approval of top civil service appointments were established in 1920. Since then the prime minister's consent has been required for the appointment or removal of permanent and deputy secretaries, principal establishment officers (in charge of personnel in a department) and principal finance officers (in charge of expenditures in a department). The procedure is that recommendations, usually of two or three names, are placed before the prime minister by the head of the Home Civil Service, who is assisted in making these recommendations by a senior appointments committee composed mainly of permanent secretaries. The limited nature of the list means that civil servants still strongly influence the shaping of the choice. Nevertheless it gives the prime minister some potential to shape the working of departments by choosing not only the ministers that run the organisations but also the top officials.

This potential is constrained in several ways. The same considerations as apply to the appointment of junior ministers are relevant, especially the need to choose competent personnel and to balance the requirements and requests of the ministers heading each department. More pertinently, the power of dismissal is seldom exercised by prime ministers; if action is to be taken, an opportunity in the form of a retirement usually has to arise. Finally, prime ministers cannot know in any detail the full range of talent that is available for appointment within the civil service, and are therefore bound to be dependent on others for advice. Yet a prime minister will necessarily form judgements about those senior members of the civil service with whom contact will have been made, and the final choice will often be imbued by personal experience and evaluation. It is clear that Thatcher often operated in this way.

For these reasons prime ministers' potential influence in this area is somewhat diluted in practice. Most prime ministers in any case have seemed not to want to become too closely involved in the overall business of appointment and have usually accepted the names and advice given to them. The oft-quoted exception here is Thatcher, who tended to take a more substantial interest in these matters than her predecessors. She also encouraged the early retirement of some civil servants, notably the permanent secretary of the Civil Service Department and his deputy before the abolition of the department in 1981.[49] Thatcher benefited from being in office for a long time, over eleven years, and thus more appointments naturally arose during her period. As it happened, because of the age profile of the top civil service a whole generation retired during these years and thus opened up the opportunity for intervention more than had been possible for her predecessors. Hennessy has calculated that between 1975 and 1983 forty-three permanent secretaries and 138 deputy secretaries retired, representing almost a complete turnover in these top two grades.[50]

It is clear that Thatcher enjoyed greater opportunity than her predecessors to exercise her powers over the appointment of top civil servants, but what is not clear is the extent to which, in practice, she exploited the opportunities available to her. Of the twenty-four senior departmental permanent secretaries in post in 1989 only two – Sir Peter Middleton at the Treasury and Sir Clive Whitmore at Defence – could, arguably, have been given their posts because of her favour. But on the other hand both were high-flyers and were likely to become permanent secretaries at some stage. If Thatcher exercised an influence, it was much more in conditioning the way in which the short list for a senior appointment was drawn up. One major change in procedure was that more names were submitted. In addition the qualities the prime minister was seeking were well known, and therefore some candidates may have been excluded at an early stage. These qualities certainly did not include the individual candidate's party political persuasion, which would not necessarily have been known or been overtly relevant; rather, it was managerial flair and energy that were being sought. Thatcher's aim was to shift the attitudes of civil servants towards a greater concern with efficient management and thus to alter the administrative culture of Whitehall. Whether by judiciously influencing the choice of senior officials she had this effect remains an open question.

The prime minister's power of appointment is in reality somewhat

49   Peter Hennessy, *Whitehall*, Fontana, 1990, p. 604.
50   Hennessy, *Whitehall*, p. 635.

restricted. In addition to points already considered, a major limitation is the tradition of a neutral civil service able to serve a government of any political colour. Thatcher may have been more active than her predecessors, but not to the point of undermining this principle. Had she done so – and this was technically possible – the outcry would probably have been overwhelming. This illustrates well not only the indeterminate character of conventions (nobody knows how far she could have pushed her authority in this area before political forces would have stopped her) but also the limitations on the growth of a presidential culture.

As the minister mainly responsible for the civil service, the prime minister potentially has a considerable impact on both its size and its organisation. However, few prime ministers have chosen to exercise this power, preferring to delegate it to a junior minister. Thatcher and Major are the exceptions. Partly this is because the effective centralisation of this function close to the prime minister's office only fully crystalised in the 1960s and partly because most prime ministers since then have either avoided or failed to push through significant reforms of the civil service.

Of the five prime ministers since the mid-1960s, Wilson and Heath were the most interested in the machinery of government questions,[51] yet both did little to alter the general staffing levels and organisation of the civil service. Admittedly the Fulton Report led to a restructuring of its administration in 1968 but, although this brought some important changes, the radical thrust of the proposals was in fact blunted and, some argue, undermined by the civil service itself.[52] Indeed one factor ensuring the limited success of the proposals (apart from the ill thought-out and impractical nature of some of them) was that the prime minister did not push the reforms vigorously enough. Heath's initiatives, especially Programme Analysis and Review (PAR), implied a considerable change in the work habits and administrative values of civil servants, but in effect the programme was colonised and stymied within the departments. It lacked strong oversight and continued thrust from the centre. Both Wilson and Heath had been civil servants and both had some sympathy with the nature and approach to problems that had become established. Heath in particular relied increasingly on his top civil servants for advice and support, especially on Sir William Armstrong, then head of the civil service. On the other hand, while sceptical of the influence of certain departments, especially the Treasury, Callaghan was not much taken up with civil service questions. His three-year period in office

51   Howell, *A New Style of Government*; Christopher Pollitt, *Manipulating the Machine*, Geo. Allen and Unwin, 1984.
52   Peter Kellner and Lord Crowther-Hunt, *The Civil Servants: An enquiry into Britain's ruling class*, Macdonald, 1980, Chapter 5.

was dominated by economic issues and the problem of running the government initially with a small parliamentary majority and later with none. Thatcher shared few of her predecessors' inhibitions. She felt uneasy with the style and culture of the top civil service, which emphasised policy advice rather than the implementation of proposals and the efficient management of state organisations. Moreover, her party was committed in an explicit way, unlike her predecessors, to rolling back the state and cutting out 'waste' in the public sector. The obvious implication of this was that the number of civil servants would be cut. This was achieved in dramatic fashion during her period in office with the personnel of the civil service being cut by 24 per cent from 730,000 to 550,000. About one-fifth of this drop in numbers was a result of privatisation, but the remainder was achieved through increased efficiency and discontinuing functions.

As well as decreasing staffing levels Thatcher also initiated significant changes in general organisation. The most important reform was proposed by the Efficiency Unit. In 1988 Sir Robin Ibbs, the prime minister's efficiency adviser, produced a 'Report to the Prime Minister', usually referred to as the 'Next Steps', which formed the basis of a new approach. Basically it involved a reorganisation of government so that tasks concerning the delivery of state services would be separated from policy functions into agencies headed by chief executives who, within policy and resource frameworks set by departments, had considerable powers over their own internal management, including pay, grading and recruitment.[53]

While initiated under Thatcher these reforms were substantially carried out under the premiership of Major. By April 1994, 112 agencies covering more than 67 per cent of civil servants had been created. The plan is that by 1998 78 per cent of civil service personnel will be employed through executive agencies. And in the long term, beyond the year 2000, the aim is to cover 95 per cent of the civil service, leaving around 20,000-25,000 civil servants directly employed by the ministries.[54] Moreover, since Thatcher's departure, the package of reforms has been extended to include a series of Citizens' Charters covering some of the main public services and a programme of 'market testing' or contracting out of some civil service functions to the private sector. All these reforms are being carried out under he auspices of the Office of Public Service and Science in the Cabinet Office. These changes certainly constitute the most important restructuring of the civil service in peace time since the Northcote-Trevelyan reforms in the latter part of the last century. What is involved is no less than a change in the

53 *Improving Management in Government: The next steps*, The Efficiency Unit, HMSO, London, 1988.
54 *The Best Future for Britain: The Conservative Manifesto 1992*, Conservative Central Office, London, 1992.

nature of the state, from being a service provider to having a more contractual and regulatory role.[55]

Overall, there have been important changes in the management of the civil service as a consequence of direct prime ministerial involvement over recent years. The Thatcher/Major reforms are a clear and dramatic example of the influence of the prime minister over the operation of Whitehall. The powers to carry out such substantial changes had been accruing over some years, but the opportunity and the will were lacking. The latter point is important, for Thatcher was determined that change be initiated and Major that it be carried through. It was both the intent and the commitment that distinguished her and her successor from other prime ministers.

The picture of change over the postwar period in the relationship between the prime minister and the government machine is one of both persistence and transformation. The evidence of continuity lies in the attempt to influence departments through the powers of appointment and dismissal. Almost the same considerations of accommodating powerful and talented candidates and producing a balanced administration apply now as applied in 1945. Equally, the over-dramatic use of the power to fire personnel can now, as it did in previous decades, greatly limit the subsequent freedom of manoeuvre of the prime minister. The ability of a prime minister to gain departmental compliance through appointment is still as problematic as it has ever been. The increase in the number of junior ministers has not solved the problem, but rather complicated it.

Change is more evident in the staff, information and advisory resources available to the prime minister. Here there has been an important extension in the prime minister's ability to know what is going on in departments and to have a view about it. The source of this enhancement is the development of the prime minister's office and the cabinet secretariat and the closer identity of the latter with the prime minister. These changes began in the 1960s and were significantly extended in the 1970s. The development of the machinery at the centre means that, in comparison to prime ministers before the 1960s, the opportunities available to the modern prime minister to intervene in departmental work are more substantial. Yet departmental work remains intricate and complex, so that these enhanced opportunities may still be insufficient for the prime minister to acquire adequate knowledge of all that is going on in a department.

By contrast, the prime minister's power to restructure the scope and

---

55   N. Lewis, 'The Citizen's Charter and the Next Steps: A new way of governing', *Political Quarterly*, vol. 64, no. 3, 1993, pp. 316-26.

functions of departments is very much a function of administrative considerations. The time this would take and the disruption it would cause remain significant constraints on what a prime minister may choose to do. Apart from the odd bit of tinkering to ensure the political balance of the government, changes in departmental functions need to be backed up by some administrative rationale and/or party commitment, and such opportunities seldom arise. They usually reflect changes in the general perception of what governments should be doing or in response to dramatic changes in the broader context. Hence the creation of the Department of the Environment reflected new thinking on the economies of scale to be had from larger organisations as well as a growing concern with matters affecting the environment generally. Equally, privatisation throughout the 1980s resulted in the inevitable decision that the Department of Energy was no longer justifiable. So the logical outcome of previously adopted policies can lead to the restructuring of departments.

On the management of civil service personnel and their work practices, the postwar period reveals a drawing together of powers and opportunities at the core of central government – another trend which has gained momentum since the 1960s. The least exercisable of these powers is that concerning the appointment of top civil service personnel. This is constrained by both the limited choices placed before the prime minister and the exigencies of staff turnover. However, as minister for the civil service the prime minister, has greatly extended opportunities to shape the manner and means whereby tasks are carried out in Whitehall. Evidence of this is the development of the Financial Management Initiative and the 'Next Steps' programme. Both emanated from personnel and advisers at the very centre of government.

Overall, the post-war trend, particularly since the 1960s, has been a strengthening of the central institutions in relation to the departments. The prime minister is at the centre of this web. However, while the centre has been strengthened, it is notable that there remain significant limitations on the extent of potential prime ministerial influence – not least the principle of departmental autonomy, which remains at the centre of the system, even though it has been compromised at the margins. However, the reforms envisaged in the 'Next Steps' programme seem almost certain to involve a radical reassessment of this relationship. A number of options will certainly be opened up. For instance, the whole range of departments as at present constituted may not be justified in a slimmed-down system. Also, a smaller cabinet could become workable, while divestment of management responsibilities should leave ministries with more time to develop longer-term policy – requiring, in turn, more overt co-ordination and leadership from the centre. These matters will certainly need to be settled in the later 1990s. In the mean time we can say that in the Whitehall game over the postwar period the hand of prime ministers has been strengthened, although it does not follow that these enhanced opportunities will be exploited. Much depends on circumstances and, even if these are favourable, on the will and ability of the individual holding the office. Some individuals may not choose to act, whole others may lack the ability to do so successfully.

It matters greatly what particular individuals make of the opportunities available to them. An obvious example of a vigorous and radical approach to government and to policy innovation was Thatcher, who tended to exploit her position and the powers established in her office. In matters concerning departments, she fell into the category of an interventionist rather than a delegator or overseer. Others, like Callaghan and Wilson, chose a different style and approach. However, Thatcher's more aggressive style was by no means always successful. She often did not get her way and in addition to her achievements, her interventionist tendency led to the development of a number of ill-thought-out initiatives, such as the 'community charge' or poll tax, the social and economic cost of which made it one of the worst policy decisions carried through by any postwar government.

The characteristics of individual incumbents are, however, played out in a wider context of economic, social and political forces which condition their responses and shape the circumstances which determine whether an opportunity to take action arises. The example of the package of management reforms contained in the Financial Management Initiative, and later the 'Next Steps' programme is instructive. Similar proposals originated by the Fulton Committee in 1967 failed to be realised, partly because of a lack of strong political support at the very centre of government. But the failure of Fulton and the successful implementation of the 1980s reforms do not simply demonstrate variations in prime ministerial purpose. By the 1980s lessons had been learned from the Fulton failure; top civil servants were far more sympathetic to change, and the idea of efficiency in government was more widely accepted among experts and commentators. In other words, the climate of opinion both *within* the civil service and *outside* it had become more sympathetic to the reform agenda. Coupled with this was an important change in the general perception of the nature of the state as being over-extended and a burden on economic development. This conventional wisdom in turn reflected the economic constraints which followed the rise in energy prices from 1973 onwards. The latter had an international impact, and governments throughout the developed world increasingly sought means of limiting state spending. So the approach to the management of government in the 1980s can be seen as partly a consequence of the desire to seek expenditure constraint, a concern developed and partly institutionalised under the 1976-9 Labour government which was then extended by its Conservative successor. The Thatcher government both reflected and benefited from changes in the climate of opinion among significant commentators and intellectual leaders. These shifts in perception helped to justify and provide an opportunity for the important policy innovations encapsulated in the Financial Management Initiative and the 'Next Steps'.

As well as personality and the opportunities provided by underlying events, attention should also be directed to the nature of the party political power-base on which prime ministers and ministers rely. Labour and Conservative administrations operate quite differently. Conservative ministers tend to accept more readily the status and authority of prime ministers and are more likely to see themselves as serving their wishes and objectives. This partly reflects the philosophy of organisation associated with the Conservative Party, emphasising the leader as the central and commanding point in the party's power structure. By contrast, Labour ministers tend rather to stress the limits on the leader and the role of the leadership group and its sensitivity to wider party interests. Consequently an interventionist prime minister is likely to be far more acceptable to a Conservative cabinet than to a Labour one. For Labour the tradition of departmental autonomy is underlined and strengthened by party traditions.

Beyond party, a major factor determining the gradual strengthening of the prime minister's position in relation to Whitehall has been administrative necessity. Not only has the business of government grown more complex in the postwar period, but the amount of cross-departmental business has also increased, making necessary both an extension and a refinement of the co-ordinatory elements at the centre. An initial impetus to this was the need to integrate overseas and defence policy in the light of changing commitments following the withdrawal from Empire. The machinery to achieve this began to emerge at Cabinet Office level in the early 1960s. Thereafter, the acceptance of the growing importance of economic policy demanded a more coherent approach, and the attempt to join the European Community and subsequent membership of it required that some means be found of uniting European issues across the field of government. These requirements partly explain the expansion in the functions of the core executive since the 1960s. And this demand for more effective co-ordination also required an extension in the advisory resources available to personnel at the centre, including the prime minster. These changes, coupled with a growing concern with the management function of the civil service, meant that some extension of core institutions was unavoidable.

In sum, the picture that emerges over the post-war period is of an extended and strengthened position for core institutions in relation to the departments. The position of the prime minister, being at the very centre, has benefited from this change. However, the system still remains to a large extent departmentally based, and in dealing with Whitehall the prime minister has to accommodate and balance the forces involved. While opportunities to exploit the machinery have grown, they are still constrained and the prime minister is more characteristically in the position of a bargainer rather than of a leader enjoying a significant power of command. Compared to those of a company chief executive in business, the prime minister's powers remain partial and limited. Whether the reforms currently being implemented will alter this situation, only time can tell.

5

PRIME MINISTERS AND THEIR PARTIES

Donald Shell

British politics is above all party politics. In their cohesiveness, their programmatic character, their ongoing national organisation and their team spirit British political parties are the dominant institutions of the political system. Wherever the activity of politics arises, party is not far away. Local government, health authorities, even school governing bodies and the management of sport, all these and many bodies besides, if not directly caught up in the party political struggle, nevertheless feel the pervasive influence of party politics. Those who call for this or that activity to be 'taken out of politics' are invariably pleading for it to be taken out of party politics. While organised groups with concerns that impinge on politics may try to avoid close or continuing identification with one political party or another, all must operate in a context in which public debate is dominated by competitive party politics.

This remains true despite some evidence pointing to the decline of parties. Their hold over the electorate has weakened in recent years; party membership has fallen and the proportion of the electorate who identify strongly with a particular party has diminished. Pressure groups have gained at the expense of parties. In the 1970s talk of the corporate state highlighted the more prominent role being accorded to organised groups of all kinds in articulating and aggregating interests within the political system. But experience of the 1980s would suggest that, whatever other forces may be helping to set the agenda of government, party still makes a difference.[1] And certainly in recruiting and socialising people into political roles, parties remain predominant.

Party leaders are the key figures within parties, and modern prime ministers are first and foremost party leaders. They owe their office to two vital achievements: first, they have forced their way to the pinnacle of power within their own party; and secondly, their party has emerged ahead of any rival in the most recent general election. To retain office prime ministers must overcome any challenge mounted to their party

---

1   See Richard Rose, *Do Parties Make a Difference?* (2nd edn), Macmillan, 1984. For a general introduction to contemporary parties, see Richard Garner and Richard Kelly, *British Political Parties Today*, Manchester University Press, 1993.

leadership and must lead their party to victory at the polls. Parties and leaders are therefore immensely important to each other. Leaders need the continuing support of their parties, and in their leader parties find their greatest single asset – or handicap. The leader's qualities and public 'image' do much to determine the party's electoral appeal. To avoid eviction from Downing Street, a prime minister needs good teamplay among party colleagues as well as the active help of a nationwide army of supporters. If a party shows signs of deserting its leader, or merely growing lukewarm in support, the leader's power can melt away as rapidly as spring snow in the foothills of the Alps. Equally, if leaders show signs of forgetting about their party, even perhaps through allowing the grandeur of the prime ministerial office to seduce them into overlooking their earthy party roots, then the party may quickly lose its ardour for them. If this happens, their days as leader may well be numbered.

The activities of parties have altered since the 1940s in all kinds of ways, not least in how party leaders operate in relation to their parties. Many changes have been important in their own way but have not altered the fundamental relationship between leaders and their parties. But other significant changes in that relationship have resulted in important developments. Before discussing these further by focussing on the role of party leaders, it is well to examine briefly the wider context of changes within the party system.

The Changing Party System

Party politics in Britain has been correctly viewed throughout most of the postwar period as two-party politics. In 1940 Labour was welcomed into the wartime national government, not as a junior partner to be rapidly relegated when war was over (as in the First World War), but as a truly equal partner. This status was confirmed by Labour's decisive election victory in 1945, when for the first time it came to power with a clear overall majority. From 1940 till 1979 Labour and the Conservatives shared almost equally the spoils of office (Appendix 2 summarises the position). Not only did the two major parties monopolise government; they also dominated parliament, and between them orchestrated debate on every subject of political significance. Underlying this dominance, at least till the 1970s, was the fact that both were sustained by an electorate divided roughly into two equal and seemingly stable halves, based largely on social class divisions. Voters on the whole remained loyal to one or the other party and largely structured their own views according to policy preferences of their favoured party.

But from the 1970s onwards the degree of two-party dominance diminished. The flirtation of voters with other parties became a persistent theme, with the electorate voting for the two major parties in a reduced proportion, and its volatility sharply increased.[2] At the same time the dominant cleavage associated with social class was undermined. These changes have caused the context within which the competitive party battle takes place to change also. Party leaders have had to adjust to a new electoral environment; the market for votes has become more fluid and has demanded new entrepreneurial skills.

The loss of electoral support by the two major parties was to some extent mirrored in the party strengths in the House of Commons. But the electoral system provides a distorting mirror, and the impact of these changes, in electoral behaviour on the House of Commons have has been relatively muted. Parliament remained dominated by the two major parties, maintaining its allegiance to a duopolistic practice and procedure, seemingly intent on offering as little recognition as possible to the presence of more than fifty MPs from minor party through most of the 1980s (compared with a dozen or less in the 1950s). But the increased strength of minor parties obliged the leaders of the two major parties to fight a more complex battle in the country at large, not only against their main opponent but also against the other parties manoevring on their flanks.

By the early 1990s the two-party system appeared under threat from a rather different direction. The Conservatives' fourth successive election victory in 1992, and the prospect of continuous Conservative rule for up to eighteen years, prompted the suggestion that Britain's two-party system had been replaced by a 'dominant party system'.[3] How far a new party model was actually in evidence in the practices of British politics was a matter of some debate. On the one hand, the electoral system itself and the conventions of British parliamentary politics still sustained a two-party system. Labour remained Her Majesty's Opposition, with a front-bench aspiring to behave just like an alternative government. Labour played the role of partner in the two-party system to the full – understandably, because if that system were to disappear, Labour was likely to be the party suffering the greater demotion. But, on the other hand, that same Labour front bench had become largely devoid of members with any former ministerial experience, and on the Conservative benches those who had any experience of opposition were an ever diminishing number. Because it appeared natural for the Conservatives to be in office and Labour in opposition, some argued

2 A brief introduction to the extensive literature on voting behaviour in post-war Britain is D. Denver, *Elections and Voting Behaviour in Britain*, Philip Allan, 1989.

3 See especially Anthony King 'The Implications of One-Party Government', in A. King (ed.), *Britain at the Polls*, Chatham House Publishers, 1993.

that expectations of the system had changed, but whether this had produced any real changes in behaviour was a moot point.[4]

The characteristics of the two-party system, as well as the threats to which it has recently been subjected, condition the relationship between parties and their party leaders. Both the two major parties have leaders, but only one of those leaders can be prime minister. The other is known as Leader of the Opposition, but may be better described as leader of Her Majesty's alternative government, leader of the government-in-exile or prime minister-in-waiting. To be the leader of Her Majesty's Opposition is to be potentially prime minister. The relationship between the leader of the Opposition and the Opposition party is shaped by the fact that this leader will be prime minister if and when the goal which the party is struggling to attain is fulfilled, namely election victory. The nearer such victory appears to be, the more the leader can and indeed must adopt a 'prime ministerial' manner. After serving longer than any of his Labour predecessors as leader of the Opposition, Kinnock in 1992 was being presented to the electorate as 'Labour's Prime Minister'. The Opposition leader not only shadows the prime minister, but is modelling for the star role, auditioning continuously in front of the electorate for the lead part: occupancy of Number 10 Downing Street.

Party Structure: The view from the top

Leaders of the major parties, whether as prime minister or leader of the opposition, are at the head of a highly complex organisation. First and foremost both have a circle of immediate party colleagues, chiefly members of the cabinet or shadow cabinet, with some of whom they must have day-to-day, even hour-by-hour, dealings. The majority of these are people they have known for many years. They include some who have become close personal friends, but by no means all can be so described. While all will have been thrust into the front rank of the party, their background and achievements within the party will be varied, as will both the direction and the prominence of their ideological outlook. Some have been close rivals for the leadership and others nurse ambitions to seize the leader's crown whenever, and for whatever reason, it becomes available.

A larger and more distant circle is the entire parliamentary party, consisting of between 150 and 300 additional MPs. This is the pool

---

4   Anthony King ('The Implications of One-Party Government') spoke of 'over the shoulder' politics, with ministers looking with greater care at their own back benchers than at the opposition. During 1993 others drew attention to ministerial arrogance and complacency; see Donald Shell, 'The British Constitution in 1993', *Parliamentary Affairs*, vol. 47 (1994), pp. 293-309.

from which a prime minister must appoint to the great majority of government posts, and from which a leader of the opposition must nowadays construct a shadow administration of similar size. This wider group contains some senior figures, including former ministers, who have spent at least as long in the Commons as the leader. Among these are some who are frustrated and even embittered at their exclusion from front- bench roles. Others are contemporaries, eager for some advancement in the party, perhaps looking to the leader for this, or maybe pinning their hopes on a potential successor. And then there are the novices, recently arrived in the Commons, anxious to catch the leader's attention, eager to impress, but still essentially untried, inexperienced and little known. To ensure the enactment of their government's policies prime ministers depend on their whole parliamentary party. Members' votes are needed week by week; that is the essential factor. If even some of this support is withheld their government runs aground; if it is withdrawn their government sinks.

Outside Parliament, but of definite importance to the leader, are the central figures in the party organisation. These include a very few professionals employed by the party. Generally of greater importance are long-term activists in key roles, such as Labour's National Executive Committee (NEC), or those who serve as leading members of the Conservative party organisation. Ideally a party leader needs to keep the party machine in good running order. At times this calls for little more than general oversight by the leader while others actually operate the machine, but at other times servicing and overhaul are necessary. The leader needs not only to set out the strategy for the organisation, but also to ensure if possible that the party attains a high degree of capability in sustaining nationwide support, especially as a general election approaches. Leaders must be prepared to intervene using their authority to ensure that so potentially fissiparous a body as a political party is drawn together as an effective election-winning machine. Leaders must lead.

Then there is the mass party itself. Party members in constituencies throughout the land send their representatives to gatherings, and leaders must grace at least some of these with their presence, rallying, mobilising and enthusing supporters. The annual party conference has a special place. But the leader can also communicate with rank-and-file party members through party publications, and the media play an important part in portraying the leader to both members and supporters. The leader must use all these resources to keep the party in good heart. Beyond the party members are the supporters and would-be supporters in the electorate. A primary function of political parties is to mobilise mass

support for their leaders. Ideally a party wants to turn voters into supporters, supporters into members, and members into activists.

Both prime minister and leader of the Opposition relate to their
parties at these various levels – immediate colleagues, party in parliament
and party outside parliament. But the way they have done so in Britain
varies, first according to whether their party is in office or in opposition,
and secondly according to which major party one is considering, since
there are some important differences of character between the two.
A leader of the Opposition is by definition someone who is not enjoying
the fruits of an election victory and may indeed have led the party
to defeat. The aura of success remains at best unconfirmed. And, although
Opposition leaders have some patronage available, this is small compared
to their potential patronage as prime minister. While leaders of the
Opposition can and in a sense must attend first and foremost to party
management, the role of prime ministers in relation to their party is
less clear-cut. The most pressing demands prime ministers face concern
affairs of state; party management cannot have the same priority as
it does for the Opposition leader – not does it normally need to do
so. The prestige of office enhances the authority of the leader. The
party would prefer the leader to be managing the nation's affairs rather
than merely managing its own affairs. Thus in a sense, and up to a
point, prime ministers are excused the latter task. But this is so only
up to a point. When the going gets tough in government, when policies
displeasing to supporters must be enforced, then the mass party needs
reassurance. To fail to give this is to run serious risks. An occupational
hazard of being prime minister is to become preoccupied with government
to the neglect of party. In expressing national interests prime ministers
can lose sight of party priorities. They can easily become too busy
to spend time with party colleagues in the House of Commons, and
modern security requirements all too readily reinforce their isolation.
Without great care they grow distant and apart from the real life of
their parties.

The second contrast is between the parties themselves. A good start-
ing-point is to acknowledge the very different beginnings of the two
major parties. Labour began as a party outside parliament, formed by
the trade unions, in order to tackle those grievances which could only
be remedied by political action taken through parliament. Not only
did Labour have a policy agenda different from that of the old parties,
but it saw itself as a different kind of party: collegial and democratic,
rather than hierarchical and authoritarian. The parliamentary wing was
there to implement the will of the party as defined by its conference;
hence the notion of conference sovereignty. But, when it first formed
a government in 1924, Labour behaved very much like the old parties.

Its chairman became prime minister and ever after was known as 'party leader'. In office, and increasingly in opposition too, the Labour leader acted like the leaders of other parties. However the party still very clearly bears its birth-marks; the arguments and changes made in the 1980s testify to this. A Labour party leader, whether prime minister or not, deals with a party which feels and acts like a federal party. It has a clear dual structure, with the trade unions, the conference and the national executive committee providing one wing of the party, and the constituency parties, the MPs and the parliamentary leadership – cabinet or shadow cabinet – the other wing. Leaders must attempt to manage the relationship between the two wings, but this task is not easy because their power over both is very limited. The party constitution makes them appear more as chief spokesmen than as authentic leaders.

The Conservative party was very different. Organisationally it appears designed for a leader to act as commander, not simply spokesman. The party has always been and remains first and foremost a parliamentary party. It existed in parliament before it did in the country, and first became organised outside parliament in order to win support among an expanding electorate. The extra-parliamentary organisation, the National Union, was both separate from and subordinate to the parliamentary leadership. Anyone reading through an account of the party organisation must be struck not only by its complexity, but by its hierarchical form. The leader has sweeping powers, to appoint and dismiss office-holders and to decide policy. Conference was an occasion for the party faithful to come and hear their leaders and indeed demonstrate support for them, perhaps offer a few views, but certainly not instruct them. The party organisation looks as if it belongs to the leader.

There remains much about the present parties, both Labour and Conservative, that can only be understood from their history. But the practice of party leadership within the same overall political system has brought considerable convergence. Robert McKenzie argued that despite the contrasting origins and formal structures of the two major parties, the distribution of power within them had become overwhelmingly similar. He suggested that this was because both had conformed to a pattern prescribed by the unwritten British constitution.[5] As soon as his view appeared it was contested, and events since suggest that at the very least significant differences between the parties remain. Yet as a political sociologist he analysed what actually happened rather than what had been assumed, and in an important sense shifted the focus of the argument away from the contrasts between the major parties, as indicated in their rule-books, to the similarities as indicated by their actual behaviour.

5   R.T. McKenzie, *British Political Parties* (2nd edn), Heinemann, 1963 (1st edn 1955); see especially pp. 635-41.

In this chapter the changing relationship between prime ministers and their parties is considered first in terms of the parliamentary parties and secondly in relation to the party organisations outside parliament. Comparison and contrast between the two main parties are shown to be of continuing significance, but contrasts between different leadership styles, depending largely on changing political circumstances, are shown to be more important. In so far as party contrasts do emerge it is argued that these have been more varied and less clear-cut than either McKenzie or most of his critics have implied.

The Primacy of Parliamentary Parties

Parliamentary parties are at the heart of the British political system. If politics in England was born with the King and his court, it grew to maturity in parliament. Some may deprecate the stifling effect of 'parliamentarianism'; others may extol the 'mother of parliaments' for the style of politics it has imposed. Whatever view is taken, the British state is a parliamentary state.[6] It is from the ranks of the parliamentary parties (themselves relatively small bodies) that almost the whole leadership, both of actual government and 'government-in-exile', must be provided. To become party leader is to become captain of a team the members of which have been playing together for many years. Whatever presidential overtones may have become apparent, British prime ministers come to office as team captains, not as winners of open tournaments.[7] The route to ministerial office lies through the Commons; top political jobs go almost exclusively to those who have run the electoral gauntlet to become members of the Commons, and then served an apprenticeship of some ten to twenty years there.

It is the parliamentary parties that in effect control party policy-making. Labour may have cherished the final authority within the party of its conference, but given the inability of conference to do anything (other than pass resolutions), it has always been the parliamentary party that actually decides what to do. Conferences can confer, manifestos can manifest, but only parliament can legislate – and only government can govern. Nor is the autonomy of parliamentary parties expressed only in a monopoly of top political jobs and policy-making. Members of parliament enjoy a high degree of security. Electoral swings may unseat the marginal, and boundary commissioners the unlucky, but the party outside parliament – locally or nationally – has only rarely been a threat.

6   See D. Judge, *The Parliamentary State*, Sage, 1993.
7   R. Rose 'Government against sub-governments' in R. Rose and Ezra Suleiman (eds), *Presidents and Prime Ministers*, American Enterprise Institute, 1980, p. 315.

While it is fair to stress the autonomy of the parliamentary parties, the point may well be made that for Labour this has always been under some question, and that for the Conservatives the significance of the extra-parliamentary party appears to have been growing. In the early 1980s changes took place in the constitution of the Labour Party which on the face of things severely undermined the collective freedom of MPs. The parliamentary party lost the sole and exclusive right to appoint the party leader, being allocated only 30 per cent of the votes in an electoral college, the other components of which were constituency parties with 30 per cent and and trade unions with 40 per cent.[8] These changes certainly altered the balance of power between the party inside and the party outside parliament.

Following its abysmal performance in the 1983 election, Labour for a time seemed to place more emphasis on fighting the political battle in opposition to the Conservatives from town halls and from trade unions rather than from the green leather benches of the House of Commons. Even for many Labour MPs, campaigning in the country was seen as more important (and as more vital to their own futures) than working in parliament. But opposition through the unions or through local government brought scant rewards. The defeat of the miners' strike in 1984-5 epitomised the general weakening of the trade union movement, while the abolition of the Greater London Council and the metro-countries demonstrated the weakened place of local government. Neil Kinnock, the new leader, seized the initiative and began to transform the party once more. The importance of putting up a 'good show' in the Commons might appear to some as nothing other than confirmation of the danger of the parliamentary embrace. But to others it emphasised the means through which ran the only road back to power. The introduction of television cameras to the Commons in 1989 helped re-focus attention on parliamentary performance. The party as a whole seemed to accept that if it wanted to remain a player in the two-party power stakes, then its parliamentary leadership had to be accorded the right to lead. Kinnock came to dominate the party more than any previous leader of the Labour Opposition had ever done. The elections of 1987 and 1992 saw a slow recovery in Labour's position. Having flirted with extra-parliamentary control, the long years in opposition in the 1980s and the fear of relegation from the two-party game propelled the party back into the parliamentary mode. The events of the 1980s will probably be seen in retrospect as having confirmed rather than threatened the pivotal position of the parliamentary party.

8   MPs also lost the secret ballot they had hitherto enjoyed for leadership elections, while at the same time constituency parties were empowered to de-select their MPs; it was assumed this would make MPs more responsive to the views of constituency activists in deciding how to cast their votes.

The traditional Conservative pattern of an independent parliamentary party and a subservient party outside parliament has also been questioned. As the parliamentary party has become more restive and assertive, so has the party outside parliament. The constituency activists have become more pushy; self-made Essex man lacks the deference so characteristic of an earlier generation of Conservatives. Leaders have had to acknowledge more openly the demands of the party rank and file. A new populism is required of leaders, and if this is not in evidence, activists then put pressure on MPs, who in turn feel encouraged and even obliged to make trouble for their leaders in parliament.

Hence in both parties the relationship between MPs and members has altered. The late 1980s saw for Labour the importance of the parliamentary party re-emphasised, and for the Conservatives a wider recognition of the need to treat the party outside parliament with greater care and respect. The implications of these changes for leaders are examined later in this chapter. But parliamentary parties remain crucial, and it is to the relationship between leaders and their parliamentary parties that we now turn.

Gaining and Keeping the Party Leadership

In politics many believe that they are called, but few are chosen, and only one can be anointed as party leader. To secure the prime position requires majority support among colleagues. It is MPs who have made that choice hitherto – they had the best opportunity to see the potential candidates in action most closely, observing them at first hand over time both in Westminister and in Whitehall.

Before 1965, appointment of a Conservative prime minister by the monarch could precede appointment as party leader, but the latter process followed the former as surely as night follows day.[9] This was because the party's choice, as defined by its most senior members, determined the monarch's decision. Selection of the leader by a small group of senior party figures, who manifestly weighed opinions (rather than simply counting votes), was consistent with a party characterised by both hierarchy and deference. The inability of this system in 1963 to produce a candidate behind whom the party as a whole could unite was evidence of the relative decline of deference within the party. The electoral mechanism then introduced gave votes to all MPs, a much more egalitarian method. Henceforth an MP who was a senior cabinet minister

9   When Churchill was appointed prime minister in 1940, Chamberlain remained leader of the Conservative Party for five months until forced to go by ill-health; Churchill then assumed the party leadership. This was in the exceptional circumstances of a wartime national government.

had but one vote, the same as the most newly elected member – a change that not only reflected changes in the character of the party but further encouraged those changes.

Labour has always elected its leaders, and before 1981 this was the prerogative of the parliamentary party exclusively. Hence all Labour leaders who have so far served as prime minister were first chosen by their parliamentary colleagues.[10] Up till 1981, the Labour party electoral mechanism involved repeated ballots until an outright winner emerged. As with the Conservatives the ballot was secret, helping to insulate MPs from outside party pressures. Only once, in 1976, has an election been held for the Labour leadership while the party has been in office (see Appendix A for details).

If the choice of party leader and hence prime minister has belonged to the parliamentary parties, so has the ability to remove the leader from office. All prime ministers have been aware that it was within the power of their parliamentary colleagues to dismiss them. Almost all have at some point in their tenure of 10 Downing Street felt the reality of this possibility. Only one, Harold Wilson in 1976, appears to have departed quite voluntarily; and only one, Margaret Thatcher in 1990, has manifestly been dismissed. But others, including Churchill, Eden and Macmillan, have departed under pressure, and no leader will dare quickly to forget Thatcher's political demise. While attention generally focuses on prime ministers' power to appoint and dismiss ministers, to structure their governments as they wish, to decide the date of an election and so on, the exercise of these powers is always within the basic context that the party might decide to sack the prime minister. It may be that using patronage skilfully to balance factions within the party, ensuring there are several heirs apparent rather than just one, and demonstrating the capacity to be flexible over policy, keeps a prime minister relatively secure. But the possibility of removal is a vital and fundamental aspect to the relationship.

Formal rules tell only part of the story, but they are important. In 1965 the Conservatives made no provision for a formal challenge to a sitting leader, but this was added in 1975. Since then at the beginning of every parliamentary session (roughly once a year) a contest has been possible. The traditional ethos of the Conservative Party placed considerable value on loyalty to the leader, just as party structures focused authority on the leader. But this has to be seen alongside the party's relative ruthlessness in discarding leaders who are perceived as failures. Before the advent of elected leaders this was done in a relatively private manner. Churchill's dictum expressed the position well: 'If [the leader]

10   Had Labour won power in 1987 or 1992 it would have come to office with a leader chosen by an electoral college wider than the parliamentary party.

trips, he must be sustained. If he makes mistakes, they must be covered. If he sleeps, he must not be wantonly disturbed. If he is no good, he must be pole-axed.'[11]

The emphasis on loyalty to the leader is a double-edged weapon, the more so since 1975. On the one hand a leader can still play the loyalty card, calling on the party to close ranks, but a leader unable to demonstrate such loyalty in almost overwhelming support at once becomes all the more vulnerable. A leader who faces a formal challenge must not only win, but win decisively. In 1989 Thatcher, three times an election-winner and with her party still enjoying a near 100-seat majority in the Commons, secured 314 out of a possible 374 votes when faced with the stalking horse challenge of Sir Anthony Meyer. For Thatcher this was barely enough; sixty MPs – or 16 per cent of the parliamentary party – had withheld support. The following year she defeated Michael Heseltine by 204 votes to 152, but with this outcome she, as a matter of practical reality, was the loser, because only 55 per cent of the party had supported her. In a party placing such value on loyalty to the leader this was intolerable. When the rules were changed in 1975, allowing the then leader of the Opposition to be removed, no thought was given to the use of this system to challenge a sitting prime minister. The fact that a leader may at the beginning of any parliamentary session face a stalking horse challenger can greatly magnify a climate of instability.[12]

In the Labour Party before 1981 no formal procedure existed for the party to challenge a leader who was in office as prime minister by forcing a ballot of the parliamentary party. But both Attlee in 1947 and Wilson intermittently from 1967 to 1969 had to cope with senior colleagues plotting their removal. When Cripps went to see Attlee in September 1947 to tell him to stand down in favour of Bevin, he had also consulted both Morrison and Dalton. Had there been general agreement among these four very senior cabinet figures, Attlee would have had to depart. But there was not, and Attlee played on that fact, with the result that Cripps came away from the meeting having himself accepted promotion from the prime minister whose removal he had plotted![13] Likewise, in 1969 conspirators within the party found substantial support for both Callaghan and Jenkins as replacements for

11   Quoted in Nigel Fisher, *The Tory Leaders*, Weidenfeld and Nicolson, 1977, p. 3.
12   At a time when Major faced intense speculation that such a challenge would take place, Thatcher herself argued that the rules should be changed to prevent a formal challenge to a party leader while prime minister. See *Sunday Times*, 3 October 1993.
13   See Ben Pimlott, *Hugh Dalton*, Macmillan, 1985, pp. 511-13; Bernard Donoughue and George Jones, *Herbert Morrison: Portrait of a Politician*, Weidenfeld and Nicolson, 1973, pp. 413-25.

Wilson; this prevented either from moving decisively against the prime minister lest the other benefit from the resulting upheaval.[14]

Curious as it may seem in a party so greatly emphasising its democratic character, Labour leaders have enjoyed a high degree of security. Attlee was never formally challenged before he retired at the age of seventy-two in 1955, after twenty years as leader. Nor was Wilson challenged when he led a disgruntled party back into opposition in 1970. Drucker puts this down to the ethos of Labour which emphasises both job security (no sackings, a good trade union principle) and those provisions which allow leaders to be freely criticised, voted against, and even over-ruled by the party, all supposedly in contrast to the Conservative party.[15] By the 1990s such differences of ethos between the two main parties had greatly diminished. But differences in the means through which formal challenges to leaders could be made had become more apparent. The process of mounting a challenge to a Labour leader had been made so ponderous, so public and so long-winded that it seemed hard to imagine such a process running its course, especially if the leader were to be in occupation of Downing Street.[16] By contrast a Conservative leader, whether prime minister or not, could be removed with relative despatch. The Labour leader of the Opposition looked much harder to remove than the Conservative leader in office as prime minister.

Prime Ministers and the Power of Appointment

The prime minister's power of appointment to ministerial office has been endlessly discussed and is usually seen as the crux of the prime ministerial versus presidential debate. There is one notable difference in practice between the two major parties. The Labour Party when in opposition has always elected its shadow cabinet, while a Conservative Opposition leader has had a free hand in appointing the shadow team. This means that a Labour leader comes to office with a shadow cabinet chosen by the parliamentary party rather than one composed of personal appointees. But the portfolios which individuals hold in opposition have been at the leader's discretion. So, although Labour leaders may have to suffer fools gladly, they can at least match individuals to ministries.

---

14 See Harold Wilson, *The Labour Government, 1964- 1970*, Weidenfeld and Nicolson, 1971, pp. 535-9; Roy Jenkins, *A Life at the Centre*, Macmillan, 1991, pp. 256-7.
15 H.M. Drucker, *Doctrine and Ethos in the Labour Party*, Geo. Allen and Unwin, 1979.
16 Even as leader of the Opposition Kinnock was insulated from a swift removal in 1987. Following Benn's unsuccessful challenge for the leadership in 1988, the rules were amended to provide that any challenge required the backing of 20 per cent (not 5 per cent, as hitherto) of the PLP. If the party were in office a two-thirds majority vote at conference is also required before a challenge can be triggered! See Garner and Kelly, *British Political Parties Today*, pp. 177-8.

And once in office a Labour premier can re-shuffle the cabinet without formal party constraint.

Concerning party management, two rather different points deserve particular attention. The first concerns the supply of posts; this had risen from fifty-eight in 1940 to eighty-four by 1990 (see Appendix C), that is more than a quarter of the parliamentary party. A steeper increase has taken place in the number of parliamentary private secretaries, from twenty-five to forty-four and although they are not ministers, appointment as a PPS involves acceptance of the convention of collective responsibility and is generally seen as the first step on the ministerial ladder. The so-called 'payroll' vote within the governing party comprises all ministers and PPSs, a total of 128 in 1990, half as many again as in 1940.

But if supply has risen, demand has increased propotionately even more. The rise of the so-called career politician to dominance in both major parties must be noted. Almost all MPs now want that which only prime ministers have it within their power to give – ministerial office.[17] This represents a significant change since 1945. In the early postwar years (and still more so earlier in the twentieth century), merely entering the House of Commons was the summit of the ambition of many MPs. The so called 'knights of the shires' on the Conservative side were matched by older trade union-sponsored MPs on the Labour side, with members of neither group pressing for appointment to ministerial office. But in recent years MPs who never attain the accolade of ministerial office are more inclined to feel that their careers remain unfulfilled. And in politics there are very few other jobs remotely comparable to holding ministerial office. MPs may join select committees, and a few can find some prominence in the chairmanship of such bodies. But this appears more like a form of training for ministerial office, or a consolation prize for the failure to hold or retain such office, than a comparable alternative career.

So the gap between supply and demand results in a greater deficit of unfulfilled ambition. This may have strengthened the hand of the prime minister: 'The career politician's ambition is the ambitious prime minister's opportunity,' comments Anthony King.[18] But it might equally be said that the rise of the career politician brings new hazards to the job of prime minister: the danger of unappeased ambition lurking ever more copiously on the backbenches in the House of Commons. The risk for the prime minister is that the disappointed start looking

17 See A. King 'The rise of the career politician – and its consequences', *British Journal of Political Science*, vol. 11, no. 2 (July 1981) pp. 249-85. Also P. Riddell, *Honest Opportunism: The rise of the career politician*, Hamish Hamilton, 1993.

18 Anthony King, 'The British prime minister in the age of the career politician', *West European Politics*, vol. 14, no. 2 (April 1991) pp. 25-47.

to the next potential leader for preferment and then seek to hasten the arrival of a successor.

The disappointed may be soothed by other means, not least the award of honours (in particular for Conservative backbenchers the award of knighthoods). Macmillan and Thatcher were both generous in this, while Heath was noticeably parsimonious. Labour leaders have eschewed political honours, but since many MPs, not least Labour ones, aspire to an eventide existence in the House of Lords, the possibility of gaining a place there through a dissolution or resignation honours list, or a list of so-called 'working' peers, must ever be kept in mind. Prime ministers also have other forms of patronage at their disposal, and these may be used at times to help with party management. The appointment of Leon Brittan to the European Community Commission in 1989, after he had helped to divert criticism from Thatcher by resigning from her government in 1986, was highly convenient for the prime minister. In 1989 Thatcher apparently reminded Lawson when he was on the point of resignation that he had earlier expressed interest in the possibility of succeeding Robin Leigh-Pemberton as governor of the Bank of England; did he really want to shatter that attractive prospect by resigning? But by then Lawson's mind was firmly made up, in favour of resignation.[19]

Management of the Parliamentary Party: Role of Whips

The expansion in the number of ministerial posts has in one important sense made party management easier. If the ranks of PPSs are included, then the so-called payroll vote has risen to almost 40 per cent of the party. Not only can no minister or PPS vote against the party whip without forfeiting office, but none can openly criticise government policy. In meetings of the Parliamentary Labour Party formal votes take place and for these too a Labour Prime Minister may demand loyalty from the entire government team, even though such use of the payroll vote has at times been greatly resented.

In sustaining party cohesion the carrot of appointment to office is complemented by the stick of party discipline applied through the whips. But the role of the whips is not merely to persuade, cajole, bully or coerce members into voting for the government. They are also there to ensure that the leader of the party is kept well informed about party opinion, although the extent to which a leader takes notice varies. In 1950 A.P. Herbert described the whips as the 'guides, philosophers and friends' of members.[20] This may have been something of a euphemism then; it is certainly not a full description of whips now.

19 Nigel Lawson, *The View from No. 11*, Bantam, 1991, p. 963.

The most significant changes in the role of the whips appear to have taken place during the late 1950s and early 1960s. Heath as chief whip from 1956 to 1959 brought a new professionalism to the job; he was the first holder of that position routinely to attend cabinet meetings, although neither he nor his successors have been full cabinet members. More significant was the way he systematically gathered information about every member of the party, and developed the art of using this to maximum advantage. He was after all responsible for piloting the Conservative party through the Suez crisis and its turbulent aftermath. When Edward Short became Wilson's chief whip in 1964 he found that it 'had been the practice to keep a "dirt book" in which unsavoury personal items about members were recorded',[21] and he immediately ordered this to be discontinued. It is probable that such stories arose simply out of the thoroughness with which Heath and his successors had gathered information. Heath himself explained his professionalism: 'I acted on the principle that the more you know about the people you are speaking for, and having to give the leader's instructions to, and the more they know about you and what you are being asked to do, the better.'[22] The growth in the number of whips, never more than nine before the 1960s, but never less than thirteen since then, reflects their increased workload in monitoring and relaying views within the party.

Information about members, about the views they hold, and about how often they speak or ask questions and in particular how effectively they do so – all this and much else is available to the prime minister from the whips' office. Whips can apparently even provide lists of the names of those MPs who have refused to sign a friendly early day motion.[23] When there is a re-shuffle of ministers, the whips provide an important part of the advice available to the prime minister. It is they who feed names to the House of Commons Committee of Selection which decides the composition of most parliamentary committees. On the Conservative side a whip attends meetings of the 1922 Committee and of every backbench committee, and thereby opinion within the party on almost every issue can be closely monitored. Different prime ministers have made varied use of the resources provided by the whips. As chief whip Heath apparently saw the prime minister, Macmillan,

20   A.P. Herbert, *Independent Member*, Methuen, 1950, p. 379.
21   Edward Short, *Whip to Wilson*, Macdonald, 1989, p. 61.
22   John Campbell, *Edward Heath*, Cape, 1993, p. 101.
23   Apparently Wilson requested his whips to provide a list of MPs who refused to sign an EDM condemning a newspaper attack on his government in 1968; no fewer than 77 names were provided, all of whom were 'marked down as audacious enemies to be punished or appeased'; see Ben Pimlott, *Harold Wilson*, HarperCollins, 1992, p. 507.

every day. But when he himself became premier, he would sometimes meet his own chief whip, Francis Pym, no more than once a week.[24]

The prime minister's parliamentary private secretary (PPS) is a further link between the leader and the parliamentary party, acting in Callaghan's words as another pair of 'eyes and ears' for the prime minister.[25] It is the job of the PPS always to be around the House sniffing the parliamentary breeze. A PPS can seek to ensure that interventions at prime minister's question time are as helpful as possible. Both Thatcher's and Major's PPSs developed the role of trying to see that those members considered loyal to the leadership won the main positions on backbench party committees. A poor choice of PPS can be a real handicap. Peter Morrison, who was Thatcher's PPS in the period leading up to her dismissal, apparently felt that his main role was to exude confidence about her re-election prospects, rather than actually working to bring this about.[26] Macmillan's biographer saw the replacement in 1959 of both his PPS (Barber by Knox Cunningham) and chief whip (Heath by Redmayne) as contributing to the prime minister's loss of touch with his party.[27]

Backbench Party Organisation

In both major parties leaders also have to relate to their backbench party organisations. Again these have been different in form and style between the parties, and many detailed adjustments have been made over the years.[28] On the Conservative side the 1922 Committee consists of all backbenchers; the leader attends only by invitation, usually once or twice a year, to make a speech to rally members. When the party is in opposition, other frontbenchers may attend but when in office they only do so by specific invitation. The 1922 Committee is envisaged not as a decision-making body but rather as a forum for the expression of views, which are then relayed to the party leader. The chairman and an executive committee are elected annually, but the turnover in

---

24 See Campbell, *Edward Heath*, p. 514.
25 Callaghan records that after the single vote defeat of his government in the no confidence vote in 1979, 'I left the Chamber with my Parliamentary Private Secretary, Roger Stott, who had been my constant companion, adviser and eyes and ears during the previous three years...We sat talking in my room until nearly midnight'. See James Callaghan, *Time and Chance*, Collins, 1987, p. 563.
26 See Alan Clark's *Diary*, Weidenfeld and Nicolson, 1993, pp. 354 and 358, where he expresses his anger at finding Morrison fast asleep when he went to see him on the eve of the election!
27 Alistair Horne, *Macmillan, 1957–1986*, Macmillan, 1989, p. 339.
28 See Philip Norton, 'The Organisation of Political Parties in the House of Commons', in S.A. Walkland (ed.), *The House of Commons in the Twentieth Century*, Clarendon Press, 1979.

these elections is usually low. Unlike the chief whip and all ministers, no officers of the 1922 Committee owe their appointment to the party leader. Particularly at times of crisis within the party it is the officers of the 1922 Committee (so often referred to in the early 1990s as the 'men in grey suits') who may have to tell the prime minister that a particular policy must be changed, or that a certain minister must be sacked, or even that the prime minister must depart.

As well as the 1922 Committee the Conservative Party has subject groups which with time have become more numerous. They are not committees in the normal sense since their meetings are open to all backbenchers. Usually only a regular dozen or so attend, but numbers may suddenly and dramatically rise at times of controversy, with ministers being summoned to defend their policies. All officers of these groups are elected, except that since 1950 when the party has been in opposition the chairman have been appointed by the leader, a change probably reflecting an increased awareness of the importance of the groups. Elections of officers on these committees, and to the executive of the 1922 Committee, have become ever more keenly contested. They are seen as something of weathervane for the party. When in 1972 Conservative MPs elected as chairman of the 1922 Committee Edward du Cann, whom Heath had earlier sacked from the party chairmanship, Heath should have seen it as a warning signal. When the following year Nicholas Ridley and John Biffen, both MPs whom Heath had dropped from ministerial office, were elected as chairmen respectively of the Finance and Industry Committees, this was recognised as backbenchers turning up the volume of complaint. But to Heath it appeared to make no difference. In the Thatcher and Major years there were signs that competition for backbench committee posts had intensified, with prime ministerial loyalists eager to capture as many as possible and thus to demonstrate support for the prime minister in the parliamentary party.

On the Labour side, whether the party has been in office or in opposition, all members, including the leader and all frontbenchers, have been eligible to attend meetings of the parliamentary party. MPs elect a party chairman who then chairs these meetings.[29] In contrast to the Conservative practice, meetings of the PLP are seen as decision-making occasions; votes are taken and the decisions reached are supposedly binding on all members. A Labour prime minister may attend and speak; Attlee did so in 1946 when members were hostile to government proposals on conscription, and his intervention was followed by a vote which ran approximately 5-2 in favour of the government, although the govern-

---

29   When the party was in opposition from 1951 to 1964 the leader was also chairman. When the party went into opposition in 1970 Wilson preferred not to revert to chairing these meetings, so since then the Party has always had a separate chairman and leader.

ment later compromised on the proposed length of service. When in 1947 the PLP expressed considerable hostility to a proposal to postpone steel nationalisation, this helped to incline ministers towards a change of mind the following week.[30] Under Wilson the PLP met more frequently than in Attlee's time, with weekly meetings becoming the norm. References to Wilson and Callaghan attending meetings of the PLP are frequent in the memoirs and diaries covering their premierships. For example, Crossman records that in June 1966 all ministers were ordered to attend a meeting of the PLP at which a motion calling for a decisive reduction in commitments east of Suez was to be debated; five-minute speeches were allowed from the floor, to which Wilson replied with a speech lasting forty minutes; the vote went 225 to 54 in support of the government, although Crossman states that he would have abstained if he had not been a minister.[31] Three weeks later all ministers were again ordered to the PLP to vote down a critical motion on support for United States policy in Vietnam.[32]

Whenever Labour has been in office since 1945 a liaison committee has been formed as a channel of communication between backbenchers and frontbenchers. After 1974 this body was considerably expanded to some fourteen members, but the experience of the 1970s suggests that the relationship between size and effectiveness was an inverse one. Backbench subject groups have had a somewhat more erratic role in the PLP than their equivalent on the Conservative side. Such groups have existed continually since the 1940s, but their tendency to proliferate and to become factionalised has at times led to a severe cull.[33] In general the Labour pattern has required PLP members to register for backbench subject committees, and only those registered for a particular group can vote for its officers – unlike voting rights for all MPs on the Conservative side. Whether the party is in government or in opposition, front-benchers are allowed to attend the meetings of these PLP subject groups.

Backbench party organisation has increased in both parties, reflecting the more participatory role sought by contemporary MPs. Within both parties, groups of a more ideological kind have also had their place.

30 See McKenzie, *British Political Parties*, pp. 451- 2; also Kenneth Harris, *Attlee*, Weidenfeld and Nicolson, 1982, pp. 339-43, and Ronald Butt, *The Power of Parliament*, Constable, 1967, pp. 192-3.

31 Richard Crossman, *Diaries of a Cabinet, Minister*, vol. 1, Cape, 1975, p. 539; see also Wilson, *The Labour Government 1964-1970*, p. 243; Tony Benn, *Out of the Wilderness: Diaries, 1963-1967*, Heinemann, 1987, p. 431; Barbara Castle, *The Castle Diaries, 1964-1976*, Macmillan, 1990, pp. 69-70.

32 See Crossman, *Diaries of a Cabinet Minister*, p. 562; Benn, *Out of the Wilderness*, p. 447.

33 See Norton, 'The Organisation of Political Parties in the House of Commons', pp. 33-49.

In 1964 Richard Rose characterised Labour as a part of factions, that is groups seeking to further a range of policies through consciously organised political activity, and the Conservatives as a party of tendencies, that is stable sets of attitude rather than a stable group of individuals.[34] Since then, the Conservatives have become much more factionalised, with groups such as the 92 group and the No Turning Back group gaining prominence. At the same time the 1980s saw a waning in the importance of factions within the Labour party, perhaps because of the exhaustion and demoralisation of the left under Kinnock's leadership.[35]

In office Labour's postwar prime ministers have varied in their approach to the parliamentary party. Attlee saw himself as its chief executive: 'In his philosophy the leader was obligated to try to carry out what the party was publicly committed to.' If the leadership wanted to vary this, persuasion could be attempted, but if the parliamentary party as a whole proved unwilling to accept persuasion, the leadership had to do as the party wanted.[36] Wilson was always prepared to give himself greater latitude, and at times this led to open defiance of the party with strenuous attempts to use the payroll vote to secure support for the government's decisions. At one stage Wilson appeared to threaten dissolution of parliament, referring to his backbenchers as dogs that should not go on biting lest they fail to get their licences renewed (see above, page 86) This drew forth newspaper editorials about 'President Wilson', but Wilson himself claimed retrospectively that he had intended those remarks as a joke.[37]

Downing Street distanced from the House of Commons

Prime ministers relate with that most vital element in the party, their parliamentary colleagues, in very varied ways. Information flows from the party to the prime minister and from the prime minister to the party via ministers, the whips and party office-holders. Superficially this seems a multiplicity of channels. But each is nuanced to do a slightly different job. What the above account indicates is that the formal linkages between prime ministers and their parties in the House of Commons have expanded throughout the postwar period. The number of ministers and whips has grown, as has the number of party office-holders. The frequency of party meetings and the range of party groups

34   Richard Rose, 'Parties, Factions and Tendencies in Britain', *Political Studies*, vol. XII, no. 1, 1964, pp. 33-46; reprinted in R. Rose (ed.), *Studies in British Politics*, Macmillan, 1966.

35   See Jack Brand, 'Faction as its own Reward: Groups in the British Parliament, 1945-1986', *Parliamentary Affairs*, vol. 42, no. 2 (1989), pp. 148-64.

36   See Harris, *Attlee*, p. 343.

37   See Philip Ziegler, *Wilson*, Weidenfeld and Nicolson, 1993, p. 275.

have increased, with periodic attempts made to review this machinery. But it is note striking that despite the widening of these various channels of communication prime ministers seem to become so easily isolated from their party backbenchers, the more so after than before the 1960s. It was Attlee's habit to go to the Commons tearoom during the afternoon when Parliament was sitting. Churchill apparently frequented the smoking room while he was prime minister, as did Macmillan. In his first government Wilson regularly spent time in the House making 'himself freely available to any Member who wanted an audience', but after the 1966 election he discontinued this practice.[38] The result was a growing distance between him and the expanded and much younger parliamentary party, in sharp contrast to his relationship with the party during his early days as leader.

Heath's whole approach to the parliamentary party was very taut and strained, and the chief whip tried to keep him away from the House as much as possible precisely because, when he did show himself, he 'alienated more good will than he engendered'! Instead Heath invited groups of backbenchers over to Downing Street, but these gatherings were not a success because he not only made no effort to listen to their views but it was also clear that he had no intention of listening to them.[39] Thatcher recognised the importance of avoiding Heath's error. Conservative backbench MPs were encouraged to go and see her if they had concerns, and in her early years as prime minister she made a point of spending time around the House. But again the habit died. By 1990 when her party chairman urged her to get on the telephone to MPs and spend time in the tea room to try and build support in advance of the first ballot in the leadership contest, she replied: 'That's not for me after eleven years.'[40] Is it simply the growing pressure on a prime minister's time that creates this distance? Or is it the outcome of a more complex shift in the priorities of leadership, with more emphasis on the need to appeal over the heads of MPs to the party beyond Parliament and the public at large? Some examination of the changing relationship between prime ministers and their parties outside parliament is necessary before we can attempt to answer that question.

Prime Minister and the Party outside Parliament

Parties nationwide present a paradoxical picture. On the one hand both major parties appear to be organisations in decline. The Conservatives boasted almost 3 million members in the early 1950s but were down

38 Pimlott, *Harold Wilson*, p. 401.
39 Campbell, *Edward Heath*, p. 513.
40 Kenneth Baker, 'The Ides of Margaret' in the *Sunday Times*, 30 August 1993.

to a little over half a million forty years later, while Labour's individual membership had dropped from around 1 million to 275,000 in the same period. Instead of 10 per cent of the electorate belonging to political parties, less than 2 per cent of an expanded electorate did so. The parties employ fewer professional staff, and their finances have become increasingly embarrassing. Yet despite this, both seem as complex as ever and both appeared to demand ever more attention from their leaders. Perhaps this simply reflected the fact that organisations in decline are more difficult and time-consuming to manage than those blessed with buoyancy and expansion.

The Conservative leader has traditionally been viewed as a figure elevated above, and deliberately distanced from, the party. Lofty separation from the lower elements lent authority and dignity to the office. The fact that Conservative leaders were not infrequently closely linked to the aristocracy reinforced this detachment. Churchill was the grandson of a duke, Macmillan was married to a duke's daughter, and Douglas-Home was the fourteenth holder of his earldom. Such men did not appear to strive in a calculating way for political advancement. Rather they seemed effortlessly to sweep into public life, and characteristically none of these three gained the party leadership through open election. The 1960s saw profound changes in the party. The first elected leader was Heath; he was not the first Conservative leader who had not attended a public school, but his social origins were a world away from those of his immediate predecessors. He had no money, no wife and no family of high status to support him. His successor, Mrs Thatcher, may be acknowledged as one of the all-time great leaders of the party, but that is certainly not how she was viewed at first. She was manifestly an outsider, a grammar school girl and a woman, and this in a party where, up till a few years earlier, almost the only women to be seen on the party conference platform were the decorously hatted wives of ministers, seated at a decent distance behind their menfolk.

It seemed quite natural for Conservative leaders such as Churchill or Macmillan not to mix with members at the party conference. They descended at the end of the two-and-a-half-day event to exhort the faithful, almost like Moses bringing the tablets down from Mount Sinai. But in 1965 it would have seemed preposterous if Heath, the newly-elected leader, had not attended the conference, and of course leaders have done so ever since. The conference itself has almost doubled in length and, although formally its powers remain advisory, its importance within the total counsels of the party is now more apparent. Perhaps, as Richard Kelly has argued, the influence of the conference has always been underrated by commentators.[41] It has never been easy to discern

41   Richard Kelly, *Conservative Party Conferences*, Manchester University Press, 1989.

beneath its rituals (the innocuous motions chosen for debate, the reluctance to press anything to a formal vote) just what was going on. But there have been obvious changes in style. One argument previously used against the leader attending the conference had been that conference members would feel too inhibited by the leader's presence, and that any kind of criticism or expression of differences would become impossible. But the arrival of Heath was a sign that the party no longer lived by such deference. And the way he treated the party ensured that within a few years the Conservative conference was looking as rumbustious and divisive as the Labour conference typically did.[42] The sight of the leader sitting studiously and attentively on the conference platform seemed to encourage rather than discourage the expression of divergent views. The arrival of the television cameras had a similar effect. Reading the memoirs covering the Thatcher years confirms the view that annual conferences were seen as important. Thatcher herself, for example, writing about the 1981 conference at a time when her position within her cabinet was very difficult (see Chapter 2, pp. 61–2), recognised the link between conference and the mood of the parliamentary party: 'A rebuff for the platform would have emboldened back bench "wets" to step up their attack when parliament resumed...a rebuff for the critics, which is what they received, would strengthen our moral authority.'[43]

Nor is the annual conference to be seen in isolation. Within the party other conferences take place, for Conservative trade unionists and for women, for Young Conservatives and for students, for Scotland and for Wales and for local government. Every spring the central council meets, with perhaps 1,200 activists present. Again, Thatcher comments: 'I soon learned that central council provided an opportunity I could never afford to miss.'[44] No previous leaders had made such deliberate attempts to mobilise support in the party nationally to boost support for their leadership within Parliament. This pattern was one further developed by Major. The bitterness within the party after Thatcher's removal and the continuing acute divisions over developments within the European Community left Major struggling to assert authority. Victory in the 1992 election under his leadership gave him a new basis upon which to build, but 1993 only proved how difficult this was going to be. In late summer, before the 1993 conference, there was increasing and intense speculation about a possible leadership challenge. Major

---

42 Especially the 1972 conference, characterised by bitter public disputes over EC membership.

43 See Margaret Thatcher, *The Downing Street Years*, HarperCollins, 1993, pp. 154, 138.

44 Ibid., p. 138. Kelly says Thatcher addressed every women's conference after she became leader in 1975; see *Conservative Party Conferences*, p. 132.

toured the country speaking to closed gatherings of the party activists trying to build his support in advance of the conference and the new session of parliament. In the event the party conference passed without any serious eruption, and so was judged a success from the leadership's point of view. But the contrast between the lofty dignity and distance preserved by Churchill, Eden or Macmillan and the sight of Major cavorting around the country courting the party faithful was striking.

Following defeat in the 1945 election Churchill asked his businessman friend Lord Woolton if he would become party chairman with a brief to 'reorganise the party and bring it to a proper state of efficiency'; Woolton found the party 'the most topsy-like arrangement that I had ever come across', but he set about drastically changing it.[45] Addressing the party conference in 1946, he admitted that this was the first time he had ever attended such a gathering, but there was no sign that members were in the least perturbed by this revelation.[46] He remained party chairman for nine years, longer than any other postwar holder of that office, and during that time became both popular and respected for the changes he made. This appointment illustrated the unfettered power of the Conservative leader to choose (as well as dismiss) the party chairman, who in turn controls Central Office (the party head office). Giving the leader this power was justified in 1949 in the Maxwell-Fyfe Report on party organisation, because it allowed the leader to have as chairman someone in whom he had full confidence, and to recruit 'an outstanding personality, not necessarily already related to the party organisation'.[47] It is not easy to imagine so bald a statement being accepted forty-five years later. It seems inconceivable that a leader would now dare to impose a chairman who had not acquired at first hand a substantial knowledge of the party organisation.[48]

Heath inherited as party chairman Edward du Cann; they did not get on well together and Heath forced du Cann out, replacing him with Anthony Barber. When Thatcher became leader she appointed Lord Thorneycroft as party chairman, the man who had resigned as Macmillan's chancellor of the exchequer seventeen years earlier in protest at what he viewed as the government's financial profligacy. When Major became leader he appointed Chris Patten in place of Kenneth Baker, the latter surviving in his cabinet only till the 1992 election. But the

---

45   See Earl of Woolton, *Memoirs*, Cassell, 1959, pp. 328 and 331ff.

46   See McKenzie, *British Political Parties*, 1963, p. 273.

47   Quoted in Ibid., 1963, pp. 272-3.

48   The Charter Group campaigning for reform within the party in the 1980s wanted an elected chairman. When in 1993 speculation about the replacement of the chairman was rife, a founder member of that group wrote a letter to the *Daily Telegraph* (10 September 1993) arguing that it was more vital that the chairman was someone the party could trust than someone the leader could trust.

freedom of the leader to appoint and dismiss has not by any means always guaranteed harmony between leader and chairman. In 1987 there was considerable tension between Thatcher and Central Office, then headed by Norman Tebbit. Rivalries and misunderstandings were aggravated during the election campaign partly because the advertising agency chosen by Central Office was different from the one used previously and known to Thatcher. But a further factor had been the prime minister's decision to ask Lord Young also to work in Central Office, reporting directly to her. On 'wobbly Thursday' there was clearly a row between Norman Tebbit and Lord Young. Changes were hurriedly made in campaign strategy. Reading the accounts of what took place, one is impressed by the degree to which the overriding concern of those involved was to please their leader, to soothe her, to calm her down and to settle matters on terms agreeable to her.[49]

The chairman once appointed has considerable freedom in determining matters within central office. One of Lord Thorneycroft's first acts in 1975 was to sack the recently appointed director-general of the party, Michael Wolff. This line of command has resulted in Central Office being described as the personal machine of the leader. Within the party the tradition has been that the leader does not take advantage of this, but respects the importance of Central Office serving the whole party. Heath was criticised for the way he used central office after losing power in 1974, and the clean sweep made under Thatcher's leadership in 1975 was justified in these terms.[50] A centralising trend has been apparent within the party. Since 1972 party agents have been organised as a national service under the direction of Central Office. In 1980 Thatcher decided the time had come to integrate the Conservative research department, hitherto and traditionally a separate organisation with its own head directly appointed by the leader, into Central Office. This caused some pain and misgivings within the party but as leader Thatcher was able to impose the decision. In 1988 Peter Brooke consolidated the lines of control at Central Office and in 1992 Norman Fowler carried this process further in another reorganisation.

The problem with the job of chairman is that the post stands between the leader, who in the party constitution is accorded an autocratic position, and the voluntary party organisation, which increasingly feels it has the right to assert itself in its own way. The party's professional staff,

49   See Lord Young, *The Enterprise Years*, Headline, 1990, pp. 235ff; Norman Tebbit, *Upwardly Mobile* (2nd edn), 1989, pp. 332-6; Lawson, *The View from No. 11*, pp. 698-9.

50   John Campbell comments that Wolff's appointment in April 1974 was controversial and tactless, 'much resented by the area agents and [area] chairmen as a snub to the long serving party professionals…it reinforced the impression of an insecure leader acting to protect his own position'; see Campbell, *Edward Heath*, p. 629.

whom the chairman controls, are the servants of both the National Union and the party leadership. Tensions are inevitable. Although Lord Thorneycroft served as party chairman throughout Thatcher's first six years as leader, she then had five different chairmen in the next nine years. Once she had become established firmly as party leader and prime minister, it seemed that successive chairmen found the role difficult to fulfil under the sharp, watchful eye of the mistress of Downing Street. Baker described the job as 'a bed of nails', and Patten said it was 'an impossible job, not to be wished on one's worst enemy'. Cecil Parkinson reckoned that Thatcher did not understand Central Office, while Tebbit thought all prime ministers would like Central Office to be very weak, because they were wary of an alternative power base except at election time when they suddenly wanted it to be enormously strong.[51]

As with appointments, so with policy. The party manifesto is the leader's responsibility. Advice can of course be sought, but it is the leader who has the last word over the content. On the 1983 manifesto Thatcher commented: 'The party leader cannot dictate to senior colleagues: the rest of the government and parliamentary party need to feel committed to the manifesto's proposals and consequently there has to be a good deal of consultation.'[52] The preference for short manifestos, 'to proclaim a theme rather than write a prospectus' in Churchill's words,[53] had certainly given way by the 1980s to length and detail. Heath argued that the public had become so cynical about politics and politicians that it was essential to spell out policies to convince electors both of their viability and of the party's intentions. Another perhaps base motive for expanding the manifesto has been the opportunity this gives a leader to shackle the party with commitments that might otherwise prove difficult to secure. The longest ever was the Conservatives' manifesto for 1987. Thatcher's determination to secure a radical agenda for a third term drove the whole process. Proposals for the poll tax, for education reform and for further privatisation were all included, having in several cases received very little discussion within the party. The changes in education were largely the work of Brian Griffiths, head of her policy unit, and not of the secretary of state for education,

---

51   These comments by four former party chairmen were all made in a television programme entitled 'The Kenneth Baker Memoirs' broadcast on BBC2 on 2 October 1993.

52   Thatcher, *The Downing Street Years*, p. 281.

53   Quoted in J.D. Hoffman, *The Conservative Party in Opposition 1945-51*, MacGibbon and Kee, 1964, p. 206. See also R.A. Butler, *The Art of the Possible*, Hamish Hamilton, 1971, p. 135, where he quotes Churchill: 'When an Opposition spells out its policy in detail, the Government becomes the Opposition and attacks the Opposition which becomes the Government. So having failed to win the sweets of office, it equally fails to enjoy the benefits of being out of office.'

Baker. A confident Conservative leader can in effect bounce the party into commitments which have only lukewarm support. Thatcher did this in 1987, and paid the price for it in 1990.

The Labour Leader and the Party Organisation

Of Labour's eight postwar leaders only three have served as prime minister; Labour's last three leaders, in addition to Tony Blair, the leader at the time of writing, have not reached Downing Street. Perhaps a Labour leader in office as prime minister is in a better position than a leader of the Opposition to exercise authority within the party. Certainly that appeared to be so under Wilson and Callaghan. But no leader became as dominant as Kinnock, the longest-serving Opposition leader of the postwar period. Perhaps this was because he followed Michael Foot, by any reckoning the least effective leader in either major party throughout this period.

One view of the Labour party has been that it is a inherently divided body. Its organisation outside parliament is capable of marching the party off in a direction that may be anathema to a majority of its parliamentary members. But if the party is to remain responsive to the opinions of the wider electorate, then it is the parliamentary members who are best placed to ensure this because they face election at the hands of that wider electorate. Keeping the two wings of the party in harmony if possible, but at least avoiding open warfare, is an important task for the leader.

Attlee had difficulties with the Bevanites, but their strength was more in the parliamentary party than outside it, and when it came to crucial conference votes the party power structure was reliable from his point of view. His cabinet began with at least nine of its twenty members having substantial trade union backgrounds. Ernest Bevin in particular was a tower of strength, ever ready to throw his considerable weight behind 'little Clem' and to bully trade unionists into lending their support. Attlee's matter-of-factness and his modesty helped win him support. Here was a leader with whom the party could feel at ease; that was why he had been chosen – after the showmanship of MacDonald – and it was a continuing source of strength. When in 1945 Attlee slapped down Harold Laski, the chairman of the National Executive Committee, no one was likely to think he was on an ego trip.

Periodically however tension between the two wings of the party has flared up. Following its third successive defeat in 1959, the then leader, Hugh Gaitskell, wanted the party to jettison some of its socialist baggage. But his efforts to secure the alteration of Clause Four, so that the party would no longer be formally committed to nationalising almost everything, failed. He wanted to re-shape the party in a social democratic direction, in order to make it more attractive to a newly affluent electorate. His endeavours were thwarted, although the outcome of the struggle no doubt helped to alter the image of the party in the public mind.[54]

In 1969 Wilson likewise found himself defeated by the party when he sought to legislate in the contentious area of industrial relations. There were many contrasts with ten years earlier. For a start Wilson was prime minister, but after five years in office much of the party felt betrayed, and it was in many ways even more demoralised than it had been a decade earlier. Whereas Gaitskell accepted that if he could not persuade conference to change its mind he would have to compromise, Wilson as prime minister appeared to feel that he had the right to defy conference indefinitely. By 1969, unlike Attlee, he had a cabinet with only two members who knew the trade union movement from the inside.[55] The two wings of the party were drifting apart and it seemed as if Wilson did not mind too much.

There was an indication of the difficulties brought about by this distancing of Wilson from his party in 1968 when the post of general secretary, in effect chief executive, fell vacant. The appointment was the responsibility of the National Executive Committee, and it was widely reported that Wilson's preferred choice had been defeated by 14 votes to 12. Although Wilson argued in his memoirs that he had remained detached from the whole process, other contemporary diarists saw the matter very much as the press did. Crossman wrote that Tony Greenwood 'would have been the PM's stooge and that's why he lost'; hence Wilson's 'gratuitous defeat'. Benn says that when the result was announced 'Harold's face was like thunder'.[56] Subsequently the gulf between Downing Street and Labour's head office at Transport House widened. Wilson felt that any information passed on to the party would simply be leaked to the press. He disliked the tone of mid-term policy documents produced by the NEC, and 'regretted that the Labour Party constitution...denied him the freedom in making party policy enjoyed by his Conservative counterpart'.[57] The distrust between Transport House and Number 10 resulted in the former preparing for an autumn election some time after Wilson had decided on a June election.[58]

54   See Stephen Haseler, *The Gaitskellites*, Macmillan, 1969.
55   Lewis Minkin, *The Contentious Alliance*, Edinburgh University Press, 1991, p. 111.
56   See Wilson, *The Labour Government,1964-1970*, pp. 547-8; Crossman, *Diaries of a Cabinet Minister*, 1977, pp. 155-6; Benn, *Out of the Wilderness*, 1988, p. 93.
57   David Butler and Michael Pinto-Duschinsky, *The British General Election of 1970*, Macmillan, 1971, p. 60. Crossman also bemoaned the fact that Labour did not have a member of its cabinet clearly responsible for relations with the party head office then at Transport House; see Crossman, *Diaries of a Cabinet Minister*, 1975, pp. 97 and 223.

When the Conservatives produced a potentially election-winning policy on industrial relations, the very popularity of this policy as measured by opinion polls propelled Wilson into action, appealing to the electorate ever the heads of the party. Toughness and firm government were to be his forte. But his party would not have it. Resistance in the unions stiffened opposition within the parliamentary party. When faced with defeat there, Wilson backed down. A year later the party lost the election. Its achievements in office seemed unimpressive. In opposition Wilson rapidly trimmed; his leadership was not formally challenged, but had he not accepted substantial policy adjustments, he would have been pushed out, as happened to the less malleable deputy leader, Roy Jenkins.

In the 1970s Labour's parliamentary leadership, in opposition till 1974 and then in office, developed a much closer relationship with the unions than it had had in the 1960s. A so-called Social Contract shaped policy. These were the years when corporatism reached its most obvious public expression. Tax changes were made conditional on votes from the Trades Union Congress in support of incomes policies. But relations between the party in government and the party in the country were hardly harmonious. In 1975 the party conference took a hostile view to continued membership of the European Community, while in the referendum of that year the government's official line was support for it. The party very nearly committed its own organisation to campaign against its own government, but Wilson averted this by threatening to resign.[59] In 1976 Callaghan at his first party conference as prime minister announced the ending of Keynesian-style demand management, and Denis Healey as chancellor began talking the language of monetarism. Callaghan as a former trade unionist employed all his skills to keep the party both together and in office.

In the latter endeavour, he failed, and in 1979, full of disappointment and bitter recrimination, the party went into opposition. Once in opposition, it was as if the party activists outside parliament, and many trade union leaders, were determined to settle old scores. Foot replaced Callaghan and led the party, but rather in the style of a fox leading a pack of hounds. The party conference asserted itself; unprecedentedly not a single member of the shadow cabinet was elected to the National Executive Committee. The two wings of the party were at loggerheads. Foot bowed to the extra-parliamentary party. The result was the 1983 election débâcle.

For the party this was shock therapy: if it was to avoid relegation in a two-party system, it had to change. With Thatcher riding high

---

58   See Butler and Pinto-Duschinsky, *The British General Election of 1970*, p. 61.
59   See Pimlott, *Harold Wilson*, p. 658.

in government and the myth (or was it the reality?) of union power shattered once the miners' strike was over, the party outside parliament was prepared to let the leader actually lead. Kinnock elbowed his way to dominance and with a secure majority on the National Executive Committee began a transformation. So-called extremists were purged and policies were turned upside-down. Kinnock secured the appointment of his own candidates both as general secretary of the party and to the newly-created post of director of communications. The new focus of power within the party was the 'Office of the Leader of the Opposition', an organisation hitherto unknown, and one on which the party constitution needless to say remained silent. But all lines of control met there.

Unlike a Conservative leader, a Labour leader has to secure approval for the party manifesto from the NEC and cabinet (or shadow cabinet) meeting jointly. Tensions between the two wings of the party have frequently emerged at the time of manifesto-making. Sitting prime ministers have usually got their way without too much difficulty; in both 1966 and 1970 Wilson dominated the process, partly by delaying serious work on the manifesto till the last possible moment, by which time, with an election campaign launched, the incentive for reaching agreement quickly was strong. In 1974 Wilson made a point of telling colleagues at the joint meeting that he had not seen a draft of the manifesto any earlier than they had.[60] But after nearly five precarious years in office, things were different. The joint meeting between cabinet and NEC in 1979 lasted eight hours, with Callaghan as prime minister repeatedly using what Tony Benn described as a 'veto' to exclude items of which he disapproved.[61] At least this produced a credible manifesto. In 1983 Foot agreed to the NEC policy document within minutes, but under the pressure of the campaign the extravagances, vagueness and self-contradictions of the manifesto were painfully exposed. Thereafter Kinnock succeeded in dominating the process, securing the abandonment of polices that were like albatrosses to Labour's hopes, such as unilateralism and re-nationalisation.

Kinnock never became prime minister, but in 1992 he came very close to doing so. Bringing the Labour Party back from the doldrums of 1983 to a position where opinion polls indicated, and politicians expected, a Labour victory was a considerable achievement. It is difficult not to conclude that a precondition of this recovery was his apparent unparalleled ascendancy, and this in the party that has traditionally kept its leader closely circumscribed by so-called intra-party democracy. Almost all sections of the party were prepared to acquiesce in this process of building Kinnock up and allowing him dominance. Initially

60   Tony Benn, *Against the Tide: Diaries, 1973-1976*, Hutchinson, 1989, p. 225.
61   Tony Benn, *Conflicts of Interest: Diaries, 1977-80*, Hutchinson, 1990, pp. 485-8.

this was seen as the price for Labour's survival in the two-party system; later it was felt to be a necessary pre-condition for electoral success.

Perhaps Kinnock exemplified the new requirements of party leadership. All the old relationships still exist, between the leader and immediate colleagues, the leader and the parliamentary party, the leader and the party professionals and the activists. But what is new is the heightened intensity of political leadership itself. This has a number of aspects. Most obvious is the relentless and irresistible intrusion into every aspect of personality, background, family life and friendships, even of appearance and mannerisms. Leaders must allow themselves to be packaged for presentation to a voracious media. Repeated photo opportunities and soundbites have become the inescapable requirement of leadership. The demands of leadership no longer allow any space for life outside the role of party leader. Month by month the opinion polls provide searching analysis, not simply of how popular or otherwise they are, but of how the public perceives their varied qualities of compassion, truthfulness, sincerity, decisiveness and so on. Leaders are not just spokesmen, but have become 'ostentatious flagships of their respective fleets'.[62]

Thatcher's populism both reflected and endorsed a changed model for leadership. She was happy to personalise the party struggle more than ever before. She claimed the party mandate as a personal mandate in a way no predecessor had dared to do.[63] Alan Clark, a former Thatcher minister and admirer, commented in his diary that her 'constituency in this place [the House of Commons] depends solely on her ability to win elections'.[64] The Heseltine leadership challenge in 1990 exemplified the same populism. Having left the cabinet five years previously, Heseltine spent his time campaigning, largely in the party in the country. The strength of his support in parliament depended on the strength of his support outside. What nearly enabled him to leap from the backbenches straight into Downing Street were opinion polls showing that a Conservative party led by him was very much more likely to win

62   The phrase is Michael Foley's; see his *The Rise of the British Presidency*, Manchester University Press, 1993, p. 121.

63   In 1984 Margaret Thatcher was quoted as saying, 'Five years ago the British people made me prime minister...last year I was re-elected with an overwhelming majority', as if her party and the House of Commons had nothing to do with the matter. And until 1990 her party did hardly dare to interfere. Following the 1992 election John Major said: 'I am delighted to have my own mandate. I think it is very important. I can now accept that the country have elected me in my own right to be prime minister'; quoted in Foley, *The Rise of the British Presidency*, p. 254. For Thatcher reference see Donald Shell, 'The British Constitution in 1984', *Parliamentary Affairs*, vol. 38 (1985), no. 2, p. 131.

64   Alan Clark, *Diary*, p. 289.

a general election than one led by Thatcher. But his challenge crumbled when polls suddenly showed that Major was seen as having a similar capacity.

Underlying this is the increasingly restless and rootless character of the electorate. Former party loyalties have weakened; political activity has become fragmented through a bewildering variety of organised groups. Election campaigns mark the culmination of several years of marketing strategy by the parties, with voters ready to opt for whatever seems the best buy at the time. In appealing to the electorate, parties find they must give place to their leader because they have nowhere else to go. No effort can be spared in presenting the leader to the public because it is through the leader that the party is perceived. From policy advisers to public relations consultants, from speech-writers to elocutionists, transport managers to make-up artists, all must be at the disposal of the leader. Parties may be slimmer organisations engaging less with society. But at the same time leaders are called upon to relate more directly and with greater immediacy to voters. This does not necessarily mean that the leader rules the party; it could even mean that the party rules the leader.

6

PRIME MINISTER AND THE PUBLIC
MANAGING MEDIA RELATIONS

Colin-Seymour-Ure

Invited by the BBC to a display of the exciting medium of television, soon after its relaunch in 1946, Clement Attlee went home unimpressed. To him the obvious comparison seemed to be with adult education, and he compared TV unfavourably with the excellent work done by the Workers' Educational Association.[1] Winston Churchill refused to appear on TV at all, except in occasional newsreels and at the first televised Conservative Party annual conference in 1954. Thirty years later, by contrast, it was becoming normal for prime ministers to adapt their style and mannerisms, their very physique, to the demands of TV. Margaret Thatcher lowered her voice and changed her hairstyle on the advice of media consultants. Politicians might not quite give their eye-teeth for television, but they would certainly cap them for it.

Prime ministers' relations with the public largely mean their relations with the news media, and it is tempting to interpret the entire period since 1945 as one of adjustment to the voracious appetites of TV. That would be to oversimplify. Even so, the first and most obvious reason for studying prime ministers' media relations is their vastly increased visibility. One reason for the success of an early studio interview with Anthony Eden (when still foreign secretary), according to the producers, was that it showed a leading politician being normal, instead of speechifying.[2] This, in 1951, was completely novel. Yet by 1993 newspaper cartoonists, for example, could habitually draw John Major wearing his underpants outside his trousers, because he had been spotted from TV pictures as someone who appeared to tuck his shirt inside his underpants rather than between his pants and his trousers. This somehow seemed revealing of his character. A prime minister's voice, face, clothes, gait, body language, laughter – and tears, as Margaret Thatcher showed

1   Grace Wyndham Goldie, *Facing the Nation: Television and politics, 1936-1976*, Bodley Head, 1977, p. 105.
2   BBC Written Archives, contributors' file: Anthony Eden, September 1951.

169

when talking fondly of her father in an interview – became commonplace on the TV screen.

Potentially, too, this living-room familiarity with the prime minister may affect how viewers cast their votes. It naturally followed, therefore, that after the premierships of Attlee and Churchill, as TV grew more popular, prime ministers had to spend ever more time, energy and administrative resources on managing their media relations. It was not surprising that as a result the prime minister's press secretary became an influential member of the Downing Street staff. Bernard Ingham, Thatcher's press secretary for all but six months of her premiership, was a constant adviser and companion. He was sniped at in the Commons, criticised for behaving almost as a minister – and was probably better known to the public than many ministers. On retirement he was knighted. While still at Downing Street, he was important enough to generate a hostile biography, serialised in the Sunday press.[3]

Bernard Ingham's closeness to Thatcher is a practical reminder of the strong link between the presentation and the substance of government decisions. This is a further reason for studying the prime minister's media relations. When a government is deciding what to do – whether in legislation, such as health service reform, or over the best reaction to events, such as the Argentine invasion of the Falklands – ministers wish to maximise the chances of success. To the extent that success depends on public acceptance of the decision, media presentation will become one of the factors in consideration of the alternatives. This point was as relevant for Attlee as for Major. Attlee deliberately chose as press secretary an experienced journalist, Francis Williams, who was known to be a Labour Party supporter. Williams had edited the Labour-controlled mass circulation *Daily Herald* before the war, but he was trusted also in Whitehall because of his wartime service in the Ministry of Information. Attlee knew that Williams's advice on press relations would have Labour's best interests at heart, but without involving the kind of kneejerk partisanship that would provoke corresponding scepticism from his newspaper clientele. In this the change from Attlee and Williams to Thatcher and Ingham was one of scale, due to TV, rather than of kind.

The link between presentation and substance in decision-making connects also with the idea of power as persuasion. For the American president, lacking a reliable majority for his programmes in Congress, power is famously 'the power to persuade'.[4] But political leadership of most kinds, unless it talks along the barrel of a gun, involves persuasion of some sort. In an early contribution to the debate about prime ministerial

3   Robert Harris, *Good and Faithful Servant*, Faber and Faber, 1990.
4   Richard E. Neustadt, *Presidential Power*, John Wiley, New York, 1976, p. 78.

power, George Jones argued that a prime minister is 'only as strong as his [colleagues] let him be'.[5] How powerful is that? His colleagues take into account such factors as their estimates of his reputation with their colleagues and with the party, both in Parliament and in the constituencies. They gauge his standing in the country – monitored in the opinion polls, from about the end of the 1950s, with the regularity of an intensive care unit – and they avidly follow the media.

All these elements of reputation reflect success or failure of persuasion. Eden failed fully to carry his cabinet – still less the parliamentary party and the Opposition – in the Suez invasion of 1956, and it cost him his job. Thatcher carried almost everyone at Westminster in the Falklands crisis of 1982. Yet she failed in the later 1980s to persuade probably a majority in the country even to call the unpopular poll tax by its official name: the community charge. And the failure of the tax was a major factor in her rejection by the Conservative Party in 1990. Thus, although a role in the mobilisation of popular opinion is not as important in the job description of a prime minister as in that of an American president, the prime minister has a need, and an unequalled opportunity, to use the 'power to persuade'. Good media management may make a crucial difference to success.

In the increasingly complex media world, and as TV has intruded further into politics, prime ministers' handling of media relations has revealed more and more about their political styles. Some incumbents, such as Macmillan and Wilson, welcomed TV; others – Home and Heath – were uncomfortable with it. Churchill tried to do without a press secretary in 1951, having earlier found one unnecessary in the special circumstances of a wartime government; Thatcher, on the other hand, made Ingham indispensable. Attlee was unenthusiastic even about having the news agency tapes at Downing Street, until Francis Williams said they would tell him the cricket scores; Wilson pored over the papers and prided himself on knowing about deadlines and journalistic insider lore. In studying Downing Street media relations, we may learn something about a significant aspect of prime ministers' whole attitude to the job, to management priorities and to the nature of power.

The more important media relations have become, moreover, the greater is their relevance also to questions about the future development of the premiership. Can we yet make claims for the influence of TV upon the pathways to the office or upon the nature of 'prime ministerial timber'? More generally, what does the development of Downing Street news operations contribute to the argument that the premiership is becoming presidential?

5   George W. Jones, 'The prime minister's power', *Parliamentary Affairs*, vol. 18 (1965), p. 185.

The subject of this chapter is important, lastly, for the pious reason of its relevance to the principles and rhetoric of democratic accountability. More than ever in the 1990s, mass media are inextricable from the processes of political competition: between parties, between the interest groups which in some ways have supplanted them, and between the individuals driving for place and preferment within them. Beyond the political activists, the electorate depends upon media for most of its information about politics. All politics is to a great extent carried on in or through the mass media. At the centre of British politics is 10 Downing Street. A study of the accountability of prime ministers, quite apart from the details of their job, necessarily includes the study of their relations with the media. The practical expression of this link is that a prime minister's political crises, great and small, frequently contain a media sub-plot. At the time of Suez (1956) it was a row with the BBC. The Profumo crisis of 1963, which drained confidence in Macmillan, grew out of press exposures. The Falklands crisis of 1982 involved more rows with the broadcasters. A *leitmotiv* of Northern Ireland policy from the 1970s was tension about broadcast coverage. Major's attempts to bolster public (and party) confidence in his administration in 1993-4, not least through a 'Back to Basics' campaign intended to stress the party's concern for traditional morality, were drowned by a spate of press exposures of ministerial peccadillos.

In taking these points further, the rest of this chapter looks first at factors affecting prime ministers' public communication: some derive from the political context, others from the media. After an account of the development of Downing Street news operations, the chapter next discusses issues that confront a prime minister in handling media relations and, finally, some issues relevant to the wider political system.

The Downing Street Context

The main factor affecting the nature and scale of a prime minister's communication task is the general standing of the government: its parliamentary majority, its reputation in the party, at Westminster and in the constituencies, its popularity in the country – reflected in the polls, in MPs' postbags and in the media – and its reputation among media commentators themselves. All these, most of them changing and intangible, make up a mood of confidence and optimism for ministers, or of comparative gloom. The mood is affected too, of course, by the prime minister's own personal standing and by external factors such as the imminence of the next general election, the state of the Opposition parties and the course of events.

In one way, this means that prime ministers are never faced with exactly the same communication task as their predecessors – nor, indeed, for themselves, as time goes by. Attlee, Wilson and Major each experienced both the cushion of large majorities and, later (earlier too, in Wilson's case), the discomfort of small ones. Major's bill to ratify the Maastricht treaty survived only through attaching the issue of confidence to the final vote in July 1993; yet before the 1992 election reduced his overall majority to twenty-one, he had won the preliminary votes on ratification quite easily. Wilson's symbolically important steel renationalisation bill in 1965 turned on the vote, ultimately, of two recalcitrants; while most of his legislative programme after Labour's big election win in 1966 passed without difficulty.

Even so, such variations happen within broadly the same Downing Street context. Prime ministers benefit, for instance, from the principle of collective cabinet responsibility. However much this may be a fiction if interpreted to mean collective ministerial involvement in decision-making, it has real force in preventing public dissent by ministers from decisions with which they disagree. The Privy Council oath, which ministers swear on taking office, binds them fearsomely to secrecy. In principle, the cabinet sings with one voice; and, if this is not always the voice of Number 10, Number 10 nevertheless is the conductor. Prime ministers can still exercise a large degree of control over the pronouncements of their colleagues. Signed newspaper articles must normally be limited to the affairs of a minister's own department, to avoid the risk of crossed wires or inaccuracy. For many years, broadcast interviews had to be cleared with Downing Street. The possibility of adverse publicity (and ridicule?) means that ministers require permission before instituting libel proceedings. In suing two magazines to clear his name and – more important as a motive, perhaps, the name of a Downing Street caterer with whom it had been linked – Major in 1993 became the third postwar prime minister to start an action for libel (the others were Churchill and Wilson).

The prime minister's authority for control, or co-ordination, of ministers' publicity derives from the status of 'first among equals'. The problem with this idea is its ambiguity: you cannot simultaneously be both first and on an identical footing to everyone else. As a device for prescribing constitutional forms, the principle may work, but in practice the ambiguity both reflects and blurs, to varying degrees, the tensions typical within political parties. Party competition at Westminster requires discipline, to keep the majority intact. Discipline requires that dirty linen be washed only in private (in the backbench 1922 Committee or the Parliamentary Labour Party committee), so as to minimise the public appearance of disunity and the scope for rival parties to score points. Disunity is bad for morale and for the party's reputation: it is likely to show up in the opinion polls.

To the constitutional requirement of secrecy, then, is added a party motive. Each should make a prime minister's public communication task simpler. In practice, however, the story of every government from Attlee to Major is to a greater or less extent the story of a struggle by the leadership to concert or maintain support for its programme. In every Cabinet there are dissenters – notables, such as Aneurin Bevan and Tony Benn, or those of lighter weight such as the 'wets' whom Thatcher was able to discard as her authority grew (for example, Norman St John-Stevas and Ian Gilmour). These will want to make sure that their perspective on events is accurately reported. The prime minister's allies will ensure, equally, that the official line is given full weight. The result, obviously, is the Cabinet Leak. Thus is the circle of constitutional form – collective responsibility – fitted to the square of political reality. In the 1990s, as in the 1940s, the rule was simple: 'I give guidance: you leak.' The nuances are well illustrated from the Wilson years in Richard Crossman's diaries: 'I wonder whether it is worth having these [Cabinet committee] meetings, with the kind of leaks we saw in the Sunday press,' Wilson grumbles (according to Crossman) on one occasion. 'This took my breath away', comments Crossman, 'because, of course, I had organised the interviews [with Lobby correspondents] and thought they had done a first-rate job.' Yet earlier Crossman himself is 'not very happy' about Tony Benn: 'To begin with, on every single occasion when he is about to bring a plan to Cabinet a leak occurs, giving the full details in advance.'[6]

Similar attitudes surely existed in other administrations. Prime ministers hate leaks, for they rightly see them as a threat. Leaks are an index of their inability to control their colleagues (most of whom, almost by definition, want their job) and to unite them behind a policy. Wilson and Thatcher, in particular, instituted bizarre and apparently excessive witch-hunts, generally by the Cabinet Secretary, in the fruitless pursuit of leakers.

The preoccupation with leaks is an illustration, too, of politicians' absorption in their own world. Few leaks can have made a significant difference to a government's record and electoral prospects. But politicians work in a world confined (more than actually enclosed) by the routines of Parliament, Whitehall, constituency and party. Words are the tools of their trade, and the flow of publicity (or its absence) is intrinsic to their position, whether as backbencher or prime minister. Media are the mirror into which politicians are for ever glancing, over someone

6   Richard Crossman, *The Diaries of a Cabinet Minister*, vol. 1, Hamish Hamilton, London, 1975 p. 551.

else's shoulder if not their own. The faintest image may assume for them, and for journalists, an intensity and significance largely lost on the world beyond Westminster.

The Media Context: Broadcasting

The political world before television is increasingly difficult to visualise, even for those who experienced it. While the organisation and procedures at Downing Street have changed greatly since 1946, these changes are trivial compared with the ones brought by television.[7]

Television's intrusion (for so party leaders often viewed it) was driven more by the needs of party competition than of government. Aptly, therefore, it was an election campaign – that of 1959 – which is the most important symbolic date in the process. Until then, campaigns received no broadcast coverage at all, apart from the reporting of results on election night and the small number of broadcasts run, as now, by the parties themselves. In 1945 these party broadcasts were a notable feature of the campaign. They took place nightly after the nine o'clock news, except on Sundays and the last few evenings before polling day. Unbelievable as it seems now, some 45 per cent of the electorate listened nightly to party leaders intoning solemnly to the microphone for up to thirty minutes at a time. Churchill's broadcast opening the series and Attlee's reply the next evening set the tone of the whole campaign. It was in a party broadcast that Churchill made his notorious 'Gestapo' charge, later regarded as tactically inept, that a socialist system could not be established without a political police.[8] The reason why the broadcasters did not build on the success of these broadcasts was their fear of breaking the election laws about fairness and impartiality. But experiments at four by-elections in 1958, led by Granada TV in Rochdale, produced no hostile reaction from the parties, and so in the following year the era of TV campaigns began.

This world of before-and-after can be further sub-divided, without fixing too firm a pattern on what was a steady, albeit jerky, progress. The premierships of Attlee and Churchill were a period of broadcasting inauguration, lasting until Eden took office in 1955, which was also the year when Independent Television (ITV) began. The lack of enthusiasm of those two prime ministers is not surprising, since they were respectively sixty-two and seventy-six when they took office. They had made their careers when political communication was an art of

7   See, e.g., Colin Seymour-Ure, *The British Press and Broadcasting since 1945*, Blackwell, 1991, Chapter 7.

8   R.B. McCallum and A. Readman, *The British General Election of 1945*, Oxford University Press, 1947, pp. 142-3.

the platform and the printed page. But TV itself in the decade 1946-55 was still very much at the heels of radio. Some senior broadcasters were still hesitant about introducing news of any kind at all, for fear that pictures would distort established news values. TV sought faithfully to portray such political activity as it actually observed, without in any way affecting it in the process and without breaching the BBC's requirements of balance and impartiality.

Attlee and Churchill were therefore hardly confronted with an aggressive medium. The best example of the broadcasters' deference was the now astonishing 14-days rule. This had been introduced by the BBC in 1944, in anticipation of postwar renewal of party competition and possible pressures on programme-makers. After 1945, both prime ministers warmly supported it. The effect was to ban all broadcast discussion of matters coming before parliament within the ensuing fourteen days. The rule survived into Eden's administration, and indeed it was confirmed by a vote of 271–126 in the Commons on 30 November 1955.[9] But it could not withstand the clamour of argument in the Suez crisis and it was suspended, supposedly for a 'trial period', in December 1956.

The obscurantism of the two party leaders did not prevent their colleagues exploring the potential of the new medium. For the Conservatives, it was a natural extension of work with newsreels that had started between the world wars. In 1950 TV showed the election night results. In 1951 came the first televised party election broadcasts. From 1952 onwards ministers occasionally appeared on discussion programmes such as 'Press Conference'. 'Panorama' began in 1953 – when the Coronation gave an immense fillip to TV sales. In 1954 came the first televised budget talks by the chancellor of the exchequer and his opposite numbers, and also the Conservatives' first televised party conference. Not till 1965, however, did a party leader, Heath, take advantage of the publicity opportunity and attend the whole conference, rather than descend on the last morning to make the traditional climactic speech.

Eden and all his successors had the advantage of becoming prime minister with experience of TV behind them. Eden's brief premiership (1955-7) marks the second stage of TV's political progress: a period of initiative and adjustment, which may be regarded as reaching a key symbolic moment in the election of 1959. Prime ministers henceforth would increasingly adapt to the potential of the medium, rather than slight it or expect to use it entirely on their own terms. Eden won plaudits and top ratings for his televised party broadcasts in the 1955 election. He was the first prime minister to address the nation face-to-camera on television, once during a visit by the Soviet leaders Bulganin and Khrushchev and twice during the Suez crisis (on 8 August and during the Anglo-French invasion of the canal, on 3 November).

In the late 1950s TV licences were growing at the rate of 800,000 a year. To Grace Wyndham Goldie, a pioneer in the production of political broadcasting, Eden's use of television in the Suez crisis was the beginning of the medium's primacy over sound. The start of ITV, more particularly of Independent Television News (ITN), was a challenge to the BBC and heralded new styles of interview and discussion. Current affairs 'magazine' programmes were introduced. Interviewing became 'journalistic rather than reverential', in Mrs Goldie's phrase.[10] ITN's crisp young newscasters, including the Olympic athletics medallist and future Conservative minister Christopher Chataway, were discouraged from calling ministers 'sir' and ducking hard questions. Viewers began to expect automatically to see their political leaders on TV during momentous events. 'Far and away' the most important finding in a quick survey of the public at one stage of the Suez crisis, the Conservative Party chairman Oliver Poole told Eden, was that he should make a broadcast as soon as he possibly could.[11]

The years after 1959 divide a little less clearly into two, but for present purposes a line can be drawn at the retirement of Wilson in April 1976. Macmillan, Douglas-Home, Wilson and Heath spanned the years when political broadcasting, both on radio and on television, reached maturity. TV was no longer an optional extra to be used, as Macmillan tended to do, for occasional dignified and statesmanlike excursions (including, in his case, a celebrated 'fireside chat' in 1959 with the visiting American President Eisenhower). If prime ministers and political institutions did not adapt, they, not TV, would be the likely losers. Thus election campaigns, for example, were increasingly shaped by the scope of television. The timing and venue of speeches changed to fit the needs of TV technology. Wilson found in 1964 that to make hustings repartee effective on TV, he had to repeat a heckler's comment before demolishing it. Douglas-Home, fighting the same election as a prime minister plainly uncomfortable with the cameras, did not learn that trick. Heath remarked in 1966 that TV coverage made his jokes stale more quickly. Leaders went on 'walkabouts' for TV more than on old-fashioned countrywide hustings tours. Already in 1966 and 1970 more than half of all broadcast election news coverage went on Heath and Wilson. By 1987 and 1992 the proportion given to the party leaders was even higher. The daily party press conferences, which had been invented by Labour in 1959 specifically for the broadcasters,

10 Goldie, *Facing the Nation*, p. 215.
11 Oliver Poole to the prime minister, 2 November 1956. PREM 11/1123. (The series of prime ministers' files in the Public Record Office is numbered with the prefix PREM.)

became an important fixture. Party leaders met broadcasters for set-piece interviews on the broadcasters' own ground in TV studios.

For prime ministers in office there were more, and more varied, political programmes with which to contend. BBC-2 started in 1964, with a specific remit for 'serious' programmes. The number of hours in the broadcasting day was extended. Commercial ('independent') radio began in 1973 and made phone-in programmes commonplace. 'Satire', introduced in 1963 with 'That Was the Week That Was' (which made David Frost a celebrity), used unheard-of mimicry and ridicule of politicians, requiring the most careful attention by BBC management to 'balance'. The actor John Bird became famous for his impersonations of Harold Wilson. Documentary programmes followed the newspaper fashion for 'investigative' reporting, much influenced by American examples. Resulting resentments burst out in heroic rows between politicians and broadcasters about fairness, impartiality, bias, trivialisation. Wilson was enraged, after the unexpected defeat of his government in 1970, by 'Yesterday's Men', a slightly frivolous inquiry into the condition of ministers thrown untimely out of office. (He disliked, in particular, the presenter's curiosity about the sums paid for his memoirs.) Meanwhile the Heath government was also enraged, in 1972, by 'The Question of Ulster', the first in the long list of programmes on that subject to cause friction.[12]

Alone among the institutions in which prime ministers traditionally encountered the media, with or without public participation too, the House of Commons was still resisting the TV cameras at the time of Wilson's retirement in 1976. A prime minister's principal regular platform, with its highly charged potential, remained the preserve of the print media. The causes were complex, but they included a feeling among many backbenchers precisely that TV would give the prime minister a weapon of publicity too powerful in relation to the House as a whole – even though, in feeble hands, it might prove self-destructive. As a compromise, radio broadcasting was permitted from 1975. This too had long been regarded with suspicion. Even during the Second World War, the idea that Churchill's inspirational speeches should be broadcast live, rather than repeated afterwards from a studio, was considered inappropriate.

Harold Wilson was in a general sense the first 'TV prime minister', for he was the first to exploit the opportunities of the medium across a broad range. For all his successors, TV has not been an instrument applied to political activity, but rather an inescapable part of the environment within which politics is carried on. The period since the

12   On both *Yesterday's Men* and *The Question of Ulster*, see Michael Leapman, *The Last Days of the Beeb*, Geo. Allen and Unwin, London, 1986.

late 1970s may thus be fairly described as one in which TV has been politically in the ascendant. However, this does not mean that broadcasters dictate to prime ministers. On the contrary, the government's statutory powers over programme content, over key personnel in the governing bodies both of BBC and ITV, and over the BBC's licence fee funding, mean that prime ministers can ultimately dictate to the broadcasters, even if the effect on public opinion may not be what they wanted. The point, rather, is that the TV medium itself is ascendant. Mildly shocking claims of the 1970s, such as that 'TV is the election campaign', were the clichés of the 1980s. It is axiomatic that party leaders should have at least a reasonable competence as TV performers and that media advisers should be prominent in their retinue.

In the 1980s the number of TV channels continued to expand, with the arrival of Channel 4 (1982) and breakfast television (1983). Later came BSkyB and a variety of other satellite channels. Broadcasting hours now extended virtually round the clock. Access to TV and radio became much easier, for citizens as well as politicians. It was widely remarked that Margaret Thatcher was more troubled by a Bristol housewife on a talkback programme in the 1983 election than by any professional interviewer, bound by the rules of the game and the need to live to interview another day.[13] Radio 4's 'Today' programme became an almost daily forum for political leaders; Mrs Thatcher once called in during the programme, when she heard an item she was determined to comment on. The House of Commons at last acknowledged that members would prefer the studio interview to the floor of the Chamber, if TV was not allowed in. Inhibitions were abandoned, and from 1989 onwards the public could see a prime minister jousting with the Opposition leader, unhorsing or unhorsed. The depiction of politicians in satirical programmes went a big step beyond mimicry with the animated puppetry of 'Spitting Image', which dressed Thatcher in a man's suit and coloured Major a monochrome grey from head to foot.

In the broadcasting world of the 1990s, – a supermarket compared to the 1950s corner store – the politicians' ability to monitor political coverage, let alone control it, was greatly reduced. Impartiality and balance remained the ideals, but the Thatcher government sought them less by tightening the rules of access than by indirect pressure. This included traditional methods of private pressure, employed since the dawn of broadcasting, and a new readiness to use the laws of secrecy and contempt. Thatcher battled with Thames Television over its documentary about the SAS shooting of alleged IRA terrorists in Gibraltar, 'Death on the Rock' (1988), and even repudiated an inquiry into the programme by a former Conservative minister, Lord Windlesham.

13   See Hugo Young, *One of Us*, Macmillan, 1989, p. 286.

Another documentary about Ireland, 'Real Lives' (1985), saw the minister responsible for broadcasting policy in the front line, but with the prime minister in support. After their criticism the programme was broadcast very slightly altered, but the row cost the BBC director-general his job.[14] The glaring exception to the use of indirect pressure was Thatcher's attempt to deny Irish extremists publicity by imposing in 1988 a legal ban on their voices. They could still be filmed, and their words reported. What the government presumably failed to foresee was that the broadcasters' riposte to this blow against their discretion could be the routine dubbing of actors' voices over the originals.

Politicians and broadcasters do not normally welcome rows with each other. But these are an inevitable product of tensions between rival powerholders. Prime ministers trade on the constitutional and political power of their electoral mandate. Broadcasters trade on the power of TV as the primary medium of communication and recreation. Each needs the others; but their objectives are not identical, and therefore from time to time they clash. Most of the time, however, a prime minister has to deal with TV as part of the daily routine. Since Churchill conducted a private experiment with the cameras, to see if he liked them (he did not), TV has become like a cuckoo in the political nest. It has invaded the established forums of prime ministerial performance, from party conference to Parliament, and has spurred the formation of new ones, such as campaign press conferences and (under Major) little sessions outside Number 10. It has fashioned interview and discussion formats of its own, with rules and conventions about who takes part, on what terms and when. These, unlike most of those others, have no purpose separate from being broadcast and take place mainly – and not always comfortably – on the broadcasters' territory. ('You have a head like a skull', said a make-up woman to Douglas-Home. 'Doesn't everyone...?', he replied. 'No', she said.[15]) If prime ministers cannot now control the broadcasters as they could in Churchill's day, they must at least work hard to manage their own relations with them to best effect.

The Media Context: the Press

Newspapers never were easy for prime ministers to squash or square (in Lloyd George's phrase). Broadcasting was a public policy area from the start. A 'free press', in contrast, has been taken by governments throughout the twentieth century to mean a press free from government legislative interference. Every prime minister from Attlee to Major has

---

14   Alisdair Milne, *DG: The memoirs of a British broadcaster*, Hodder and Stoughton, 1988.
15   Michael Cockerell, *Live From Number 10*, Faber and Faber, 1988, p. 105.

had to deal with a press whose chief political characteristic is partisanship. The main variation in fact has been in the degree of overall support for the Conservative Party. Labour and Conservative prime ministers have thus faced distinct problems. For Attlee, Wilson and Callaghan the task was damage limitation in an overwhelmingly unsympathetic set of mass circulation national daily and Sunday papers. At the same time, they had to keep a much smaller number of sympathisers – latterly the papers of the *Mirror* group – lined up behind the leadership and its policies.

For Conservative prime ministers the problem was the other way round. Until Rupert Murdoch bought the *Sun* in 1969 and turned it into a Conservative tabloid, steadily overtaking the circulation of the *Daily Mirror*, Conservative prime ministers could reach working-class voters only through the *Daily Mail, Daily Express* and *Daily Sketch* (until its demise in 1971). These papers had a minority of working-class readers. Even so, Eden reached in this way a much larger proportion of what Labour thought of as its natural class constituency during the divisive Suez crisis, for instance (not to mention election campaigns), than a Labour prime minister was able to reach, correspondingly, among middle-class voters reading a Labour paper. In the 1945 general election the Labour-supporting *Daily Herald* and *Daily Mirror* accounted for about one-third of total national daily newspaper circulation, while Labour's share of the vote was nearly half. The Conservatives, in contrast, had 52 per cent of the circulation and 40 per cent of the votes. Since then, Conservative circulation has never fallen below 50 per cent at a general election; and since 1974, due to the irruption of the *Sun*, it has stayed between 67 and 78 per cent. The Conservative percentage of the votes, on the other hand, has generally been in the mid or low forties. For Labour the ratios, broadly, have been reversed.

Circulation figures conceal the even greater imbalance in the number of titles. In the practical business of press relations, this may be the more important figure. Since 1945 Labour has never had more than two mass-circulation dailies on its side. The *Daily Herald* was closer to its heart, because closer to its pocket: through the Trades Union Congress, Labour actually owned nearly half of its shares. Odhams Press owned the rest, but its owner had agreed in 1929 that Labour should control editorial policy. Throughout his premiership, therefore, Attlee knew that the *Daily Herald* was obliged to support his government. This was not, of course, the clear-cut relationship it might seem. The paper's editor had to render an account of his work to the annual party conference, and the conference was in theory the Labour Party's sovereign body. The *Daily Herald* was the party's paper, not the government's. Even so, proprietorship gave Attlee a different relationship than he

had with the *Daily Mirror*. Falling readership made the paper un-
economic; it was relaunched as the *Sun* in 1964, having passed into
Mirror group ownership, before being unwisely sold to Murdoch.

Harold Wilson could not directly control the Labour *Sun*, nor the
daily and Sunday *Mirror* papers. Instead he had to woo them. One
time-honoured method was the use of honours. At one point in the
later 1960s the management of those papers included four or five Life
Peers. The chairman, Cecil King, who did not take a peerage, knew
the importance of his support and was said to be interested in a government
post. When he criticised Wilson too strongly, in 1968, he was unseated
in a boardroom coup.

For Conservative prime ministers the use of peerages and knighthoods
for proprietors and journalists was routine. The growth of mass-circulation newspapers in the twentieth century had made direct party
control generally unfeasible, so party loyalty had often been secured
in that way. In Churchill's postwar premiership several of these elderly
barons – Kemsley (*Sunday Times* etc.), Camrose (*Daily Telegraph*) and,
above all, his crony and wartime ministerial colleague Beaverbrook
(*Daily Express, Sunday Express* and *Evening Standard*), were still active.
When a party manager chided him in 1953 for not taking more trouble
with the press, Churchill defended himself by naming a string of such
men whom he had recently seen.[16] This was not at all what his colleague
meant: he wanted Churchill to talk to journalists. All Churchill's successors have continued to deal directly with proprietors and, more than
in the past, with senior editors. They have seemed almost to ladle out
honours to stalwarts – if they wanted them. Some, such as Murdoch,
did not.

From Eden's premiership onwards, however, there was a shift of
emphasis. The old barons had not usually wanted political office, as
had Beaverbrook; but they liked public office. As the business of running
newspapers became more complex, partly because (by Thatcher's time)
almost all the national papers were part of international conglomerates,
proprietors seemed to be more detached than their predecessors from
public life in general. This made it even more important, not less so,
for a prime minister to cosset them. The interest in British politics
of a man such as Murdoch, with a global empire, must surely be potentially
less deep-rooted than those others'. Thatcher's policies on industrial
relations, media concentration and satellite broadcasting all helped Murdoch. While she remained in office, his support strayed strong. After
she went, his papers' support of Major vacillated.

Conservative prime ministers thus had to work increasingly hard
at cultivating the half-dozen or so dailies, and a similar number of

16   James Margach, *The Abuse of Power*, W.H. Allen, 1978, pp. 68-9.

Sunday Papers, which formed the core of the Tory press at any time since 1945. Their controllers expected to be cultivated and might take umbrage if they were not. Closest to an 'official' paper, while it remained in the hands of Lord Hartwell, until 1985, was the *Daily Telegraph*. Most maverick, initially because of Beaverbrook's anti-European, pro-Commonwealth vision, was the *Daily Express*. Most lively was the Murdoch *Sun*, especially during the Thatcher years, when it developed a style of self-conscious cheekiness.

While they could be relied on to fall into line during election campaigns, all these papers were willing to criticise prime ministers and, still more readily, their policies. Already before Suez, the *Daily Telegraph* jabbed at Eden for not providing 'the smack of firm government'. The press did much to undermine Macmillan in 1962-3, first by dubbing a major cabinet reshuffle in 1962 'the night of the long knives', not as a welcome reconstruction; and secondly by hounding him over the sexual peccadillos and deceptions of the Profumo and Stephen Ward affairs in 1963.[17] Heath's leadership was often questioned by Conservative papers. A prime minister remaining in office as long as Thatcher was bound also to be attacked; and the newspapers were openly calling for Major's replacement within about eighteen months of his election victory in 1992.

The true advantage of the Tory press to a Conservative prime minister, in sum, is its sympathetic predisposition. The *Daily Telegraph*, even in its most loyal phase, carried above its editorial column the phrase 'Independent of all groups'. This meant 'of all newspaper groups', but it suggested political independence too. Automatic party support should not be assumed. A broadsheet, in particular, saw itself contributing to, and not just reflecting, the evolution of policy. All postwar Conservative prime ministers could say of the press, for longer or shorter periods, 'With friends like these, who needs enemies?' But they could assume, as Labour prime ministers could not, that the moment would pass.

Two other aspects of the press need mention. One is the changing nature of the product. Attlee and Churchill read papers (except that Attlee rarely did) emaciated by war. Newsprint rationing, which kept pages down to ten or fewer, survived till 1955. Political columnists and feature writers, in particular, could not spread themselves. Proportionately, there was more parliamentary news than later. Only in the 1960s did the huge expansion of supplements, specialist writers and investigative, analytical journalism, epitomised in the *Sunday Times*, take place. At the same time, the press began to polarise. The middle-market broadsheet papers either disappeared, like the *Daily Herald*

17   Colin Seymour-Ure, *The Press, Politics and the Public*, Methuen, London, 1968.

and *News Chronicle*, or lost circulation and went tabloid, like the *Daily Mail* and *Daily Express*. By the time of Major's premiership four readers out of five were getting their news tabloid-style. This meant less of it – personalised, simplified, sensationalised and with more pictures and graphics. The change reinforced the trend, led by television, towards the dominance of the visual over the verbal in the conduct of politics.

The second aspect is the system through which most political reporting about the prime minister is organised. This is 'the Lobby' – a confusing term for those who use the word, especially in North America, to describe pressure group activity. When Attlee was prime minister the Lobby journalists were a small, discreet, closeknit, mostly anonymous and long-serving group, almost more parliamentary in their attachment to Westminster than the parliamentarians, many of whom had not worked there for as long as they had. Membership was strictly limited to one person per paper (except *The Times*, which for historical reasons had two). Weekly and Sunday journalists and broadcasters were excluded. The emphasis was on hard news. This was acquired by individual sleuthing in the bars and corridors of Westminster and the Members' lobby outside the Commons chamber itself (hence the name); by advance copies of documentation; and by collective briefings twice daily from the prime minister's press secretary. Relationships with politicians and Downing Street were marked by clear territorial and procedural rules. In the Lobby's own turret room at Westminster, the press secretary (and other less regular briefers, such as ministers) appeared 'by invitation' and the proceedings began and ended at the journalists' initiative. Elsewhere the Lobby behaved as 'guests' and, essentially, had to mind their manners. The absolutely fundamental rule was that anything learnt 'on lobby terms' must not be sourced to the person who disclosed it but to some such abstraction as 'Westminster circles' or 'feeling in the party'.

It is easy to mock the old Lobby and its rules. But the rules were the price newspapers paid for getting access to sensitive information (if only, in advance of official release, for things such as White Papers). Increasingly the system came under criticism from broadcasters, political journalists on the weekly and Sunday papers, and even from backbenchers and Opposition MPs who thought it too much open to manipulation by Downing Street briefers. When Harold Wilson tried to cultivate Lobby journalists as no prime minister had done before – to overcome the problem of 'the Tory press' – the system even became an issue in politics. What he hoped was that a cadre of think-piece columnists, on Washington lines, would breathe some of the white heat of Labour's technological revolution (a Wilson phrase much repeated in the 1964 election campaign) over an electorate befuddled by the misconceptions of Conservative newspapers. Sessions with selected Lobby journalists took place over whisky and wreathed in pipesmoke at Downing Street. The reality, however, was that the journalists remained interested in hard news, and the Lobby collectively did not like the apparent favouritism shown to what was acidly called the 'White Commonwealth' of privileged reporters.[18]

Callaghan, Thatcher and Major dealt with a Lobby that had lost much of its mystique. Numbers swelled, anonymity declined and turnover reduced the intimacy and confidence between members and politicians. The nuances of 'Lobby terms', 'background' and 'off the record' may have been lost. Even so, the system remained open to criticism. The collective briefings encouraged 'pack journalism', with stories being inflated as reporters competed for details and a distinctive angle. The continuing practice of non-attributability enabled papers to trade gossip with the same conviction as hard fact, and it enabled politicians to 'fly kites' and sow news on a basis of 'deniability'. But attention shifted in the Thatcher years away from the reporters and on to the substantial (and undeniable) personality of the Downing Street press secretary himself, Bernard Ingham. At this point, therefore, we can look briefly at the way in which prime ministers have organised their relations with media.

Downing Street News Operations

Prime ministers can largely write their own job description. Public communication has been an inescapable element, and the previous sections have sought to show how the growth of television, especially, has made it hard for a prime minister, literally and figuratively, to hide. The communication roles which the Downing Street office must be organised to assist can be divided into three parts. First, prime ministers are producers of news for the media, by their daily activities (chairing the Cabinet, meeting foreign statesman, visiting factories) and the results of those activities. In the TV age the scope for activities having no other purpose beyond publicity has grown enormously. Already in 1966 Wilson made sure of appearing in the royal box when England won the World Cup. Would Attlee have bothered (for the same reasons, anyway) in 1946?

Prime ministers, secondly, are public performers, mainly as speechmakers. Wilson played golf, which was not a photogenic game in the days before colour TV (1975). Heath exploited the public impact of being centre-stage as an orchestral conductor, as well as the picturesqueness of sailing. Image-building was a factor in his decision to take

18   Marcia Williams, *Inside Number 10*, New English Library, London, 1972, pp. 184-5.

up the sport, and in the 1970 general election campaign he was photographed with a young woman on board, to help soften his bachelor image.[19] Major took a turn in the cricket nets on occasions such as Commonwealth prime ministers' conferences. Thatcher was able to cut a dash, in a way that a male prime minister could not, by driving a tank; and she could use to advantage the fact that women vary their clothes more often than men (Bernard Ingham called her the fastest dresser in the west). Despite the obvious daily search for good visual material, talking is what prime ministers spend most time in public doing.

In Attlee's day the public places in which prime ministers talked all had some specific political purpose beyond publicity, an example being Question Time in the Commons. TV prompted the growth of a different kind of performance, such as the studio interview, which is an end in itself. But what has not yet developed at Downing Street, except in embryo, is the prime ministerial press conference. Prime ministers in other countries have them (Australia, Canada), so why not in Britain? Heath experimented with a few rather grand press conferences in the spacious surroundings of Lancaster House, a stone's throw from Buckingham Palace, but they were not a success. Print journalists disliked being stooges for the cameras, and MPs regard all such occasions as tending to distract from the Commons chamber as the forum in which prime ministers should say anything of importance for the first time in public. The enclosure of Downing Street for security reasons during the Thatcher administration created a controlled space and an opportunity for brief and more informal public exchanges between press and prime minister. Gus O'Donnell, Major's press secretary, developed the practice of marching the prime minister out of Number 10, sometimes with a visitor (for example, the Irish prime minister in December 1993), and placing him opposite the press behind a microphone. These occasions did not last long. They focused on a specific topic and were therefore fairly easily managed. But they had the potential to expand into something rather more wide-ranging.

More often prime ministers meet the press collectively in private, or they delegate the task to a ministerial colleague or to their press secretary. Such decisions exemplify the prime minister's third communications role. This is as a manager of media relations, whether cajoling the chairman of the BBC or deciding to go on a Radio 2 chat show. Attlee did not want to be bothered, and he let Francis Williams get on with it. Williams, to one observer, 'seemed to have the status almost of a minister' – and 'most of the cabinet' were indeed, as he wrote, 'old friends of mine'.[20] Churchill so disliked the idea of deliberate

19   Cockerell, *Live From Number 10*, p. 157.
20   Francis Williams, *Nothing So Strange*, Cassell, London, 1970, p. 218.

media management that he tried to do without a press secretary altogether when he returned to office in 1951. After a few months, however, one of his old associates, Lord Swinton, talked him round.

Since Churchill's premiership the press secretary's office has become institutionalised, specialised and diversified. What Francis Williams did virtually single-handed was done by Gus O'Donnell with five assistants and clerical backup amounting to a staff of a dozen or more. The essence of the job has remained the same, and to some extent it mirrors the communication roles of the prime minister personally. The press secretary is spokesman (never yet spokeswoman), adviser on media relations, intermediary (or agent) with news organisations, and co-ordinator of government information services. Just as the prime minister is 'first among equals', so the press secretary acts for the Cabinet as a whole. Attlee's formal letter appointing Williams referred to him 'acting on behalf of the government generally'.[21] As spokesman the press secretary briefs journalists singly or in groups, almost invariably without personal attribution. These briefings, mainly at 11.00 a.m. in Downing Street for the regional and evening press, and at 4.00 p.m. in the turret room at Westminster during the parliamentary session for the national press, give a rhythm to the work of the press office. Much of its daily routine in built round them.

The press secretary is involved, as adviser, with the preparation of prime ministerial speeches and broadcasts, including Question Time, and with the tactics of presenting government policy in the best light. As intermediary he negotiates with journalists and news executives about interviews and TV appearances. As co-ordinator, he liaises with the Whitehall departments to ensure that government spokesmen play the same tune.

These activities have changed in scale and emphasis within the group of offices in Downing Street described in Chapter 4. By the 1990s there were four offices serving the prime minister, with a total staff of about eighty under Thatcher and seventy, including the press office, under Major. A fifth office, the Cabinet Office, managed cabinet business and thus served the cabinet as a whole. But it, too, was infected by the 'first among equals' ethos and had arguably come to perform functions primarily for the prime minister.[22] In addition prime ministers have often liked an individual adviser at hand, a parliamentary private secretary, to be eyes and ears in the Commons; and specialists, typically, in economic or foreign policy. Beyond that, but formally quite distinct

21   Francis Williams's papers. Attlee to Williams, 27 September 1945.
22   George W. Jones, 'The United Kingdom', in William Plowden (ed.), *Advising the Rulers*, Basil Blackwell, 1987, p. 39.

from Downing Street, are the professionals in the Conservative Party
Central Office and the Labour party.

From these latter, most press secretaries have kept a clear distance.
William Clark, secretary to Eden and a former *Observer* journalist (and
therefore implicitly pink, at least), was dismayed by Central Office
attempts to put him 50 per cent on the party's payroll, so that he could
blur the non-partisan boundary which press secretaries hitherto had not
crossed. But the other Downing Street offices share to some extent
the prime minister's communication roles and are necessarily involved
with the Press Office. Most important is the prime minister's Private
Office, 'the core of Number 10', with a staff of half a dozen.[23] Its
head, the principal private secretary, is the nearest official in the system
to a prime ministerial Chief of Staff, and is bound to become involved
in at least the broader issues of communication strategy. More specifically, the office has speech-writing responsibilities, handles prime
ministers' public correspondence and prepares them for their performances at Question Time.

The prime minister's Political Office, even smaller, with a staff of
two or three political appointees, helps prepare political speeches, in
which civil servants can play no part, and liaises with the party organisation. Again, communication strategy can never be far from its
thoughts. The third office, instituted by Wilson in 1974 and kept by
his successors as a useful source of ideas, is the Policy Unit, with
a staff of about ten appointees. Major appointed as its head the economic
journalist Sarah Hogg, wife of a junior minister. The range of her advice
surely included public relations matters.

When also taking into account prime ministers' individual advisers,
the line may become blurred between formal, full-time staff, such as
the parliamentary private secretary, and those who are friends or cronies
(the word used of Churchill's associates) without official status. Wilson
was unique in appointing formally in 1965 a Parliamentary Press Liaison
Officer. The reason for this mouthful title was that his press secretary
tended, as Wilson's secretary Marcia Williams later wrote, 'to shrink
from any connection with any part of the work of the government
which could in any way be regarded as political'.[24] Wilson wanted
a press adviser uninhibited by non-partisanship, and thus the future
MP and frontbencher Gerald Kaufman, then working for the weekly
New Statesman, was appointed. His salary was paid out of party funds.

Thatcher took advice from media specialists of various kinds, without
incorporating them full-time into the Downing Street staff. Three, whose
importance is measured by the knighthoods given them when she

---

23   Jones, 'The United Kingdom', p. 49.
24   Williams, *Inside Number 10*, p. 48.

resigned, were Tim Bell, a senior advertising executive (whose influence eventually depended on friendship and not on formal office), Gordon Reece, a TV producer, who groomed her for sound and vision, and Ronald Millar, playwright turned speechwriter.

Considerations of public image and communications thus permeate the atmosphere of the modern Downing Street. The contrast with the 1940s, apart from scale and specialisation, is symbolised in the fact that Francis Williams found even the name 'Press Secretary' distasteful and preferred to be styled 'Press Relations Adviser'. Williams was anxious mainly about the taint of partisanship which his title might carry. He had to tread a fine line between the 'broad sympathy' for Labour, to which Attlee's job description had alluded, and the lack of perspective implicit in party zealotry. Williams trod the line very well, and when he retired the Lobby journalists gave him a tobacco jar made of stone from the bombed House of Commons. To Attlee he was invaluable – particularly as Attlee started from a low base of awareness. Williams called him 'allergic to newspapers'.[25] His successor, Philip Jordan, had to explain what the phrase 'off the record' meant.[26] We have seen earlier his dislike of television. With Lobby journalists he was dutiful, meeting them occasionally to discuss such matters as the date of Indian independence in 1947.[27]

'Why do we need this peepshow?', grumbled Churchill about television.[28] 'I am informed that at the moment Churchill is very reluctant to appear in [sic] television because he was handled badly by newsreels at the time of the last Election,' reported one BBC executive in 1951.[29] Churchill was a craftsman with words and took great pains with his speeches, dictating draft after draft. No doubt he could have adapted to the new medium if he had wished and had been younger. But his relations with print journalists too remained distant during his postwar government. His press secretary, when eventually appointed, was not given an office in Number 10 and was effectively responsible to other Cabinet ministers.

Eden's positive attitude to TV has already been noted. Apart from one Suez broadcast, for which he reluctantly wore glasses that paradoxically hampered his ability to read the script, his problems were less with performance than with managing his media relations. He took a direct interest in senior BBC appointments. He lent his authority to Conservative party complaints about programme

25 Francis Williams, *A Prime Minister Remembers*, Heinemann, 1961, p. 224.
26 Attlee papers. Philip Jordan to Attlee, 10 December 1948.
27 Attlee to Secretary of State for India, 29 May 1947. PREM 8/551.
28 Asa Briggs, *Sound and Vision*, Oxford University Press, 1979, p. 424.
29 BBC Written Archives. Grace Wyndham Goldie to Controller of Television Programmes, 5 September 1951.

'balance'.[30] He took to Cabinet the question whether ITV should be subsidised temporarily, after its poor financial start in 1955; 'I have always been against ITV', he minuted; 'I think it a national misfortune just now and could not agree to spend a penny on it.'[31] As press secretary he appointed a journalist, William Clark, who was a pioneer performer on political TV programmes and a diplomatic specialist, not a Lobby correspondent. Eden met reporters from time to time, and brought Fleet Street editors together in August 1956 to win their co-operation in playing down news of troop movements in the Suez crisis.

All this was effective. But when Suez became a shooting war Eden was astonished and then enraged to discover that he could not, at a word, command the airwaves. The laboriously agreed rules about ministerial broadcasts left discretion clearly with the broadcasters about the issue, particularly, of a 'right to reply'. As British troops proceeded to invade Egypt, Eden found his own statesmanlike address to the nation on 3 November followed next day by a comparably grave but dissenting address by the Opposition leader Hugh Gaitskell. He put in hand inquiries about commandeering the BBC, but before they got anywhere the crisis was over, and Eden's premiership with it.[32]

Macmillan, succeeding Eden early in 1957, already had several years of experience as a performer, including the first televised Party Political Broadcast in 1953. 'From a strictly professional point of view', commented a senior BBC producer to the Downing Street Press Secretary, 'there is no doubt that the prime minister has perfected in a comparatively short time a fine television technique.'[33] TV brought out the showman in him; he was quick to spot the publicity value of a gimmick, such as the outsize white fur hat which he took to Moscow in 1959. Photographers and cartoonists seized on it. The hat gave a touch of swagger to a visit which, at the height of the Cold War and before the days of shuttle diplomacy, was an unusual and critical event. But Macmillan explored the potential of TV in grander ways, taking the cameras into Downing Street for his chat with President Eisenhower.

Also there has been no other prime minister except Macmillan, before or since, to appoint in effect a Minister for Public Relations. The first appointee was Dr Charles Hill, who was probably the first politician to build a political career on a reputation as a broadcaster – as 'the Radio Doctor'. He handled media strategy for the prime minister and briefed journalists regularly on political questions which Macmillan's civil service press secretary, Harold Evans, would have found embar-

30   Correspondence between Eden and Dr Charles Hill, Postmaster General, 15-26 June 1956. PREM 11/1212.
31   Eden to Private Secretary, 25 April 1956. PREM 11/1728.
32   Cockerell, *Live From Number 10*, pp. 48-51.
33   BBC Written Archives. Anthony Craxton to Harold Evans, 7 March 1957.

rassing. When Hill left the government in 1962, William Deedes, himself a journalist as well as an MP, did the job on the same basis.

Douglas-Home's premiership of almost exactly one year did not allow time to make a mark in media relations. His significance is rather in being the first prime minister whom TV was widely believed to have helped destroy. His performance may not really have affected voters in the close-run 1964 election as badly as his party colleagues judged, but it was their judgement which mattered, and it weighed in Home's decision to stand down as Conservative leader in 1965.

Wilson and Heath were the two prime ministers associated with the period described earlier as that of television's political maturity. With Wilson, therefore, standards of performance and media management changed. More than anyone before him he was prepared initially to meet media on their own ground. He appointed the Lobby correspondent of his local Liverpool daily paper, Trevor Lloyd-Hughes, to be press secretary, in the hope that this would ensure a good understanding with the Lobby journalists, rather in the manner of Attlee's success with Francis Williams. He was far more accessible to the Lobby collectively and individually than former prime ministers. He was informally accessible to TV too, 'breakfasting' on the air with David Frost (who at that time was mainly on the 'showbiz' side of TV), and being interviewed in relaxed and casual surroundings. Such apparently irrelevant factors as the bigger size of jet aircraft made a difference too, for the press began to accompany Wilson abroad and the Press Office found itself becoming a travel agency.

But when his policies ran into trouble Wilson, like many politicians, blamed poor communication and thus the media. Lloyd-Hughes was supplemented by Gerald Kaufman and then replaced by a Labour loyalist, Joe Haines, who eventually stopped collective Lobby briefings altogether. The experiment of group meetings between Wilson and the more reflective Lobby journalists was derided and abandoned. Wilson began to see himself as the victim of the media.[34] He punished the BBC for alleged unfairness, through such gestures as the selective denial of interview requests and, more substantially, by appointing Charles Hill as chairman of the BBC governors – he had previously held the corresponding position with their arch-rival, the Independent Television Authority.

Wilson certainly tried harder at media management than his predecessors, and learned from American experience. But it is difficult to judge exactly how much difference this made to his government's fortunes. By comparison, Heath was a much less effective TV performer, and he organised his media relations somewhat differently. The Conservative

Party has always had closer links than Labour with the advertising industry. Heath was groomed in Opposition by party advisers with marketing skills, but in office he largely discarded them. Heath chose as press secretary a senior civil servant from the Foreign Office, Donald Maitland – a choice which reflected the importance Heath attached to getting Britain into the European Community. Maitland had worked with him on the abortive negotiations for entry in 1963 (later he became Ambassador to the EEC). Maitland could not have the rapport with Lobby correspondents that would come from having been one of them, but on the other hand he had intimate knowledge of the world of Whitehall. In practice, his appointment worked well: he modernised and expanded the Downing Street Press Office, and encouraged Heath in experiments, even if they did not always work well, such as the big Lancaster House press conferences mentioned earlier.

Wilson's second term provided no new developments; nor did Callaghan during 1976-9. Like Heath, Callaghan chose a civil servant as press secretary. As a performer he proved adept at handling interviewers, but he lacked Wilson's general sensitiveness to the potential of media relations as an instrument of political management.

Margaret Thatcher was in office for so long, and at a time when TV was so well established, that her public communication was bound to have distinctive features. As a performer, she was summed up in the words of a former ITN editor, Sir Geoffrey Cox, as 'an extremely effective screen figure, who uses actions as an alternative to words'.[35] She enjoyed studio triumphs over interviewers such as Robin Day, who was famous for exposing politicians' inadequacies. She went readily on to children's programmes, gardening programmes, celebrity programmes. She made sure of reaching beyond the politician's natural channel, Radio 4, to appear regularly on Jimmy Young's Radio 2 talk show. In or out of election campaigns, she joined with a will in contrived and sometimes surreal picture opportunities (picking up litter in the park, for instance, which had been scattered immediately beforehand for the purpose).

In managing media relations, Thatcher charmed or pummelled publishers and TV executives. She used her patronage to reward the Conservative press with peerages and knighthoods, and to instal persons who were 'one of us' in key positions such as the chairmanship of the board of governors of the BBC. She had regard to the interests of press moguls when framing the industrial relations legislation which made possible the breaking of the old, restrictive production unions and the introduction of cheaper publication methods. She broke up the

---

35 Cockerell, *Live from Number 10*, p. 255.

old ITV system in the 1990 Broadcasting Act, although the consequences were not what she foresaw.

In general, little in those methods was new. Wilson had used many of them (obviously to different ends). But TV especially had changed the scale, scope and pace of media relations. International summits, for instance, became much more frequent in the Thatcher years, partly with the thaw in East-West relations but mainly with developments in the European Community. Every summit meant at least one press conference. Major traumas such as the Falklands war in 1982 required energetic media management – both of a positive character, to win the argument with public opinion (which Eden had failed to do during the Suez adventure), and for damage limitation (trying to avoid the broadcasters being too 'detached' or showing ghastly film). The year-long miners' strike of 1984, similarly, needed skillful media steerage, starting with the government's insistence that the miners were in dispute with the Coal Board and not with the government. The conflict in Northern Ireland was at constant risk of provoking clashes between the government and the broadcasters. Broadcasters persisted in interpreting their 'public service' role to extend beyond what Thatcher liked. TV exposure for terrorists, to her, was 'the oxygen of publicity'. The rows culminated in the 'broadcasting ban' of 1988.

For advice in handling crises and routines alike, Thatcher relied heavily on her press secretary, Bernard Ingham. Although he was not as visible in the Falklands crisis, for instance, as the Ministry of Defence spokesman Ian Macdonald (much derided for his automaton-style delivery for the benefit of non-anglophone journalists), Ingham played an important part at Downing Street. None of his predecessors as press secretary served for anything like so long (the closest was Macmillan's secretary), and Ingham became one of two or three key staff at Number 10. Equally, his closeness made him increasingly suspect. Officially a civil servant, originally in the information officer class, he seemed more like a partisan, even a minister. Paradoxically, as a journalist he had had Labour sympathies and had worked on the *Guardian*. But he had the perfect press secretary's quality of getting inside the prime minister's mind. Journalists knew that when briefed by him, they could tell what the prime minister was thinking. This very quality could cause resentment among ministers, one or two of whom first learned of their impending demotion from Ingham's off-the-cuff remarks. John Biffen, the House leader, was famously dismissed as 'a semi-detached member of the Cabinet'.[36]

---

36   For a sustained criticism of Bernard Ingham's role, see Robert Harris, *Good and Faithful Servant*, Faber and Faber, 1990. Ingham's own account is *Kill the Messenger*, HarperCollins, 1991. The quotation about Biffen is at p. 327.

With Ingham in charge, Thatcher certainly had no need of a minister for public relations on the Charles Hill/Bill Deedes model. His indispensability was soon highlighted by the very different strategy pursued by Major, who chose as press secretary Gus O'Donnell, a Treasury economist who had been in the same relationship to Major when he was chancellor of the exchequer. O'Donnell never became a public figure like Ingham, nor did he have Ingham's experience, as journalist and information officer, in dealing with the Lobby correspondents. After the 1992 election, Major's government suffered an almost continuous series of public relations failures: ministers forced to resign because of incidents in their private lives; mismanaged policy announcements, such as a pit closures programme which had as a result to be delayed; bad media coverage about Major's relations with his chancellor, Norman Lamont; the mismatch between the slogan 'Back to Basics' and the private morality of Conservative MPs.

Major seemed by 1994 to have a kind of anti-Midas touch: everything he touched turned to dross. In judging the part played by an inadequate media relations strategy, the link between substance and presentation is central. How much difference to Major's predicament could an Ingham have made? O'Donnell returned to the Treasury in 1994 (even his farewell dinner at Number 10 got bad publicity, because of the selective guest list). No one suggested he was going earlier than he might have done: a three-year stint was, if anything, above average for the job. He was replaced by Chris Meyer, a Foreign Office high-flyer. To judge by appearances, however, Major badly needed not another mandarin as press secretary but a strong partisan figure or, preferably, a cabinet minister with special responsibility for media relations. No prime minister since Churchill, arguably, seemed so unaware of the need for an active communications strategy, or else so incompetent.

Issues for the Prime Minister

The main issue for a prime minister is precisely the one which Major apparently failed to tackle: how much priority to give to public communication in all its forms, and especially to the mass media. In the pre-TV age, Parliament was the prime minister's natural publicity base, with the convenient advantage that it was the base also for managing the parliamentary party. The party outside Parliament made time-consuming demands of publicity too, through weekend speeches and great rituals such as the annual party conference. The arenas of political broadcasting have been added to these bases, but without anything else being taken away.

In these circumstances, a prime minister has no option but to follow an active communications strategy. It may not be successful, of course. He may fail to get his agenda and his interpretation of events adopted by the media. But even if he succeeds in doing this, the results may fail to impress the public, parliament, party, pressure group – or whoever else it is, whose support is necessary to the achievement of his objectives. The history of electioneering, for instance, shows how difficult it is for politicians to predict, let alone manipulate, the influence of mass media. Media tend to reinforce opinion more than to change it. Yet reinforcement is itself an effect and can be equally critical to an electoral outcome.

For a prime minister who neglects communications strategy the alternative is drift – or the surrender of initiative to rivals and the Opposition. One thing that facts do not do in the 1990s is 'speak for themselves'. To some prime ministers (Macmillan, Wilson) an active communications role has come naturally. To others (Douglas-Home, Heath, Major) it has caused discomfort. Central to any strategy must be the press secretary, in himself and in his role as director of an office reaching out to, and co-ordinating, information services throughout Whitehall.

Experience suggests that the job is difficult to do well. Probably more than anyone else in the prime minister's entourage, the press secretary is subject to cross-pressures. If he does not enjoy the confidence of his master, he is of no use to the press; yet if he does not enjoy the confidence of the press, he is no use to his master. Churchill, Eden and Wilson each had problems of this kind. One of the factors affecting the balance is partisanship. 'Broad partisan sympathy', as ascribed to Francis Williams, is a fudge, like 'first among equals'. But like that fudge, it has sometimes worked, particularly in small matters such as speech-writing, and for symbolic things such as party conferences. Ingham insisted that he should not attend the Conservative conference, for instance. If sympathy can be sufficiently restrained, it has the advantage of enabling the press secretary to be recruited from the civil service, with undoubted benefits of the kind of inside knowledge that Donald Maitland and Bernard Ingham brought to bear on matters of co-ordination.

One drawback to a non-partisan press secretary, on the other hand, is that there has to be some other link to the party organisation. Indeed it is surprising that Downing Street communications seem nearly always to have been kept quite far apart, indeed almost isolated, from the parties. A second probable drawback is that a non-partisan press secretary cannot brief so freely on political rows in cabinet, especially if these involve personalities (as they often do). This difficulty links to a third source of tension in the press secretary's job: the number of masters he serves. He is explicitly press secretary for the cabinet as a whole. His co-ordinating responsibilities apply both at official level and in such activities as the discreet orchestration of ministerial radio and TV broadcasts. Ingham explained to the Lobby journalists that for this reason he preferred being described in print as 'government sources', not as 'Downing Street sources'.[37] Yet the press secretary is a personal appointment of the prime minister and his office is only a step away: he is very much the prime minister's person.

To what extent serving the prime minister and serving the cabinet amount in practice to the same thing depends on how far the cabinet behaves, as constitutional convention would have it, as an entity. To the extent that it does not, the press secretary risks getting caught up in the tensions and the inevitable rival leaks. If he distances himself, he may lose credibility and, with it, the capacity to influence the news agenda. If he gets involved, he may be seen too uncompromisingly as the prime minister's agent.

Part of the importance of this particular balancing act is that news operations have become an increasingly useful instrument with which prime ministers can manage their cabinet colleagues and their parliamentary support. Most of the time, ministers are occupied with their own departments. Apart from gossip, they depend for their knowledge of what else is going on inside the government upon information circulated about cabinet business, or reported via the civil service network. Several former ministers have described their ignorance of the progress of policy (for which implicitly they shared collective responsibility) because the existence or the composition of certain cabinet committees was unknown to them. An early and contentious example was Richard Crossman's claim that Attlee deliberately concealed information about the committee concerned with authorising the manufacture of British nuclear weapons.[38] Decisions about what to release to journalists, and in what circumstances, are simply an extension into the public domain of the same practice. Each testifies to the truism 'Knowledge is power'.

In the Thatcher era, an unusually public example of cabinet management was the prime minister's handling of the Westland crisis in 1986, described by Philip Giddings on pp. 66-7. This was an issue nominally about the future of a small helicopter company but actually about Thatcher's authority in Cabinet. It was brought to a head dramatically by Michael Heseltine, Minister of Defence, walking out of a cabinet meeting – and his job. In the subsequent rival explanations of events, Heseltine gave seventeen broadcast interviews within the first twenty-four

37   Ingham, *Kill the Messenger*, pp. 203-4.
38   Richard Crossman, 'Introduction' to W. Bagehot, *The English Constitution*, Fontana, 1963, pp. 54- 5.

hours. Thatcher sought to establish her own version, and to keep the initiative, through the agency of Ingham and her private office. This involved the controversial leaking to the press of a damaging letter to Heseltine from the attorney-general. Thatcher survived the crisis, but her reputation in the parliamentary party was badly shaken.[39]

Daily Downing Street news operations involve no great crises. But the press secretary's routine tactics in encouraging some stories to be played up and others down, some ministers to speak up, others to keep quiet – all the realities of co-ordination – give him an unrivalled role not merely in maximising the appearance of coherence and consistency in government, summed up in the notion of collective responsibility, but also in ensuring that the pattern bears so far as possible the stamp that the prime minister wishes. But while the Press Office is crucial, an effective communications strategy must go beyond Downing Street itself. It requires effective communications machinery in the party organisation, with special emphasis on election campaigns; opinion polling and advertising; and arrangements for dealing with top broadcasting executives and newspaper publishers. Churchill may have been distant from the Lobby, but he did have close personal relations with most of the press barons, who at that period still had closer association with the party organisation than their successors.

Is there anyone other than the prime minister who can pull together those separate strands into a coherent strategy? At first sight it is puzzling that no one has followed Macmillan's practice of having a minister for media relations (Deedes's actual title was minister without portfolio). Traditionally the leader of the Commons, under both parties, has given weekly press briefings about the parliamentary programme. The minister responsible for broadcasting has handled rows with the broadcasters about political bias and other alleged outrages on the air, if the prime minister has not wished to do so. Under the Conservatives the party chairman (often a cabinet minister) has handled opinion polling and advertising.

If prime ministers were to give responsibility for overseeing all such activities to one of their colleagues, the job would either be a sinecure or it would impinge too closely for comfort on a prime minister's own role as leader of the government and party. The political weight of ministers without substantial departments is notoriously vulnerable, unless their standing in the party is unchallengeable (like William Whitelaw under Thatcher). A communications supremo by his very nature would not have a substantial department; but if he did have political weight, his functions might give him, looked at from the prime minister's viewpoint, an uncomfortably strong position as a potential rival.

39   On Westland see, e.g., Hugo Young, *One of Us*, Chapter 19.

Issues for the Political System

The intrusion of television into all the public political arenas (the Cabinet counting as a private one), and the creation of its own arenas such as the studio discussion or interview in addition, have gradually drawn prime ministers away from their parliamentary bases. This tendency raises three questions, which may be discussed in conclusion. Who is the 'real' prime minister? Do media have the potential to rival Parliament as the pathway to party leadership and thence to the premiership? Is the premiership becoming in a definite sense more presidential?

The prime minister's 'reality' is not the philosophical question it might seem. The point arises from the existence of TV's own arenas. Daniel Boorstin coined the word 'pseudo-event' in 1961 to describe activity carried on solely for the purpose of getting media coverage.[40] Such events may have had no other purpose, but they did have an existence independent of the media. The studio interview, chat show, phone-in, discussion programme – endlessly variegated and with inter-changeable-sounding names – have no such link with an independent reality. The temptation is to say that a prime minister who changes accent, clothes, hairstyle or manners for the sake of TV perpetrates a 'deception': the TV version is not the 'real' person. If such devices are used, say, on the floor of the House, then they are related to the purposes of that specific forum and to the political reality of parliamentary behaviour, entirely separate from television. In such a forum the prime minister's need to satisfy both TV and the immediate audience tends to keep the two kinds of reality at least in touch, if not identical. But the more important the TV arenas become, relative to others, the greater the tendency for the screen reality to dominate the public perception of the prime minister's character and capacities. How far this would matter depends, in the present context, on whether the leaders who benefit from the TV arena perform their tasks as prime minister elsewhere (in Cabinet, for instance) at least no worse than leaders who emerged in the pre-TV age.

This argument anticipates the second question. An unchallenged power of the House of Commons throughout the period since 1945, when commentators have often perceived a decline in Parliament, has been the need for a substantial parliamentary apprenticeship to qualify for prime ministerial office. Even Major, the baby in these terms, had served eleven years. In practice, too, this means a party apprenticeship. In the future could these requirements prove vulnerable to TV? When Major became prime minister, Australia and Canada – two parliamentary systems steeped in Westminster values and practices – had prime ministers (Hawke and Mulroney) who served respectively two years

40   D. Boorstin, *The Image: A guide to pseudo-events in America*, Athenaeum, New York, 1961.

and one year in their federal legislatures before becoming prime minister. TV has the potential to give someone prime ministerial timber, creating a ready-made national candidate who could step smoothly into party leadership. Major absolutely did not emerge in this way: Heseltine, on this analysis, should have done so. But might the day come?

That speculation in turn anticipates the argument about presidentialism. In the United States, if we take that as a model, party and Congress have had no monopoly over the pathways to the White House (or more accurately to the nominating conventions). The American president is characterised by having sole, rather than shared, responsibility within the executive; and by popular authority conferred independently of the legislature. He also attaches a high priority to the leadership of public opinion, and he doubles as Head of State.

Much of this chapter could support the conclusion that the office of prime minister has indeed been moving in that direction. The conventional view of Thatcher is certainly consistent with it. Dominance over her colleagues was a frequent refrain; and her skill as performer and (with Ingham) media manager was one of the instruments. In general elections she attracted far more broadcast coverage than her colleagues. Her prominence between elections is less easily documented but was undoubtedly great. Her popular support (as opposed to her actual popularity) owed little to her relations with the legislature. Indeed she spent significantly less time in the Commons than her predecessors. Her radical and largely unanticipated success in educating public opinion away from the consensus orthodoxies of the postwar era undoubtedly resembled the opinion-mobilising role of American presidents. A developing habit of publicly using the royal 'we' (most famously in 'We are a grandmother now') drew the jibe from critics that she was acquiring queenly trappings.

So long as prime ministers depend for office on the support of a majority in the House of Commons, their base must obviously be there, and their public communication will ultimately be directed at keeping that majority in being. The cutting of that constitutional tie would be more likely to follow from the growth of European integration, say, than from any conceivable development in news media. Even so, in the last resort all politics is carried on through the communications technologies of the day; and these, though socially determined, are 'bigger' than political forms and procedures. To quote, appropriately, an American president (and political scientist) Woodrow Wilson, 'News is the atmosphere of politics.' The half-century after Attlee took office saw the making and management of news permeate the atmosphere of Downing Street with growing intensity. Managing media relations has become an intrinsic part of the prime minister's job.

41 P. Dunleavy, G.W. Jones and B. O'Leary, 'Prime Ministers and the Commons: Patterns of Behaviour, 1868-1987', *Public Administration*, vol. 68 (1990), pp. 123-40.

7

THE PRIME MINISTER
AND INTERNATIONAL RELATIONS

J.M. Lee

The conduct of international affairs since 1945 has had a dramatic impact on the office of prime minister. The increasing influence of international forces on the form and implementation of domestic policies has given the prime minister a wider range of co-ordination problems. Prime ministers are expected to provide the leadership which will find solutions to domestic problems against constant pressures in the management of foreign policy. External forces have both reshaped the roles which prime ministers play and introduced new constraints upon their exercise of power and influence.

Distinctions between foreign and domestic policy have been blurred, as have the conventions of managing them in fairly separate spheres of action. There is no longer the dividing-line that there once was between 'home' and 'colonial' or between 'domestic' and 'imperial'. Instead prime ministers are for ever considering the interweaving of domestic and international affairs. Estimates of the allocation of prime ministerial time suggest that all incumbents in the office now spend more than half their working hours on matters arising from external questions. The cabinet secretary thought that James Callaghan spent at least 60 per cent of his time on international affairs; many commentators thought that towards the end of her period in office they were occupying 80 per cent of Margaret Thatcher's time. The consequences of the intergovernmental conference which drew up the Maastricht treaty in 1992 loomed large on John Major's daily agenda.

There are three aspects of the roles of the prime minister which are strongly influenced by events overseas. First for most practical purposes, the prime minister as head of government in a constitutional monarchy is seen to be sharing with the head of state the role of embodying the nation. The phrase 'relations with the palace' – that domain of delicate negotiation and convention which determines what the monarch and what the prime minister shall do – has to be understood by foreign governments. Ambassadors are accredited to the Court of St James but the representatives of foreign powers expect to enjoy access to Number 10 Downing Street. If these expectations are modified in any way, there are repercussions upon the practice of negotiations as well as upon diplomacy and protocol. Secondly, as chairman of the cabinet and of its principal committees, the prime minister is responsible for co-ordinating the actions of different government departments whenever a national policy or a national stance is required. Foreign governments need to appreciate how the issues of foreign policy impinge on the relationships between departments and on domestic opinion as a whole. Any shift in a national order of priorities may have an effect upon the relationships between British and foreign governments. Thirdly, the prime minister is the only member of the government who can give a lead in policy and effectively bring together the sources of intelligence about what is happening overseas, and at the same time regulate access to the deductions and diagnoses which are presented. All governments try to intercept and decode the traffic between different parts of other governments, so that they can judge the alternative lines of action which are being considered and prepared. Any change in the conventions determining who 'needs to know' the secrets of state can influence what government decides.

Since 1945 there have been developments in the conduct of relationships between governments which impinge directly upon these three aspects of the prime minister's roles. One of these is the transformation of the role of head of government by the increasing use of summit meetings for negotiation. The practice of convening meetings between the fountainheads of authority from different systems goes back into antiquity. It was given a particular significance during the Second World War by the Western Allies, who brought together the supreme representatives of the Big Five, the Big Four and the Big Three.[1] The British Empire had developed its own form of summitry in the conference of prime ministers from the self-governing dominions. Indeed it has been argued that British civil service practice set the tone of all the international secretariats in the League of Nations, because the British Cabinet Office was accustomed to handling such international meetings.[2] Since the 1970s all major Western governments have accepted some responsibility for co-operating in the management of the world economy. The abandonment of the Bretton Woods system for regulating currency rates has led to the greater institutionalisation of meetings between heads of government, such as those of the Group of Seven. In addition, improvements in air travel have encouraged an increasing number of

1   The major powers were the United States, the Soviet Union and Britain. When they met with France there was 'four' and with China 'five'.
2   John B. Hattendorf and Malcolm H. Murfett (eds), *The Limitations of Military Power*, Macmillan, 1990, pp. 95-110.

bilateral discussions. Heads of government in the Western world nowadays expect regular visits from their opposite numbers. In Britain the head of government is as likely to receive invitations to make official visits as the head of state. Britain's entry into the European community has meant participation by the prime minister in the European Council meeting of heads of government and in intergovernmental conferences.

There is also the added complexity of the role of co-ordinating the business of government departments brought about through the impact of international discussions or agreements on nearly every aspect of domestic policy. Foreign policy and domestic policy are even more closely intertwined. Some commentators have even used the word 'intermestic' to describe what they see as the high degree of inter-penetration between the two spheres.[3]

A third factor is that the role of collecting intelligence from different sources and of regulating access to its interpretation has given an increased importance to the prime minister's functions in what might be called preventative diplomacy, the anticipation of events and the preparation of contingency plans. The expansion of preventative measures against international terrorism and the technological improvements in the interception and decoding of messages passing between other governments have taken place under the prime minister's supervision. By definition, the modifications in this role which result from changes in the covert strategy and tactics of all governments cannot be readily studied. But it looks as if each head of government has to develop a communications system which is as secure as possible. In addition, much greater attention has been paid to campaigns which target information to specific audiences. Governments employ public relations experts to identify significant groups of people abroad. Heads of government sometimes need to know about the pressures being applied on their own domestic opinion by outside agencies.

National Leadership

The increasing use of summit meetings between heads of government has encouraged the development of new variations on the deep-seated British traditions which assign pride of place to the prime minister for national leadership in time of war. Nowadays the battles are more likely to be 'fighting one's corner' in the rough and tumble of international negotiation rather than the marshalling of troops on the ground. They are also likely to be performances in front of the world's media. The potential for leadership now appears in fresh guises.

The office of prime minister sprang in the eighteenth century from

---

3   Peter Byrd (ed.), *British Foreign Policy under Thatcher*, Philip Allan, 1988, pp. 28-33.

the task of creating and maintaining a majority of MPs in the House of Commons in support of the government of the Crown. The prime minister ensured that the Bills presented to parliament by the executive secured the necessary votes to provide an adequate revenue for the civil and military services which the Crown employed. The evolution of political parties depended initially on a contest over who was to be chosen and rewarded for the Crown's service. Prime ministers then held together 'political parties'; they have more recently been characterised as 'elected monarchs'.

International affairs shaped the office of prime minister because the legitimacy of William and Mary, Anne and the Hanoverian monarchs who followed them was tied to the parliamentary régime which, after 1688, sanctioned a Protestant succession to the Crown in spite of hostility from Catholic monarchs in Europe.[4] The security of both the régime and the country came to depend on maritime power, and on occasional interventions into the dynastic wars of continental European powers. British identity was conceived as an expression of Protestantism against Catholic powers.[5] The premiership was expected to embody the national will in time of war. The main sources of revenue for national defence were the customs levies and excise taxes approved by a parliamentary majority under the prime minister's direction. The epitome of both national security and national maritime strategy was William Pitt the Elder, Earl of Chatham, who became premier and leader of the House of Commons in 1756.

The domestic and international context in which the office of prime minister was formed has meant that successive premiers have always been involved in some degree with the making of foreign policy. In an historical perspective, therefore, it is inappropriate to think of 10 Downing Street as 'interfering' in the work of the Foreign Office. The office of prime minister predates that of foreign secretary. Britain's relations with other countries were traditionally conducted by the two secretaries of state, one for what came to be referred to as the north and the other for the south. The northern secretary took charge of relationships with Europe and the United States, and the southern secretary with the colonies.

The office of secretary of state for foreign affairs was created from the southern department in 1782. Before that date prime ministers tended to take all major responsibilities for foreign policy. In the 1720s and 1730s Sir Robert Walpole was sensitive to the dangers of intervention in European wars, because of the risk that foreign powers would support

---

4   J. Brewer, *The Sinews of War: War, money and the English state, 1688-1783*, Unwin Hyman, 1989.
5   Linda Colley, *Britons: Forging the nation, 1707-1837*, Yale University Press, 1992.

the claims of the Stuarts to the Crown. He was convinced that it was impossible to separate domestic and foreign policies if the régime were to survive.[6] The costs of war which the Treasury could calculate were a vital factor in developing judgement in the formation of diplomatic alliances.

These interdependences, real more than 250 years ago, have left a lasting mark on the relationships in cabinet between the prime minister, the foreign secretary and the chancellor of the exchequer. The Foreign Office and the Treasury are the two key central departments which every prime minister has to consider; the incumbents of these two great offices of state are sometimes rivals for succession to the premiership, and premiers appoint cabinet colleagues to these offices with great circumspection. They may themselves have passed through these positions of influence, and be aware from that experience of the simultaneous strength and vulnerability of individual prime ministers. Such vulnerabilities are the subject of much political gossip: it is often rumoured that a premier has chosen a particular colleague to fill one of these two offices principally because that colleague can be guaranteed to remain reasonably subordinate. Selwyn Lloyd (foreign secretary 1955-60) was no threat to Macmillan, and Michael Stewart (foreign secretary 1968-70) was unlikely to challenge Wilson. There can be a degree of ambivalence in such subordination. Lord Carrington claimed that he spent 80 per cent of his time as foreign secretary (1979-82) repairing the damage caused by the rhetoric of Thatcher as prime minister.[7] Of the nineteen incumbents of the office of prime minister in the twentieth century only five never served as either foreign secretary or chancellor (Campbell-Bannerman, Attlee, Wilson, Heath, Thatcher). Of the others, five were foreign secretary, although Balfour did not serve as such until after his premiership; six were chancellor, and three have been both (Macmillan, Callaghan and Major). Major entered the premiership with the most rapid translation through the other two offices; three months as foreign secretary and thirteen months as chancellor.

There have been prime ministers who have so enjoyed their apparent influence in world affairs that they have resisted pressure to retire and give way to possible successors. Churchill, for example, was convinced he could engineer success in talks between the heads of government of the four major powers, as he thought he had done during the Second World War, and therefore postponed inviting Eden to succeed him as most of the parliamentary Conservative Party expected.[8]

Civil servants in Number 10, the Foreign Office and the Treasury

6   Jeremy Black, *British Foreign Policy in the Age of Walpole*, J. Donald, Edinburgh, 1985.
7   Patrick Cosgrave, *Carrington: A life and a Policy*, Dent, 1985, p. 155.
8   Robert Rhodes James, *Anthony Eden*, Weidenfeld and Nicolson, 1986, pp. 400-3.

are obliged to take account of such personal ambitions and rivalries. The principal private secretary in Number 10 and the cabinet secretary are mindful of the political capital which senior ministers can gain from foreign affairs. Since 1916 senior officials in the Foreign Office and Treasury have been seconded to the Cabinet Office for periods of service, and since 1945 one of the principal private secretaries in Downing Street has been seconded from the Foreign Office. The latter might be deemed the person who manages the relationships between the Foreign Office and Number 10. How that role is conceived and practised can be important; it has normally been described as a 'channel of communication'.[9] Increasingly, however, prime ministers have come to seek advice on foreign policy from outside this channel and so enhanced their independence.

In the twentieth century the classic examples of personal ascendancy and rapid adjustments in the official management of the machinery of government have been the war cabinets and coalition governments of 1916 and 1940. Lloyd George succeeding Asquith and Churchill succeeding Chamberlain were expressions of the tradition that a prime minister as war leader needs to have the support of the House of Commons. These national governments allow suspension of the parliamentary conventions of contest between the two front benches, and sanction prime ministers to manage the war and, by extension, all the major issues of foreign policy. Prime ministers thus commissioned rely on others to manage 'the home front'.

Prime ministers may on occasions lead the country into war without securing a new base of power through coalition. In 1956 Eden devised the Suez invasion with great secrecy and with the connivance of the French and Israeli governments. In 1982 Thatcher insisted on sending a task force to evict the Argentines from the Falkland Islands, in spite of dissent from both ministerial colleagues and leading officials. Prime ministers are in a strong position to launch such overseas ventures because they manage the cabinet and determine the shape of the machinery of government.

Some commentators ascribe these changes in prime ministerial leadership to technological improvements in air transport and electronic communication. Heads of government have found it much easier to meet in person since the advent of jet travel. Political reporting from foreign capitals via diplomatic bags has been largely superseded by telex, television pictures and fax. The leaders of the Western Allies during the Second World War met after cruises in battleships or gruelling trans-Atlantic flights, with refuelling in Greenland and Labrador. There

9   See, for example, Lord Armstrong writing an obituary of Peter Moon in *The Guardian*, 8 July 1991.

appears to have been a quantum leap in the accessibility of British
leaders between Eden's visit to the United States in the liner *Queen
Elizabeth* in January 1956[10] and Macmillan's arrival by plane in the
Soviet Union in February 1959. During the 1960s the time spent by
prime ministers out of the country increased. In 1965 Wilson's advisers
thought that three overseas visits within five months was an excessive
absence from the daily round of Number 10.[11] Wilson also conducted
in person rather fruitless negotiations with the leaders of the breakaway
Rhodesian régime aboard battleships on the high seas, HMS *Tiger* in
1966 and HMS *Fearless* in 1968. Since the 1970s prime ministers have
normally undertaken visits by chartering an aeroplane from the RAF.
Thatcher regularly used a VC-10; in May 1992 Major announced that
he was taking measures to secure an official Downing Street plane.[12]

The agenda of international alliances tends to demand the presence
of heads of government. British prime ministers have participated in
the institutionalisation of regular consultations. Some of the principal
negotiations, however, have been at a lower level. The finance ministers
of leading industrial countries and their central bank governors meet
informally, usually in the days which precede the larger gatherings
of the International Monetary Fund and the World Bank. Such informal
meetings can fluctuate in their composition. There have been the Group
of Five, the Group of Seven and the Group of Ten. There is always
a risk that the 'core' states at these meetings – the United States, Germany
and Japan, which have the strongest economies – will wish to create
a Group of Three. The most stable of these groupings consisted of
these three powers meeting with the representatives of Britain and France
as the Group of Five. This was extended in 1985 with the addition
of Italy and Canada at the finance ministers' level to form the Group
of Seven after agreement at the Plaza Hotel, New York, to reduce
the value of the American dollar. Meetings of finance ministers continue
to risk expressing different levels of status. For example, the Louvre
Accord of 1987 was devised by five powers, announced by six, and
endorsed by seven.[13] Although there may be no formal structure, the
expectation of these regular meetings has transformed the way in which
international disagreements are mediated and the issues addressed.

The meetings of the heads of government of the Group of Seven
take their origins from the 1975 proposal of President Giscard d'Estaing
and Chancellor Helmut Schmidt on behalf of France and Germany.
These leaders had both been finance ministers at the beginning of the

---

10   Rhodes James, *Anthony Eden*, p. 426.
11   Marcia Williams, *Inside Number 10*, Weidenfeld and Nicolson, 1972, p. 52.
12   *The Independent*, 29 May 1992.
13   Nigel Lawson, *The View from No. 11: Memoirs of a Tory radical*, Bantam Press,
     1992, p. 557.

Group of Five, and they wanted to create a world forum at which heads of government could discuss limiting the possibilities of an international trade war. These meetings were often designated 'economic summits' and by 1977 had been institutionalised for heads of government from the seven countries which later assembled their finance ministers. Representatives of the European Community were also included. Thatcher's long tenure of office meant that she attended twelve such summits, a record only surpassed by President Mitterrand.

The admission of Britain into the European Community in 1973 has increased the formal co-operation, since it has entailed the attendance of British representatives at many different levels. Prime ministers attend principally through the regular meetings of the European Council for heads of government which was created in 1974 at the suggestion of Giscard d'Estaing. They also play a prominent role when Britain takes its turn to provide the presidency of the Council of Ministers (for six months in every six years), and on the three occasions when there has been an intergovernmental conference to discuss or to negotiate modifications of the treaties. In 1990 Major took over from Thatcher between the two European Councils held in Rome in order to prepare for the intergovernmental conferences which were set to consider further moves towards economic and political union. The British prime minister has been president of the Council of Ministers in 1977, 1981, 1986 and again in 1992. Other ministers in British government also meet their counterparts in the different 'formations' into which the work of the Council of Ministers is broken up. This reflects the internationalising of almost all policy areas, but the structure of the European Union places the critical authority in the hands of government, thus emphasising yet further a prime minister's formal pre-eminence.

These wider forums of negotiation have also encouraged an additional proliferation of bilateral meetings. Leaders of government invite each other for state visits with greater regularity, and test each other's bargaining positions in advance of formal engagements. For example, Britain's membership of the European Community has stimulated Franco-British summits and consultations between prime ministers and German chancellors. The state funerals of heads of governments have also provided opportunities for bilateral talks among the mourners. Attendance at state funerals can become a delicate matter of protocol. Thatcher secured tangible benefits from attending the funerals of President Tito in Yugoslavia in 1980, President Andropov in the Soviet Union in 1984, Indira Gandhi in India in 1984, and President Chernenko in the Soviet Union in 1985. For diplomatic reasons she did not go to Moscow for the funeral of President Brezhnev in 1982. There were doubts about the inferences that might have been drawn if she had attended the funeral of Emperor Hirohito of Japan in 1989. Britain was then represented by the Duke of Edinburgh and the foreign secretary.

Another dimension of the increased mobility of prime ministers has been the publicity they can attract to promote the export of British goods. 'Selling Britain' has become a prime ministerial function in a strictly commercial sense. Before Callaghan became prime minister, he 'felt not so much a Foreign Secretary as a multiple grocer'.[14] Thatcher attended a number of trade fairs, and used the opportunities presented by such occasions to secure further invitations for official visits. She liked to be present for the signing of some key contracts. Such agreements included examples of foreign firms investing in Britain. Britain's European partners saw a certain hypocrisy in combining proclamations of national sovereignty with setting up 'screwdriver factories' by foreign firms. In 1986 the Italians objected to Honda/Rover cars being considered British; in 1989 the French similarly objected to the products of Nissan assembly lines in north-east England.

Thatcher made careful use of these increased opportunities for direct contact with other heads of government. Not only did she play a major part in the meetings of the EC and the Group of Seven, but she developed the habit of allocating time for foreign visits, often in September before the House of Commons was reconvened. Her accumulated experience became an important asset in her development of policy. When she was elected leader of the Conservative Party in 1975, her immediate colleagues doubted her ability to make a mark in foreign affairs.[15] Between the success of the Falklands war in 1982 and the retirement of Whitelaw from the cabinet in January 1988 she developed a seemingly almost manic drive in the pursuit of foreign policy questions which her colleagues and senior officials did their best to contain. At the time of Whitelaw's retirement she was planning to visit at least ten countries within the next ten months.[16] Cabinet colleagues were less and less convinced of the benefits accruing to government from her style of presentation. The personal slight inflicted on Sir Geoffrey Howe with his removal from the foreign secretaryship in the cabinet reshuffle of July 1989 confirmed party feelings that her leadership would have to be challenged.

The immediate effects of these modifications in the prime minister's role have been to raise questions both about the machinery of government itself and about the character of the advice which is tendered by officials on foreign policy. There have been a number of enquiries into the structure of the Foreign Office and the functions of the diplomatic

---

14 James Callaghan, *Time and Chance*, Collins, 1987, p. 304.
15 William Whitelaw, *The Whitelaw Memoirs*, Aurum Press, 1989, p. 209.
16 *Sunday Times*, 10 January 1988, p. A2e.

service. The most far-reaching was initially sanctioned by Callaghan as prime minister as part of the reviews undertaken by the Central Policy Review Staff; the publication of its report in 1977 led the Foreign Office to conduct a campaign in favour of the *status quo*.

This debate on the administrative support necessary for foreign policy was a major influence in the increased interest in the idea of making a 'prime minister's department' from an amalgamation of Number 10 and the Cabinet Office. Sir John Hunt, the cabinet secretary, encouraged speculation about this possibility. Sir Kenneth Berrill, the retiring director of the Central Policy Review Staff, argued in favour of a greatly strengthened 'prime minister's department' to sustain the increased administrative load which summit meetings and official visits demanded.[17] The sheer scale of government hospitality and the added costs of providing adequate security for visiting diguitaries had to be quantified. The idea of a prime minister's department was again explored in the quality press during the winter of 1982-3, but no major structural changes actually followed.

In the absence of any formal restructuring of the centre of government, attention then shifted to the increased briefing on overseas affairs which prime ministers now required. The cabinet secretary took on the task of being the principal 'Sherpa', one who prepared for the climb to the summit. In preparing the prime minister principally for EC and economic summits, he developed greater functional expertise in the Cabinet Office, where the administrative work was delegated to a number of deputy secretaries, each in charge of a set of committees. The deputy secretary in charge of the new European Secretariat was given the special privilege of direct access to the prime minister, without having to await the permission of the cabinet secretary, and he continued to enjoy direct access to the foreign secretary through the Foreign Office division on the EC. This secretariat had its own direct link with British officials in Brussels and held weekly meetings with the British member of the Committee of Permanent Representatives (COREPER), the ambassadors of all member-states.

Thatcher's contribution to the increased requirements of overseas briefing was to extend the expertise available within Number 10 outside the confines of the established civil service structure. She appointed diplomats to be her personal policy advisers. Sir Anthony Parsons, who before his retirement had been Britain's Permanent Representative to the United Nations, became a special adviser in 1982-3, and Sir Percy Cradock, who had been Ambassador in Beijing, succeeded him in 1983. Sir David Wilson, who was appointed Governor of Hong Kong, also

17   Sir Kenneth Berrill, 'Strength at the Centre: The case for a prime minister's department, in A. King (ed.), *The British Prime Minister*, 2nd edn, Macmillan, 1985.

became an important adviser. These advisers were attached to the Number 10 Policy Unit and were joined by advisers on defence and on the security services. Thatcher never went as far as some of her supporters, who recommended the creation of a special foreign affairs unit to serve the prime minister directly; this, they hoped, would prevent the Foreign Office from 'frustrating government policy'.[18]

The functions of the principal private secretary for foreign affairs in Number 10 acquired a fresh importance. Charles Powell became the longest-serving member of the private office; his two predecessors, David Goodall and John Coles, served for only two years each. Powell took up his position in June 1984 as a Grade 5 officer, but by 1990 on Thatcher's resignation had been promoted to Grade 3, the rank of the principal private secretary. He was retained in his functions by Major till March 1991. He became known as the 'official who facilitated the expression of Mrs Thatcher's foreign policy ideas'; for example, he drafted the speech on Europe which she delivered in Bruges in September 1988 by making substantial changes to a Foreign Office submission. Powell has been compared to Horace Wilson who served Chamberlain and to Jock Colville who was intimate with Churchill. He was seen by others as a usurper of the Foreign Office's influence and as a kind of unofficial national security adviser.[19] On his retirement from the post and from public service after Major's summit with President Bush in Bermuda he was succeeded by Stephen Wall,[20] who had been Major's principal private secretary during his three months at the Foreign Office. The special intimacy of the post remains important.

The prime minister's enhanced role in the regular business of international affairs was a natural consequence of developments affecting all countries, not only the United Kingdom. Precisely how to respond to the globalisation of politics and to the technological advances which made meetings of heads of government so much easier was very much a British concern and was, ultimately, the prime minister's personal choice. Although the supporting personnel have increased in number and scope, there has been no institutionalised department, as often happens elsewhere, to provide assistance. The response to the changed nature of national leadership in this area has been a personal one, in which prime ministers have felt most comfortable with a small coterie

---

18 John Dickie, *Inside the Foreign Office*, Chapmans, 1992, p. 283.
19 The quality press speculated on the influence of Powell, e.g. *The Observer*, 18 February 1990, p. 17; *The Economist*, 3 November 1990, p. 72; *The Independent on Sunday*, 24 March 1991, p. 16; *The Financial Times*, 9 September 1991, p. 30. Powell (born 1941) joined the Diplomatic Service in 1963, serving in both Washington and Brussels.
20 John Stephen Wall (born 1947) joined the Diplomatic Service in 1968, was seconded to Number 10, and also served in Washington.

of individuals whom they can trust and with whom they relate well personally.

Co-ordination of Policy

The second aspect of the prime minister's roles which can be modified by changes in international politics is the management and co-ordination of cabinet itself. The interpenetration of domestic and international affairs is most apparent whenever public expenditure plans have to be modified to meet movements in the pattern of trade or of currency value. International agreements, most notably the Treaty of Rome and its successors, also impinge on the formation of domestic policy.

Historically, the office of prime minister came to encompass responsibility for determining the ways in which the royal prerogative was exercised. It also included making recommendations on the exercise of royal patronage. Some of the great offices of state, such as the lord chancellorship, could be traced back to the medieval court, but the disposition and structure of ministerial portfolios became matters which only successive prime ministers could decide. They determined what offices there should be and then recommended who should fill them. They also developed conventions governing the size of cabinet by distinguishing between those holders of the offices of state who were deemed worthy of the right to participate in the supreme deliberations of the executive and those who were not.

International affairs impinged directly on these functions because some of the major decisions which cabinet was asked to take were choices between different approaches to defence and foreign policy. In the eighteenth century quite a number of important policy decisions were taken by the secretaries of state without reference to their colleagues, and sometimes without reference to the prime minister.[21] But decisions which required the raising of revenue entailed broader consultation and parliamentary support, and so nineteenth-century governments became more collegiate in their decision-making.

The classic problems of managing the executive involved its three key members: the prime minister, the chancellor of the exchequer and the foreign secretary. The Treasury was in effect the central department since it had an overall view of the revenue needs of government and was responsible for preparing the estimates of parliamentary supply. Treasury officials saw the expenditures proposed at home and overseas. Since it was axiomatic that the British taxpayer could not be expected to pay for the direct costs of imperial administration, colonial armies were supposed to be financed from local sources. On the other hand,

21   Black, *British Foreign Policy in the Age of Walpole*, pp. 62-7.

British revenues supported the Royal Navy, and the Army when it was posted overseas. Therefore the principal costs of foreign policy, apart from the secret vote, were those incurred through the posting of ambassadors and other diplomats accredited to foreign governments. British power came to be expressed in fairly luxurious and well-appointed buildings in the major capitals of the world.

The prime minister's influence in the management of defence and foreign policy rested in part on the necessity to reconcile the application of different strategic doctrines considered by the armed forces. The service departments (the Admiralty, the War Office, and later the Air Ministry) were often at loggerheads over the most appropriate funding for different strategies. So long as the Royal Navy played the dominant role in the administration of a 'blue water' doctrine (the control of the world's major sea-lanes and particularly the route to India), the prime minister was little involved in policy co-ordination for defence. But, with the 'continental commitment' of the Army in Europe for the First World War and the creation of the Royal Air Force, the prime minister, chancellor and foreign secretary came to play more important roles in policy conciliation. Treasury officials, in noting the alternative costs, were also influential; Sir Warren Fisher, for example, played a major part in considering rearmament during the 1930s. It was at that time that the idea of creating a ministry for the co-ordination of defence arose, but the first incumbents in 1936 and 1939 carried little weight in cabinet.[22]

Churchill became his own minister of defence during the Second World War, and the 'defence side' of the Cabinet Office under Ismay became an important adjunct to the prime minister's management of the war effort. The development of nuclear deterrence strategies during the 1950s, which seemed to suggest that missiles launched from submarines might make the Royal Air Force redundant, compelled a revision of administrative provisions. Macmillan invited the cabinet secretary and the chief of the defence staff to begin planning for a new 'federal ministry' of defence which would incorporate all three service departments. The establishment of that new department in October 1964 was accompanied by a rearrangement of cabinet committees. The cabinet had an Overseas and Defence Policy Committee to co-ordinate decisions taken; it was served by a newly appointed deputy secretary and it marked the beginning of Cabinet Office functional specialisation.

The Ministry of Defence was initially a fairly loose structure. Internal reforms in the 1970s and 1980s increased the degree to which strategies

22   Robert Paul Shay, Jr., *British Rearmament in the Thirties*, Princeton University Press, 1977; George Peden, *British Rearmament and the Treasury, 1932-1939*, Scottish Academic Press, Edinburgh, 1979.

and costings were considered on the basis of inter-service co-operation. The prime minister was nevertheless from time to time drawn into decisions about the structure and strategies of the armed forces. The chiefs of staff remained an important part of the machinery for cabinet government and retained the right of direct access to the prime minister.[23]

The prime minister had also regularly been called upon to reconcile the different positions taken by 'overseas departments'. Until the creation in 1968 of the Foreign and Commonwealth Office, which symbolised the 'end of Empire', successive prime ministers had created different ministerial portfolios for overseas work. In addition to the Foreign Office (1782) there were the Colonial Office (1854), the India Office (1858), the Irish Office (1801), the Dominions Office (1925) – later (1947) the Commonwealth Relations Office – and the Department of Overseas Trade (1917). The Board of Trade (1696) was also regarded as an overseas department. Each of these collections of responsibilities and functions was capable of developing a view which might be at odds with the others. For example, during the Second World War the Foreign Office's conduct of discussions with the Americans on the postwar settlement risked the wrath of the Colonial Office if it appeared to be committing the British government to some kind of phased timetable for granting independence to selected colonies.[24]

The evolution of the prime minister's role as policy co-ordinator depended on the extension of government responsibility into social and economic legislation and on the greater formalisation of cabinet committee structures through the cabinet secretariat. Recent prime ministers have learnt how to manipulate the agenda of different cabinet committees and how to decide on the point at which to take the chair. These lessons have developed slowly.

There have been two main stages in which international affairs have played a major part. The first is embodied in successive attempts to manage the economy. Between 1918 and 1939 cabinets had been encouraged to think in terms of public works and of imperial preference in order to counteract the damage inflicted on the economy by trade cycles. The Treasury was gradually converted to the principles of demand management which seemed to stem from the theories of J.M. Keynes. After the Second World War cabinets were influenced by the model of French indicative planning.[25] Successive governments in the 1960s set up the National Economic Development Office and then the Department of Economic Affairs. The major shift in opinion in the 1970s followed the abandonment of the Bretton Woods system for fixed cur-

---

23   The position of the chiefs of staff is explained in Stephen Shipley Wilson (ed.), *The Cabinet Office in 1945*, HMSO, 1975.
24   Wm. Roger Louis, *Imperialism at Bay: 1941-1945*, Clarendon Press, 1977.
25   Jacques Leruez, *Economic Planning and Politics in Britain*, Martin Robertson, 1975.

rency exchange rates and the OPEC decision to raise the price of oil. Perhaps the best illustration of the transformed political climate in Britain was the 1976 currency crisis. For the first time, the British government agreed to accept a loan from the International Monetary Fund together with the stringent conditions attached.[26]

All domestic policies are manifestly subject to the overall economic strategies which attempt to shape the balance of trade, the level of the currency exchange rate and the rate of inflation. The prime minister's personal role in economic management became the subject of more comment in the 1980s than in earlier decades, as the government was committed to improve the international competitiveness of British industry by promoting deregulation and privatisation. It was difficult to pursue a strategy of retaining firms as 'national champions' in a given sector if such companies could not improve their shares of the world market. Since government policies now influence corporate strategies in so many ways, prime ministers are constantly being approached by industrialists and by foreign multinationals which seek alliances with British firms. Some projects, such as the building of the Channel Tunnel, require direct prime ministerial involvement.

The second stage was an acknowledgement of the general truth that domestic policies have to be regularly reconsidered within the general turbulence of the world economy. Britain's entry into Europe was the major step in response to this understanding. The prime minister came to act as some kind of 'minister for the affairs of the European Community'. The decision to place the European Secretariat in the Cabinet Office, and not to transform the EC division of the Foreign Office, was a statement that only the prime minister was in a position to clarify the government's position on EC issues. Heath was prime minister in 1970-4 during the course of the negotiations for Britain to sign the Treaty of Rome and he sanctioned an investigation of the arrangements made by the French government in the Secrétariat Général du Comité Interministériel (SGCI) which handled its relationships with the Community. He then confirmed that the team which negotiated Britain's entry should constitute the embryo of a new Cabinet Office secretariat. The latter devised ways for getting departments to reach agreement on the draft directives and draft legislation emerging out of the European Commission. Departmental representatives came to brief their respective ministers on the line which had been agreed through the committees serviced by the European Secretariat. The latter also commented on the draft briefs prepared by the Foreign Office for the foreign secretary

26 Martin Burch and Michael Clarke, *British Cabinet Politics: Public Expenditure and the IMF*, Hesketh, Ormskirk, 1980 (Merlin Series 1). This is a case study of the 1976 1MF crisis.

to take to the Foreign Affairs Council of Ministers. The deputy secretary of the European Secretariat was able to inform the prime minister from day to day on negotiations in each of the different fields of policy. The Secretariat combined the handling of both internal domestic policy co-ordination and European diplomacy, thus enabling a prime minister to keep a close eye on a wide range of discrete issues.

Interventions by prime ministers, as the earlier chapters indicate, are not necessarily limited to the machinery of cabinet or the Cabinet Office. They can bring pressure to bear by correspondence with ministers and by holding *ad hoc* meetings which fall outside the cabinet machinery. Thatcher frequently preferred to secure agreements without having recourse to formal committees. One such example of this (the Westland affair in 1986 in which the prime minister appeared to be favouring a buy-out by an American firm) drew public attention to prime ministerial freedom of action; but, as this showed, such bilateral negotiations are not always without cost.

A combination of internal and external considerations also arose from the issues emerging from the discussions of the Group of Seven and with other 'summits' conducted by Western nations. The main purpose of the Group of Seven was originally to consider the possibilities of policy co-ordination between leading industrial powers in the fields of trade, exchange rates and inflation. The meetings have frequently been close to the rounds of negotiation on trade liberalisation through the General Agreement on Tariffs and Trade (GATT). After the meeting at Rambouillet in 1975, Callaghan set up a working party to keep watch on 'the interplay of our domestic fiscal and monetary policy with that of overseas countries'.[27] The prime minister, instead of being regularly drawn into questions of strategy and armaments, became more and more involved with the differences between departments concerned with domestic matters, such as the Ministry of Agriculture or the Department of Trade and Industry. In addition to the direct contacts with Brussels engendered through the Treaty of Rome, large numbers of departments concerned with domestic affairs were obliged to develop their own forms of overseas representation and reporting. Departments were aware of the European Court and of the increasing tendency for national lobbies to make representations in Brussels as well as in London.

Outside the forum of the Group of Seven and that of the European Community, prime ministers also considered the impact of domestic policies on other international régimes. For example, the government's policy on licensing television companies could not be separated from the growth of transnational media conglomerate companies or from the allocation of radio spectrum and satellite positions made by the

27 Callaghan, *Time and Chance*, p. 476.

International Telecommunications Union. Thatcher made her own contacts with the entrepreneurs concerned. Similarly, government policy
for the coal industry could not be separated from changes in power
generation technology and in the world markets for energy supply. The
outcry against the announcement in 1992 of the intended closure of
many coal pits, a decision precipitated by the availability of cheaper
imported coal, required prime ministerial intervention.

Prime ministers came to recognise both that they were compelled
to play a prominent role in international negotiations at head of government level and that at the same time officials and ministers were themselves
constantly engaged in negotiations at lower levels. They learned how
and when to intervene, sometimes when the media made them feel
obliged to take visible action and sometimes when there appeared to
be important differences to reconcile between departments. Problems
calling for prime ministerial intervention were produced by both institutional and non-institutional processes of policy making.[28] The most
glaring cases of institutional problems were those arising in the European
Community. Thatcher found that the government's privatisation programme
occasionally fell foul of agreed European procedures, such as those
on policy harmonisation for transport and water. Major was faced with
the difficulty of preventing the social chapter of the Maastricht Treaty
being applied to Britain. But there were also regular difficulties outside
the European institutional framework. Prime ministers sometimes intervened in negotiations about defence procurement contracts. Making
defence procurement more cost-effective carried the price of opening
up defence contracts to foreign suppliers.

Thatcher made particular play with the opportunities of being a kind
of minister for European affairs. Her most spectacular deployment of
rhetorical pressure was in her negotiations on British contributions to
the EC budget. She did not achieve what she wanted until the summit
at Fontainebleau in June 1984. Thereafter her role in European meetings
became more conciliatory, at least until the issue of European monetary
union came to the fore. The speculation against the pound in January
1985, and particularly Bernard Ingham's role in managing the publicity
for the prime minister's views,[29] began to shift opinion within the Conservative Party towards some kind of accommodation with the European
monetary system. This change of heart, particularly in the person of
the chancellor of the exchequer, Lawson, led to criticism of the stance
which Thatcher was taking. The success of domestic anti-inflation policy
now seemed to depend on some closer association with Europe; the

28   Michael Clarke, *British External Policy-Making in the 1990s*, Macmillan, 1992,
     Chapters 5 and 6.
29   Robert Harris, *Good and Faithful Servant: The unauthorised biography of Bernard
     Ingham*, Faber and Faber, 1990, pp. 123-6; Lawson, *The View from No. 11*, pp. 467-71.

linkage between the essentially domestic and the new globalisation of politics could not have been clearer.

By contrast, the biennial meetings of the Commonwealth heads of government did not afford the same opportunities to mix domestic and foreign concerns. They were soured whenever British prime ministers found them inimical to British interests and were often marked by long-running differences of opinion over the validity of economic sanctions against South Africa. The agenda could not be managed by Britain after the creation of the Commonwealth Secretariat. After the bitter policy clashes over Rhodesia at Singapore in 1971, Heath had to be persuaded that there were any subjects which could usefully be discussed at the level of heads of Commonwealth governments. Thatcher succeeded in using the Commonwealth machinery in order to effect an adequate peace settlement in Zimbabwe, and it appears to have been instrumental in persuading Britain to arrange a constitutional conference rather than recognise the government of Bishop Muzorewa.[30] But she tended to find that the Commonwealth meetings presented few opportunities for pursuing British interests.

Thatcher also inherited the increasing public concern over environmental issues. Heath took over from Wilson in 1970 the plans then in train to create a Department of the Environment, which was intended to achieve a better reconciliation of domestic policies on housing, physical planing, transport and energy by amalgamating ministries and pushing the task of co-ordination down from cabinet. But domestic policy reconciliation became insufficient as soon as there was evidence of countries 'exporting' their own environmental damage. Oil slicks on the high seas, acid rain and radio-active fall out from nuclear power stations raised questions of immense political importance. Thatcher was criticised for coming late to a consideration of 'green issues'; Sir Crispin Tickell is credited with converting her to an interest in climatology. She gave a speech on the environment in September 1988 and hosted a conference in London on ozone depletion in March 1989. Her lecture to the Aspen Institute in Colorado in August 1990 was an important statement of the degree of her commitment to the study of global problems.[31]

International affairs presented the prime minister with other opportunities for combining domestic and foreign policies. Only a month before her departure from office Thatcher attended the UNICEF 'summit for children' in New York. Throughout her premiership she looked for the issues which the evidence accumulated in international conferences suggested she ought to be anticipating. Her advisers gained

30 For an assessment of Thatcher's record by one of her advisers, see Sir Anthony Parsons in Dennis Kavanagh and Anthony Seldon (eds), *The Thatcher Effect*, Clarendon Press, 1989, pp. 154-65.
31 *The Times*, 8 August 1990, p. 8a.

from some of the meetings hosted in Britain, such as the British-German Bilderberg meeting held in Scotland in April 1986 or the Inter-Parliamentary Union meeting on drug trafficking held in London in September 1989. In this way international gatherings affected the domestic agenda.

One consequence of the expansion of the prime minister's traditional role was the sheer political value in domestic affairs which could be gained from co-ordinating the publicity given to international appearances. It has long been the case that all leaders abroad cast half an eye on the public at home. But the combination of more regular summits and of a world with rapid access to television screens has extended the importance of the management of publicity. For example, Macmillan in 1959 and Thatcher in 1987 visited Moscow in election years, reaping benefit from the photographs that resulted.

Summitry is now accompanied by carefully developed attempts at media management, each leader bringing an appropriate team of journalists and photographers. The protection afforded by security arrangements provides the means for regulating access to pictures, and the opportunity for feeding the press with material at special conferences with official spokesmen. British prime ministers are following the customs of international gatherings. Callaghan has noted how the character of summits has changed: '[Leaders] seem to regard summits as media events or as opportunities to enhance their election prospects...the leaders make speeches to each other which are intended for public consumption back home'.[32] An apparently direct consequence of greater reliance on summitry was 'herd journalism', a gathering together in one place of large numbers of press and television reporters, each competing to secure a story to feed to the media at home. All international leaders cultivated their own media entourage, and prime ministers paid considerable attention to the manner in which stories were managed. The armed forces learned how to manage public relations in war. Thatcher in the Falklands in 1982 and Major in the Gulf in 1991 made carefully staged appearances. Thatcher in 1985 appealed to the media not to give to terrorists 'the oxygen of publicity'. Management is not always perfect, either in its coverage or its effect. The 1987 attempts by the British government to prevent the publication of Peter Wright's book *Spycatcher* (1987) backfired badly.

Bernard Ingham, Thatcher's press secretary, came to public notice, just as Charles Powell had gained considerable notoriety as her principal private secretary for foreign affairs. Ingham's presentational skills, in which Thatcher placed considerable trust, meant that he was invited to advise cabinet committees as well as to indicate the character of

32   Callaghan, *Time and Chance*, p. 497.

the prime minister's thinking when he met the Lobby. He crafted her international appearances, and set the tone of appreciation for her sometimes lonely stances in international negotiations. He embodied 'British sources' after meetings of the European Council of heads of government or of the Group of Seven. Indeed, he extended his influence across Whitehall by being appointed the head of the Government Information Services, thus vicariously extending Thatcher's influence over all departments.[33]

Successful publicity which creates favourable images makes it more difficult to judge the effectiveness of interventions made by prime ministers in the conduct of international diplomacy. For example, it was in the interests of both Thatcher and President Reagan to disguise the degree to which one could influence the government of the other. They cultivated each other as much for the photo opportunities which their meetings provided as for the substance of their negotiations. Thatcher visited the United States at least once a year during most of her premiership, even addressing Congress in February 1985. Reagan visited Europe on four separate occasions.

As public policy issues became less easy to contain within a single country, all states found themselves discussing in international fora matters of distinctly domestic significance. Britain was no exception. The European connection not only institutionalised this; it involved a wide range of ministries at several levels. One consequence has been to increase the importance of co-ordination and, as a consequence, the position of prime minister. This is additional to the perceived advantage which playing a major role on the international scene is thought to give heads of government. Prime ministers have thus seen instrumental and political reasons for playing an increasingly visible role in matters with an international dimension.

Intelligence Collection and Analysis

The third aspect of the prime minister's role which can be affected by international affairs is the control of information which can be used to anticipate events and to prepare for certain foreseeable contingencies. The Foreign Office and the Ministry of Defence have long experimented with forward thinking and intelligence assessment. But it is the prime minister and the advisers in Number 10 who are usually in the best position to recommend preventive action.

The prime minister's guardianship of the secrets of state entails responsibility for deciding who shall be privy to what kind of information. The main elements in this responsibility are the protection afforded

---

33   Harris, *Good and Faithful Servant,* passim.

by the privy councillor's oath, which is administered to all holders of high office, and the imperative of collective responsibility for cabinet decisions which limits the degree of dissent that ministers can express in public. These elements are more important for government than the formal provisions of the Official Secrets Act. Whatever reform may be introduced in order to modify that statute and whatever the effects of allowing complaints to be made against the security services, the prime minister is the only person in a position to make changes in the pattern of access to the intelligence available to government and to its analysis. Prime ministers are responsible for expenditure in this delicate area; they have the most secure communications system. The cabinet secretary ensures continuity between different prime ministers, whether they are of the same party or of different political persuasions.

The impact of international affairs on this role is by definition impossible to assess in detail. The subject is shrouded by the royal prerogative and by a long tradition of government secrecy. But certain features are worthy of comment. Freedom of information legislation elsewhere in the world has had its effects on Britain. The major modification made to widen access to the public records, the 1967 statute reducing the period after which they should normally be open to public inspection (from fifty to thirty years) was introduced after British historians had been using copies of British records in United States archives. American journalists were also among the first to reveal the names of the heads of the British security services. Threats by British authors to publish books on state secrets in the United States also brought knowledge about the wartime system for the interception of radio signals into the public domain. Dissent within the United States Central Intelligence Agency during the Vietnam war spilled over into the governments of the United States' partners in intelligence co-operation. Events overseas were largely responsible for raising general public awareness in Britain of the character of official secrecy.

The main responsibility of the prime minister for official secrets is ostensibly not concerned with covert intelligence collection and analysis. From time to time cabinet government requires the prime minister to issue directives to all ministers about actions which might be deemed imprudent. For example, ministers should not hold shares in private companies which might benefit from the exercise of ministerial authority. These directives are normally collated into a single document, *Questions of Procedure for Ministers*, now issued by all prime ministers at the beginning of their administrations. Following the haphazard procedures before the Second World War, Cabinet Office officials recommended that the practice of the wartime coalition government should be 'consolidated'. Two documents from 1945 were conflated to make the first version of 'questions of procedure' in 1946. In 1986 a House of Commons Select Committee was shown in 1976 version of this document which had been issued by Callaghan when he became prime minister in April.[34] Thatcher's 1979 version with its amendments was not placed in the public domain but Major, in line with a general opening up of secrecy, has now placed it on the public record.[35]

Questions of Procedure does not deal with the conventions for circulating secret and confidential despatches or confidential prints. Nineteenth-century prime ministers and foreign secretaries, after the invention of telegraphy, decided which ministers should see the decoded telegrams from British representatives overseas. They defined the boundaries of 'inner cabinets' according to the circulation of papers. The Foreign Office, and later the Cabinet Office, developed the practice of reproducing key documents in a series of confidential prints. Ministers who were not included in these circulations would from time to time complain that they were insufficiently informed about events overseas. Prime ministers invited foreign secretaries to make oral statements in cabinet. Since 1927 the cabinet agenda has provided a formal slot at which the foreign secretary can speak.

Prime ministers have been obliged to move beyond what is prudent for the protection of the collective responsibility of cabinet by the technological advances in signals intelligence (SIGINT) and by parallel improvements in other forms of interception. They were constrained by the system of intelligence co-operation between major Western powers which is dominated by the United States. The British security services took charge of the Government Code and Cipher School (later Government Communications Headquarters in Cheltenham) during the Second World War when the signals broadcast by the German armed forces using Enigma machines were successfully intercepted and decoded. These decrypts, given the name ULTRA, provided a select number of Allied commanders with verbatim accounts of what their enemies were saying. The Germans believed that the Enigma codes could never be broken. The Americans shared this knowledge of German intentions through the Office of Strategic Services, and after the war established the Central Intelligence Agency and the National Security Agency. The 'Cold War' against the Soviet Union consolidated the practices of Western intelligence co-operation. Britain provided sites for American listening stations and accepted specialised tasks.

Prime ministers have also become involved in what appear to be breaches of intelligence co-operation. Considerable evidence has been brought to light suggesting that British security services have intercepted

---

34 C (PR) (76) 1 of 23 April 1976; see also HC 92-ii/1985- 1986, pp. 142-52.
35 J.M. Lee, 'Cabinet procedure', *Public Administration* (1986), vol. 64, pp. 347-9.

and decoded the messages being sent to and from the embassies of friendly allies in London. On this the revelations of Peter Wright in *Spycatcher* are highly suggestive.

British governments appear to be under pressure from the Americans when intelligence co-operation is deemed to be in danger. The methods of vetting recruits to the Civil Service were designed after Americans had expressed their concerns. There may be a connection between American complaints and the decision of the prime minister in 1984 to ban trade unions from the Government Communications Headquarters (GCHQ). By that date the prime minister was seen to be generally responsible for covert operations, although MI5 was reporting to the home secretary and MI6 to the foreign secretary. The Joint Intelligence Committee, which marries intelligence from overt and covert sources, was brought within the Cabinet Office in the late 1950s and then in the late 1960s placed under the supervision of a co-ordinator for security who reports to the prime minister. An assessments staff in the Cabinet Office within this section is responsible for preparing reports on different regions and different problems.

The principal modifications in the prime minister's functions in this field have been due not only to American pressure and the presence of the co-ordinator but also to the rise of what has come to be called 'preventative diplomacy'. Like preventative policing, preventative diplomacy is action which anticipates future trouble by removing potential sources of threat. It relies to a significant extent on secret intelligence. Its principal objects of surveillance are subversives such as international terrorists and international drug traffickers. Its exponents pride themselves on their ability to penetrate organisations which may be sources of political instability. The Prevention of Terrorism Act (1976), which stems from the necessities of countering the campaign of the Irish Republican Army (IRA) in Northern Ireland, can provide legal cover for official action. Technological improvements have extended the scope for preventative action. Computers can monitor the appearance of specific words or numbers used in telephone conversations which are intercepted. Thatcher's government experienced the benefits of the improved SIGINT collection systems which followed the launchings of Rhyolite satellites in the 1970s and then of the Magnum satellites in 1985.[36]

These aids also give support to governments wishing to be informed of more overt operations. Overseas governments, as well as private organisations, are developing ways of targeting propaganda or privileged briefing documentation. The House of Commons, for example, has witnessed since the early 1980s much more direct approaches to MPs

---

36   Jeffrey T. Richelson and Desmond Ball, *The Ties that Bind; Intelligence co-operation between the UK/USA countries*, Geo. Allen and Unwin, 1985, pp. 177, 180-1.

from overseas interests, which are prepared to pay for the staff of lobbying organisations and to provide speaking notes. MPs' daily postbags contain pamphlets and handouts from foreign sources; foreign embassies have parties, dinners and introductions; ambassadors address backbench groups. The prime minister and foreign secretary can when necessary be told about the connections which MPs are cultivating. Foreign firms will pay retaining fees to MPs in the hope of securing contacts. The revelation in 1990 that an MP had received money from Saudi Arabia which he had not registered provided a reminder that overseas interests could purchase parliamentary time for the presentation of their causes.[37] Since then, however, MPs with their own consultancy firms have been obliged to submit details of their contacts to the register of MPs' interests.

The effects of these developments have been to encourage prime ministers to be more interested in the techniques of preventative diplomacy, to call for the evidence of surveillance, and to conduct negotiations on secure communications system. Summit meetings which require so much preparation by officials beforehand may represent only a minor part of the results which each leader hopes to secure. Behind the publicity there may be opportunities for securing advances to more longterm goals. Number 10 and the Cabinet Office are manifestly more deeply involved in the conduct of diplomacy. The briefings provided by the prime minister's press secretary are designed to fill the press and television with favourable impressions. Prime ministers' officials are looking for examples of success which can be attributed to their intervention. But they are also aware of the value of helping the prime minister to build up confidence and respect in the minds of other world leaders.

Modifications in the role of the prime minister since 1945 are largely part of the country's adjustments to its middle-power status. At the beginning of this period, Churchill envisaged Britain as being at the centre of three overlapping circles of geopolitical power: the Commonwealth, the Atlantic Community and Europe.[38] This vision could not survive the decline in Britain's position as an industrial power, and British prime ministers in the 1990s no longer enjoy the resources of great power status which Churchill knew. Although it is still possible to think of foreign policy in terms of the same three sets of interrelations, their relative importance and Britain's importance within each has shifted.

The less the degree of British influence in world affairs, the more

---

37 Charles Carstairs and Richard Ware, *Parliament and International Relations*, Open University Press, 1991, p. 59.

38 Martin Gilbert, *Winston Churchill*, vol. 8: 'Never Despair', Heinemann, 1988, pp. 354-5, an address to the Conservative Party conference, October 1947.

a prime minister is obliged to be conscious of international influences on *domestic* affairs, to be visible in 'selling Britain' economically, and to be interested in anticipating problems and preventing their impact on domestic affairs. This globalisation of international affairs has in any case ensured that all states view the domestic and foreign as interrelated; but this reconceptualisation is exaggerated in Britain's case because of its changed status in the world community.

When British power could be exercised relatively unhindered through the naval strategy of controlling the high seas, British interests looked as if they could be objectively defined and normally protected. Without this kind of hegemony, British interests have needed constant recalculation. Only the prime minister, as the head of government and visible personification of Britain, can do this. Yet redefinition is itself constrained by the need to meet new public expectations of government and the increased difficulties in the management of the national economy. As more and more issues, the responsibility of different ministries and an increasing number of politicians and bureaucrats take on an international dimension, it is the prime minister and those closely attached to Number 10 who necessarily play a more significant part in policy co-ordination and reconciliation.

Perhaps the difficulty now of exercising any kind of hegemony means that the very concept of national interest is itself less tenable as a guide to action. The prime minister's role has been modified both by the greater interdependence between nations and also by the changing relationships between prime minister and people. In one perspective, the prime minister is less powerful and more subject to international developments abroad and popular prejudice at home; in another, the prime minister is more important as co-ordination and preventive action become the central requisites of any effective government.

8

THE PRIME MINISTERSHIP, 1945-1995

Richard Hodder-Williams

There have been few general books devoted to the office of the prime minister.[1] Indeed, there is no widely accepted term for the office in the same way that scholars talk about the American presidency as a distinct institution: 'prime ministry' and 'prime ministership' have both been tried. This suggests, perhaps, that the attempt to distil the essence of the office is doomed to failure; Asquith was correct to write that the office of the prime minister is 'what its holder chooses and is able to make of it'.[2] Such a view is excessively defeatist. As Donald Shell shows, there are sufficient common requirements of the office to give it form and substance and yet still retain the truth that prime ministers are its major definers. This book, however, is not an attempt to delineate the contours of the office in the mid-1990s, but to examine how it has changed since the 1940s. There have been so many fundamental and momentous changes in the world during this period that it would be extraordinary if the prime ministership had been exempt from change.

Nobody can doubt that there have been many changes; but whether there has been any clear development of the office is another matter. All alterations are changes; development, on the other hand, implies a number of changes which move in one perceptible direction, building up, for example, a new set of expectations which are passed on in a durable form from one prime minister to the next. There has been change (although even that is sometimes exaggerated) in the office of the prime minister, but an almost total lack of development. The underlying sources of prime ministerial power remain as they were in Churchill's day.

It is interesting to start from the perspective of scholars who study

---

1   Byrum Carter, *The Office of the Prime Minister*, Faber and Faber, 1956; F.W.G. Benemy, *The Elected Monarch*, Harrap, 1965; Humphrey Berkeley, *The Power of the Prime Minister*, Geo. Allen and Unwin, 1968; Robert Blake, *The Office of the Prime Minister*, Oxford University Press, 1975; Anthony King (ed.), *The British Prime Minister*, Macmillan, 1969 and 1985.

2   Quoted in Harold Wilson, *The Government of Britain*, Weidenfeld and Nicolson, and Michael Joseph, 1976, p. 1.

the British system as a foreign system rather than one of which they are themselves part. Two Americans recently began their analysis of the British prime minister by observing that it was 'obvious that the prime ministry is the central institution in British politics'.[3] It may seem obvious; but it may also be illusory. In the first place, there are problems of conceptualisation when thinking of the prime ministry as an institution. It is defined neither by constitution nor by statute. It is best conceived of as a combination of roles or relationships. These link prime ministers with the members of their cabinets, with Parliament as a whole, with the party of which they are leader, with Whitehall departments, with the British public at large, and with the wider international community. These are broadly similar to the seven structural factors which Patrick Weller proposed as significant in helping to shape the capabilities of prime ministers in any parliamentary system.[4] In each set of relationships expectations are built up on both sides about the behaviour appropriate to that particular linkage. These expectations are effectively the sources of power exercisable by each side in the relationship and they alter over time. Any prime ministership is essentially the sum of these fluctuating relationships.

Secondly, while prime ministers may be the focal point of the national political system, it does not necessarily follow that they are the fundamental *source* of power. As this collection of essays shows, the relationships listed above play differently according to different contexts and different prime ministers. Even within the span of a single prime minister's experience of office, the relationships may alter; this was obviously true of Margaret Thatcher's long period as prime minister, but it was also true, for example, of Harold Wilson. The flexibility of the uncodified constitution certainly allows prime ministers some considerable freedom to make of the office what they will. Each prime minister since the Second World War entered office with a set of expectations very similar to that enjoyed by their predecessors when they took office; how they develop the resources available to them depends on their skill and their luck. During a term of office, the expectations shift and power is accordingly restructured. Such change, moreover, is not always unilinear; to take Thatcher's case again, her power waxed and waned. The reasons for this can also be deduced from the earlier chapters, but they will be sketched out again at the end of this chapter.

3 Craig V. Wilson and Andrea L. Bonnicksen, 'The British Prime Minister', in Taketsugu Tsurutani and Jack B. Gabbert (eds), *Chief Executive: national political leadership in the United States, Mexico, Great Britain, Germany and Japan*, Washington State University Press, 1992, p. 148.

4 Patrick Weller, 'Prime minister/prime ministerial government', in Vernon Bogdanor (ed.), *The Blackwell Encyclopaedia of Political Institutions*, Blackwell Reference, 1987.

The major determinants of power have remained essentially unaltered, but nobody would deny that the context in which prime ministers must operate has greatly changed since Churchill's day. Although he would feel comfortably at home in many aspects of the position, as these essays have shown, he would also notice some developments which alter the way in which a prime minister's various roles can be performed. This contextual revolution is, of course, not the same as institutional change and there is considerable evidence from the chapters in this book that the fundamental features of the prime minister's office have endured remarkably unaltered in spite of the major changes in the broader political environment.

Nearly all the chapters suggest that three distinctive and decisive contextual changes have taken place. The first is technological. The developments in communications, both the tangible aspects (such as transport improvements) and the intangible (such as the electronic media), have dramatically expanded the public visibility of prime ministers and their opportunities for short-term travel outside the United Kingdom. In foreign affairs, as J.M. Lee in particular emphasises, there is now no excuse for a prime minister not to attend a major international gathering, and indeed funerals of important political figures have become occasions for personal diplomacy. Ministers with responsibility for foreign affairs sometimes find that they are not merely advisers to prime ministers (that was always the case) but are sometimes personal assistants as well. There are variations, and tensions, in these relationships and no consistent pattern; but the opportunity for prime ministerial dominance has been increased. While the Major-Hurd relationship has plenty of earlier precedents, the Thatcher-Major relationship illustrated in extreme form the consequences of the new balance of concerns. Foreign policy issues have necessarily become more central to a prime minister's agenda, especially in attention time, at the expense of the domestic scene.

Even more obviously, the media (television in particular) have come to dominate much of a prime minister's working day. This is the central theme of Colin Seymour-Ure's chapter, but the point recurs regularly in all the others. It is ever more difficult for a prime minister to remain silent on an issue which the media have decided is one of national interest, and it is impossible for prime ministers now to avoid their performances being appraised, evaluated and criticised daily in the news media. Whatever the reality of their responsibility for specific government policies (and speeches), the presumption is that they are masters of their governments and that ministerial action reflects their priorities and choices. They must be ready with a good phrase, a plausible defence or a potent riposte whenever they are approached by journalists. As a corollary of this, prime ministers have tried to ensure that they dominate the agenda rather than react to questions posed by the media; the Lobby system and calculated off-the-record briefings are intended to ensure that the issues which the media address are those which the prime minister favours. This is not always possible, but it reflects a major change in the context of a prime minister's political life.

The intrusion of the media into so much of the minutiae of prime ministerial work may be new, but the media have always taken a close interest in the occupant of 10 Downing Street. The world of politicians and journalists has long been incestuous, each depending upon yet also influencing the other. In the competition for preferment and advancement, ambitious politicians are ready to use the media to proselytise their positions, just as the media are constantly seeking a good story to add spice to their reportage. The prime minister's press secretary and the chairman of the party are both concerned to massage the message and use their journalistic contacts to help the prime minister of the day. But journalists are not subservient and it is not always possible to manipulate the press and television, which have their own agendas and their own culture. Whatever the balance of influence, however, the world of Westminster and Whitehall, perhaps slightly less than the world within the Washington Beltway, is a hothouse, rich with rumour and judgement, in which the players are almost as much interested in what is being said about them as about the very real policy problems that face them. *The Times* has not been the only newspaper whose editor has played a significant political role or whose opinions have affected the standing and policies of individual ministers and governments. What is new is the intensity, the continuity and the sheer triviality of so such political comment. That is why Colin Seymour-Ure argues that this is a qualitative change in the political environment in which prime ministers now have to operate.

The second major change has been in the international status and power of Britain itself. This has been played out in two distinct ways. On the one hand, the country's economic problems have necessitated governments taking a close interest in the economic well-being of the nation in a period when the objective indicators of national economic power have been waning. The Keynesian and neo-Keynesian presumptions that national policy can affect the country's economy have made it extremely difficult for politicians to persuade their electors that much of the malaise may be due to external factors beyond any government's ability to control. The nature of the world economy has shifted the United Kingdom from being a dominant player in a game with few meaningful participants to a player struggling to assert influence in a game with many other players, all deeply affected by the consequences of globalisation. This malaise epitomised by the financial crisis of 1976, spilled over into a generalised discontent with institutions and their personnel. The failure of the national economy was vicariously attributed to the failure of political leaders, responsibility for which the public tended to shift on to the prime minister. Inevitably this weakened prime ministers, standing and thus their influence.

Together with a weakening economic status there has been a reduced political and military status in the world. The decision to withdraw from east of Suez epitomised the end of the imperial era. It has been difficult for prime ministers to manage the move from the status of a world power, in which Churchill revelled, to that of a major regional power, with which Major must contend. Macmillan's African tour in 1960, the first occasion on which a serving prime minister had set foot in Africa, epitomised the leader in command, even though in fact his message presaged the retreat from Empire. Imperial leadership slipped almost imperceptibly into domination of the Commonwealth; both relationships united people across divisions of party and class. But by the 1970s Britain found itself merely one major player in an enlarged grouping of sovereign states signally lacking in deference, as is clear when one compares the experience of Macmillan with that of Heath or Thatcher at Commonwealth heads of government meetings. Popular expectations of national status were dented. The European adventure, while instrumentally necessary, could not recreate the grandeur of the past and it failed to absolve a prime minister from the appearance of weakness. There was thus a tension between expectations and reality, a tension which weakened the status of prime ministers as it also frustrated them. The middle-power status which Britain now enjoys makes the British prime minister a figure of significantly reduced power on the world stage but, as J.M. Lee argues, the increased significance of external affairs and the possibilities for a prime minister to posture on the international scene seem initially to enhance the appearance of power.

Being at the centre of things, however, is not of itself the same as being influential. Simple popular expectations and realistic possibilities for the exercise of national power increasingly fail to mesh. Thus, for as long as the electorate believe that governments, and above all the individuals who lead them, can protect the daily well-being of the British people as well as their status in the world, all prime ministers will be faced with a gap between what can actually be done and what they feel obliged to promise. This may be thought of still as the residue of Empire. But it is a reality on which hitherto no political party has had the courage to educate the public, and it places severe strains on all prime ministers. In the jargon, there are no uniquely foreign policy issues (and increasingly few purely domestic issues), only intermestic ones; and these are precisely the kind, dependent as they are on political actors beyond the United Kingdom's shores, which the British government can no longer confidently influence.

Thirdly, the political divisions within the United Kingdom have become more fluid and less easy to manage. In the early 1950s two major parties dominated the electorate's loyalties and the argument between them was relatively straightforward, economic in nature, and cumulative in form. A consequence was that each party could rely on a strong base of committed supporters. The 1960s weakened the economic divisions and introduced new issues which cut across parties, such as relationships with Europe, the assimilation of immigrants from the New Commonwealth, the problems of Northern Ireland, the growth of nationalism in Scotland and the revitalisation of regional awareness in Wales. None of these nestled comfortably along a traditional Conservative versus Labour line of fission. Relative affluence compounded the difficulties facing the parties that arose from such cross-cutting issues. Prime ministers were faced with less cohesive blocks of voting supporters and from the 1970s with a large mass of voters who deserted both of the major parties, especially at by-elections, to bolster a third party (variously Liberal, Social Democrat and Liberal Democrat) whose votes were reflected less in seats then in a general impression once again of governmental malaise.

A modern prime minister must fight on all fronts, distancing the government party from what are now two opposition parties, each of which draws its support from across the country and often criticises from a quite distinct angle. The media are quick to notice ambivalences and contradictions; but these are inevitable given the need to appeal in different parts of the country to different constituencies with different priorities. Dealignment reduces the political cement of ideology and increases the need to build coalitions of groups who are energised more by their position on specific issues which are frequently personal and relatively local. The structure of post-modern society is not well prepared for the overlapping dualities which underlie an enduring two-party system. The consequence is that prime ministers appear too often to be subject to the pressures of special interests and too infrequently the confident directors of public policy. The paradox is that a prime minister like Thatcher who does stake out a strong leadership position alienates significant groups within the polity and loses support.

These contextual changes have not affected the structure of the prime ministership, although they have clearly adjusted the relative significance of some of the relationships (for instance with the people at large) and the ability to employ the resources of the office for the exercise of power. On the one hand, they have weakened the capacity to institute and administer successful public policy. Opinion polls have tended since the 1960s, regardless of the party in government, to show majorities disapproving of the government of the day, critical of its policies and pessimistic about the prospects for the future. It is simply more difficult to meet the new popular expectations with a portfolio of policies which enrich the citizenry. The 1950s, with their growth and their residual deference to government, are history. On the other hand, prime ministers have the means to appear major international figures, strong leaders and commanding personalities. Although the media are much less obsequious towards prime ministers than they were in the early 1950s, they still provide a ready stage upon which leaders can perform, and so encourage the image of the presidential figure.

Indeed, there have been some who see the prime minister becoming more like a president. In the late 1970s Quintin Hogg wrote, from the uncomfortable perspective of opposition, about an 'elective dictatorship', and Michael Foley published a book in 1993 arguing that there has been a presidentialisation of the office.[5] In some ways the analogy is beguiling. The dominant position of a prime minister in the media, both during an election campaign and between elections, is obvious; the growth of multilateral heads of government meetings, such as the Group of Seven or the European Union, again place a prime minister on the same level as presidents; the distance between prime ministers and backbenchers (and even junior ministers) adds to the impression of a disjunction between the prime minister and the rest of the political process. Compare the parliamentary appearances of Churchill and Attlee with those of Thatcher. Too busy, perhaps, to join the parliamentary throng and to participate in anything except set pieces (such as the highly theatrical twice-weekly question time drama), the modern prime minister, after the first well-meaning months of cultivating support, descends upon the House from on high just as a president in other countries deigns irregularly to come to the legislature. However, there is a danger in confusing this image with the substance. Prime ministers may now get more attention, a more searching spotlight, a more demanding schedule than they did in Attlee's day, but their effective powers remain much the same. This seems to be the central conclusion to be drawn from these essays.

At the heart of any explanation of this apparent paradox is the constitutional system itself. The British system remains obstinately parliamentary, not presidential. The precise style and form which it takes may have changed over the years, but its central principles have not. Parliament may not be a collective body which initiates laws or arbitrates upon laws presented to it by the executive (and it probably

---

5   Michael Foley, *The Rise of the British Presidency*, Manchester University Press, 1993.

never has been), and in this it remains a pale image of the Fourth French Republic's National Assembly or the American Congress. Furthermore, the growth of the visual media and the access of television to the Houses of Parliament have widened the political community whose views and actions affect public life. At first sight, it might seem that Parliament's importance has declined. But it should never be forgotten that Parliament, or the House of Commons to be more accurate, continues to provide the legitimation for governments, the parliamentary party which gives – or takes away – support for the executive, and the chamber which provides the crucible in which reputations are forged. (The vision offered by Colin Seymour-Ure of a party leader whose reputation is built upon media skills rather than parliamentary support, for which Italy may provide an early illustration, has not yet been realised; but politicians vying for position are more conscious than ever before of their performance and image in the media.) Prime ministers, of course, need the national electorate in order for them and their parties to be placed in power; but it is Parliament which made them leaders and can end their tenures, even at moments when the party activists in the country might prefer otherwise.

It must be emphasised that prime ministers have no formal political bases of their own. The central institution, in terms of power, remains Parliament. Presidents by contrast have usually been elected, and then proceed to exercise power, in their own democratic right. Prime ministers are merely MPs who have the temporary and, be it noted, the voluntary support of their parties to be leader; they have no legally based right to the position and can find that support withdrawn. More than this, although colleagues may owe their specific positions within the government to the prime minister, they not only have an equal legitimacy as MPs and often personal support of their own within the party, but they have also shared common experiences and, of particular importance, the responsibility for common policies with the prime minister. During the initial period in office, prime ministers have little room for policy manoeuvre because they are committed, as are their colleagues, to past positions, and those who come into power replacing party colleagues inherit the future promises set out in the most recent manifesto. Prime ministers are, in effect, captains of their teams, but they owe their position (and its very real powers) not to a manager or outside directors but to the team itself.

But in a different perspective one might note how in recent years some prime ministers have attempted to make general elections into plebiscites for their personal goals, and some have interpreted general elections, after the fact, as mandates for their leadership. Thatcher 'bounced' the 1987 Manifesto (the longest in Conservative Party history) through her colleagues, and in 1992 Norman Tebbit was quick to remind the doubters that Major had won a personal mandate. Are these presumptions fragile illusions? The prime minister may indeed be the chief executive (and the structure of government unquestionably gives a prime minister every chance to become the dominant figure), but the other members of the executive enjoy a democratic legitimacy of their own and can join together to obstruct or even remove the titular leaders. But such obstruction takes time. In the early aftermath of election victories, prime ministers are in a strong position to impose their will, but this honeymoon period (as in the United States) is shorter than it once was, given the unyielding attention of the media and the policy-focused base of so many politicians' interests.

Contrast the prime minister's independent sources of power with the situation of the United States president. His authority has a basis in the Constitution itself and is legitimised through national elections. The executive branch, separated from the legislature, is his creation and ultimate responsibility; he choses his political partners from the whole citizenry, and their continuation in office is at his discretion; he enjoys not only the efficient powers of the executive branch but also the dignified status of head of state. Within his sphere (and it is very much limited by the federal structure and the separation of powers), he enjoys the full powers of the executive branch sanctioned by the Constitution and electoral legitimacy.

There is another instructive comparison. To this day the shadow of Franklin Delano Roosevelt lies across the White House in two distinct forms. Although there had been presidents before him who stretched the executive power, most notably Abraham Lincoln, Theodore Roosevelt and Woodrow Wilson, none had used so many powers together or concerned themselves with so large a range of issues. It was the cumulative nature of Franklin Roosevelt's use of presidential powers which marked his term of office, as well as its length, as something unique up to that time. The modern presidency may be said to have been invented by him. There is no equivalent in the history of the prime ministership, not even Churchill in the Second World War.

Furthermore, the presidency which Roosevelt created provided, as it were, a base-line upon which successors subsequently built. Harry Truman inherited an office to which, for example, a structured Central Intelligence Agency (CIA) and National Security Council (NSC) were added. These were passed to Eisenhower, and the Executive Office of the President grew in numbers and significance. That in turn became part of John F. Kennedy's inheritance; Kennedy may have used the NSC differently, but it remained and further accretions were made to the office. Thus the presidency has developed like an irregular staircase, each holder of the office starting his term on the step left by his predecessor. Resources and, indirectly, power have accordingly grown incrementally. The office of the prime minister has not developed in this way.

But Roosevelt's shadow has lain over all his successors, with the possible exception of Kennedy, in another way. Not only the institutions but the practice and style of the man lived on after his death, as Bill Leuchtenberg has so fascinatingly recorded.[6] Encouraged by the media, a set of expectations has been established to which presidents are expected to conform; the myth of the first 100 days is just one example. Most presidents, too, are well aware of that begetter of the modern office, measure themselves against his performance, and often try to wrap themselves in his mantle. This is not limited to presidents of his own party; Ronald Reagan, for example, retained his admiration for the man even when he became a Republican president, and constantly related his own ideas and actions to a mythologised vision of FDR's tenancy of the office. There has been no such model for the British prime minister; Thatcher, often thought of as establishing a new level of dominance for a prime minister, bequeathed to Major nothing more than she had herself inherited in 1979.

The lack of developments can be exaggerated; nevertheless, it is the most striking aspect of the half-century under review. It is fascinating to read Byrum Carter's 1956 study of the office today.[7] As in the 1950s and 1960s, a large number of the most perceptive books published on British politics were written by our transatlantic cousins. Carter concluded that it was 'evident…that the office of the prime minister has been undergoing fundamental changes'[8] and pointed to five major developments since the beginning of the century. Modern prime ministers are required to do so much more; they enjoy the advantages of disciplined parties in an essentially two-party system; their powers and status have been enhanced by leadership in two world wars; the increase in government responsibilities has reduced individual ministers' time for general overview; and the emphasis on committees for decision-making and good public administration has increased the prime minister's supervisory and co-ordinating roles at their colleagues' expense. What, then, is new? In short, the modern prime ministership was in place when Britain returned to civilian mode after its wartime experience.

But this is not quite accurate. Soon after Carter wrote, there was a generational change in British politics. In the early 1960s the baton of leadership passed from those who were in politics before the Second World War to those who had entered the House of Commons after

6   William E. Leuchtenberg, *In the Shadow of FDR: From Harry Truman to Bill Clinton,* Cornell University Press, 2nd edn revised and updated, 1993.

7   Carter, *The Office of the Prime Minister.*

8   Ibid., p. 331.

1945. The shift was not merely concerned with formative experiences (the Great Depression or the Crisis of 1931) but with political assumptions. It ran along two related axes, as the system became more democratic and less deferential. The enhancement of democracy was most obvious in the changes instituted by the Conservative Party in the method designed to select leaders. Power shifted from unnamed senior politicians to the parliamentary party as a whole. Without such changes it is probable that Heath would not have become prime minister and certain that Margaret Thatcher would not have achieved the leadership. Somewhat later, the Labour Party also altered its rules, extending even beyond Parliament the people entitled to be involved in the selection of leader and potentially, therefore, of a prime minister.

Widening the electoral colleges for the selection of party leaders was accompanied at almost the same time by a more open coverage of the prime minister's personal life and public performance. As the newspapers, and not only the tabloids, cheerfully embraced prime ministers by their first names, prime ministers consciously went to the people to express their commitment to the democratic principle of accountability. Thatcher's readiness to go on the Jimmy Young show was merely one instance of this. Politics at the highest level simply became more popular – in its discourse, in the values employed in its interpretation, and in the instant nature of its descriptions and judgements.

Becoming prime minister and performing as prime minister thus became much less an intra-party, intra-Westminster happening, involving a select few, upon which the citizenry were allowed irregular glimpses. The opportunity only every four or five years to pass electoral judgement was enhanced by the regular taking of the political temperature not through the old conception of public opinion – élite, informed, expressed – but through the new democratic means of the opinion poll, with a very different basis. Bringing the prime minister closer to the people was part of the decline of deference. It was at this same time that satirical television programmes like 'That Was the Week That Was' and magazines like *Private Eye* became popular and the mimicry of actors caricatured individual politicians to raise laughter and puncture self-importance. The tests to which prime ministers were subjected thus increased and with it the likelihood of failure.

The deference that prevailed in political life in the immediate postwar years, especially in the Conservative Party, was closer to the style of the 1930s than the 1970s. The 'class of 1945', however, having experienced the democratising influences of active participation in war and the beginnings of imperial dismantling, brought a new competitive individualism to politics. The contrast should not be pushed too far. Typically, the 'new' culture was not really new; Stanley Baldwin had experienced some sharp personal attacks. As Robert Blake observed and Donald Shell's introductory chapter reiterates, the basic parameters of the prime minister's power were set long ago.[9] Nevertheless, there have been changes; criticism of senior politicians became more normal, and acceptable; intellectual or specialist qualities carried more weight; the backgrounds of members shifted to a new meritocracy, to lawyers and accountants among Conservatives, teachers and professional politicos among Labour. Prime ministers could not rely on the loyalty of those behind them with the same confidence as before.

Professionalism might be represented by the increase in the size of the prime minister's office and in the attention given to it. Martin Burch suggests that this has provided a significantly enhanced capacity at the centre – probably by intention. Yet ministerial autonomy survived almost unscathed and no Prime Minister's Department was established. Perhaps the real reasons were connected less with prime ministerial wishes to strengthen their own positions and more with a need for professional assistance at a time of ever-increasing business in a complex world. Affected by the country's entry into Europe (a European section was located in the Cabinet Office) and by a growing feeling that policy-making needed a more structured and formal gestation, first the Central Policy Review Staff and then the Policy Unit were established and attempts (ultimately unsuccessful) were made after the publication of the Fulton Committee's Report to shift the ethos of the civil service away from an intellectual amateurism to a knowledge-based profes-sionalism. Meanwhile prime ministers became ever less visible within the Palace of Westminster and backbenchers became more insistent and involved. It appeared to some after the Heath government that the very conventions on bringing governments down had to be revised. But, yet again, appearances deceive; Ramsay MacDonald had made it clear that he would not resign on every parliamentary defeat, and the supposed convention that defeat in the House of Commons was the prelude to governmental resignation was in reality untested and unsettled. John Major lost an important vote on Europe, but demanded a vote of confidence the following day, won it and remained in office. The presumed changes were more apparent than real; in any case these were not developments of an incremental kind but the adjustments made necessary by a revised political culture.

Ultimately, however, despite these changes relating to the office of the prime minister, the essential principle of prime ministerial power remained unchanged. So long as party leaders enjoy the support of colleagues in cabinet and in the parliamentary party, they remain in office until a general election removes their party and therefore them-

9 Blake, *The Office of Prime Minister.*

selves from power. This was just as it had been at the beginning of the twentieth century. As Donald Shell asserts, 'British politics is above all party politics.' However, the forces affecting the building, consolidation and dissipation of a prime minister's support have altered. Ultimately, because a politician's career depends in the first instance on victory at a general election in a particular constituency and victory for the party as a whole, MPs relate their support for prime ministers closely to an estimation of their likelihood of being victorious at a general election. However positive in policy matters, however ruthless in the making and breaking of individual careers, prime ministers cannot ultimately survive a feeling in the party that their continuation at the helm is likely to result in electoral defeat.

The link between a leader's popularity and the likelihood of electoral victory has not remained static. Prime ministers have increasingly been prepared to go over the heads of the intermediaries to relate directly both to their party rank and file and to the electorate more generally. To some extent Gaitskell's determination to challenge his party on the policy of unilateralism and 'to fight and fight again' for what he believed to be a more responsible policy was a determined effort to use the leader's status to exert pressure, through ordinary party members and voters, on his parliamentary colleagues and union supporters. Heath's attendance throughout the Conservative Party conference in 1965 was a signal that the tradition of *'de haut en bas'* reflected in previous leaders' attitudes to the Conference was dying; his open criticism of Thatcher's policies at the 1981 conference seemed to encapsulate the collapse of deferentialism (although an ex-prime minister might feel no need to defer to anyone). The relentless publication of, and attention to, public opinion polls evaluating the standing of prime ministers has a profound affect on their standing within the parliamentary party. This more democratic judgemental process has diminished the importance of an inner circle of leading party figures in supporting, or undercutting, a prime minister.

This has proved a two-edged sword. At times when prime ministers are experiencing disagreements with major figures in the party, they can reach out beyond their rivals to a wider, more democratically legitimate community to garner support. This was Major's necessary tactic in 1994. At other times, however, that same public – shrewd or fickle, according to choice – may turn against prime ministers and their weaknesses are at once magnified. Thatcher's rise and fall followed her rating with the public at large rather than in Parliament or among the party faithful. Earlier prime ministers had less opportunity to dominate the relationship between prime minister and public, since their exposure was less direct, and more mediated by newspaper commentators whose readership was élite rather than popular. To be seen and heard regularly is not enough to ensure popular support (for the performance may be unimpressive and the daily experiences of voters incapable of being assuaged), but it is a necessary condition and an opportunity which leaders take with care and professional advice. The likes of Saatchi and Saatchi, the advertising agency that worked closely with the Conservative Party, were not conceived of until the late 1950s.[10]

Another significant change has been the increased professionalisation of MPs.[11] In the early years after the Second World War, a substantial proportion of the Conservative Party's parliamentary representation consisted of a dutiful group – the lower squirearchy and retired military – for whom public service was coterminous with party support and barely touched matters of public policy. The Labour Party, too, had its consistent 'lobby fodder', worthy union leaders whose reward for years of stalwart service lay in an unchallenging spell as a MP. By the 1970s, and increasingly in the 1980s, those who entered parliament were more career-oriented, more consciously and permanently involved in politics; they had structured their lives from a relatively early age to develop a *curriculum vitae* of political service and political contacts, building on time spent as personal advisers or members of the party's extra-parliamentary policy units. They wanted to participate fully in policy-making; they sought power.

They too proved a two-edged sword, as Borthwick's chapter spells out. On the one hand, they were less deferential ideologically, more prepared to pontificate on policy matters and to join like-minded groups within the parliamentary party; they posed problems for unity and cohesion. Yet, on the other hand, ambition made them particularly susceptible to prime ministerial patronage and their numbers made prime ministerial choice a real power. They blew hot and cold, at one moment uncritically supportive of the fountain of all worthwhile jobs, at another caballing to calculate who might advance their political agendas, both personal and ideological, more effectively. The fragility of personal support was something with which the leaders of the 1950s and, to some extent, the 1960s did not have to grapple.

The role of cabinet has been a third area of change; and this too has a Janus-like quality. The quantity and complexity of matters on a government's agenda has resulted in the development of committees, a growing tendency towards multilateral (even bilateral) relations between prime minister and departmental ministers, and other developments which, from the cabinet's point of view, have fragmented its collective

10   Richard Rose, *Influencing Voters*, Faber and Faber, 1967.
11   Anthony King, 'The rise of the career politician in Britain – and its consequences', *British Journal of Political Science*, vol. 11 (1981), pp. 249-85.

power. Although the conception of cabinet meetings as the primary collective decision-making body was only applicable to a brief period in the nineteenth century, it is clear that the cabinet's role is, in the normal course of events, essentially a confirming and perhaps a legitimising one, its function being to inform (so that collective responsibility can be a real possibility) rather than to seek views. There are exceptions (for example, those at the time of the 1976 IMF negotiations, analysed by Giddings in Chapter 2), but they have a public impact precisely because of their abnormality. In a system of policy-making through subgroups, the power of the most active player and co-ordinator – the prime minister – is considerable. Knowledge is not of itself power, but it is an essential prerequisite. Here the prime minister enjoys an advantage probably unknown to Churchill or Attlee. With ministers overwhelmed by the minutiae of departmental matters filling their ministerial boxes with unremitting regularity and civil servants filling their diaries with meetings, they have little chance to participate knowledgeably on matters outside their remit. Alan Clark's diaries are peculiarly evocative of the drudgery consequent upon promotion to a position of presumed power; Richard Crossman's lament that the big issues could not be raised seriously in cabinet is surely a different side of the same coin.

The structure of decision-making in conjunction with (indeed, a consequence of) the expanded concerns of government itself seems at first sight to enhance prime ministerial power. But there is an obverse consequence. The practice of collective responsibility is less easy to ensure. When cabinet ministers could genuinely feel that they had participated in decision-making, they would naturally feel personally committed to the decisions taken. But, when in effect cabinet ministers merely approve decisions taken by colleagues without their participation, they do not have the same degree of commitment. The increase in leaks, in off-the-record briefings that publicise disagreements, and in breaches of the pure principle of collective responsibility are natural consequences of the new structure of decision-making. They weaken the public sense of government competence and hence the standing of the prime minister. Another consequence of the specialisation and diffusion of decision-making is that cabinet contributions must be couched in terms more of principle than of detail. Assertions of broad principle require little acquaintance with facts; they are the resort of people short of facts. Thus the fault-lines within each of the governing parties are exaggerated. And the prime minister's powers of group leadership are sorely tested.

As has been repeatedly emphasised in this book, the British system of government remains profoundly parliamentarian. A prime minister survives by the grace of the parliamentary party and, above all, a parliamentary majority. Since 1945, the relationship between survival and parliamentary majorities has undergone two important changes. In the first place, the myth that any defeat could result in resignation has been exploded; only when the issue of confidence has been quite explicitly attached to a vote will defeat require a government's resignation. Heath's treatment of his party provoked a change in behaviour which resulted in the new convention. Dissent, which had been largely limited to the relative privacy of the 1922 Committee and other party forums, could henceforth be expressed more openly. Perhaps this gives prime ministers a little more room at the margin; but this does not diminish the fact that several defeats, or seriously depleted majorities even on insignificant issues, can have profound political consequences of an intangible kind, reducing the sense of authority and the impression of power attributable to the prime minister. So this alteration in the 'rules of the game' may have given the prime minister more room for manoeuvre. Thatcher could remain unshaken through the experience of being the first prime minister possessing a clear majority to lose a major bill – the 1986 Shops (Sunday Trading) Bill – at second reading in the twentieth century, but she would later be the first to lose office as a result of a decision made by her own party.

If in the past a prime minister's fear of the dire consequences following a defeat in the House of Commons has been exaggerated, so too has the fear backbenchers might have had from the prime minister's power to call a general election. This power had long, and implausibly, been seen as a potent weapon in a prime minister's arsenal. But it is, of course, 10 Downing Street's nuclear device, more likely to eclipse the whole party than surgically remove troublesome dissidents, most of whom enjoy large and safe majorities. The relations between constituency associations and their representatives have mirrored the greater professionalism and seriousness of politics and, although support for the party leader is a most desirable trait, it is clearly not required. The assumptions behind Harold Wilson's 'dog license' speech were ill-judged, even at the time when he uttered it and even if, as he claimed, it was intended lightheartedly.

The chapters in this book tend to confirm the astonishingly enduring quality of the prime ministership as an institution, regardless of party. The central significance of party in British politics might suggest that prime ministers would therefore operate differently according to their party affiliation, but this has not been so. It was R.T. McKenzie's thesis more than thirty years ago that, despite the formal differences in the locus of power between the major parties, the imperatives of the parliamentary system actually forced them in practice to become more similar to one another.[12] The same forces provide prime ministers of

12   R.T. McKenzie, *British Political Parties: The distribution of power within the Conservative and Labour Parties*, Heinemann, 2nd edn, 1963.

either party with similar resources and similar constraints. As so many examples throughout these chapters illustrate, there is no discernible pattern in which party affiliation is the critical factor. Who would have immediately presumed, for example, that the Conservative (and dominating) Thatcher consulted extensively over cabinet appointments while the Labour (and reticent) Attlee did not?

The reason for this is that the office is based on no specific grants of power and no direct line of democratic legitimacy and is inherited by each prime minister in what might be termed its pristine state. This is to say that there has been no accumulation of powers, no incremental growth in size or authority which is handed on complete to each prime minister. Prime ministers can, and do, build up power over time as their leadership role and the logical consequences of the dispersion of responsibilities across the government structure gradually draw the threads of co-ordinating power into their hands. This is the nature of the job.

Such an observation suggests that the job of prime minister is self-defining. It is true that there is no specification, and that no constitutional provisions set out the duties and responsibilities of the office, but time and common sense have built up the outlines of one. Anthony King has set down seven functions which a prime minister must perform.[13] This obligation derives essentially from the lack of any other sensible line of responsibility. Thus prime ministers (and only prime ministers) must appoint and dismiss ministers, appoint the top civil servants, chair meetings of the cabinet and important cabinet committees, attend the House of Commons twice a week to answer questions, act as the head of government in international meetings of heads of government, be the minister for security services and decide on the date of general elections. Donald Shell develops this point by suggesting that any job description would contain a hierarchy of tasks. He notes too that the functions enumerated by King must be performed and that they can only be performed by the prime minister. But he adds that there are others which a prudent prime minister would elect to perform and others again which a prime minister is free to take on, or not, as the mood demands. It is at this end of the continuum that Asquith's famous remark quoted at the beginning of this chapter becomes apposite. Each prime minister, having normally served under his or her predecessor, develops a style and a set of priorities as a response to that experience; there is normally a clear wish to differentiate and to alter patterns of behaviour (authoritarianism or long-winded collegiality). In this way, prime ministers determine the nature of their term of office. Philip Giddings's

13   Anthony King, 'The British prime ministership in the age of the career politician', *Western European Politics*, Vol. 14 (1991), pp. 31-3.

case studies show that similar situations are dealt with differently by different prime ministers and the extent, for example, to which cabinets are relatively collegial is a function of a prime minister's preference. Prime ministers enjoy enormous discretionary power, especially when their party is popular, they have recently been victorious in an election, and their colleagues respect them both personally and professionally. But these are indeed variables, and are subject to the fluctuating moods of the British public and those who interpret those moods. In the last analysis, it is precisely because, in Michael Foley's telling phrase, prime ministers are 'the ostentatious flagships of their respective fleets'[14] that their colleagues may desert them if there is a danger of running aground; prime ministers have no power other than that granted to their party by the electorate and to them personally by their parliamentary colleagues.

The roots of prime ministerial power thus remain deeply embedded in the notion of parliamentary sovereignty. Prime ministers who neglect this aspect of their multi-faceted job find that the solid pillars which supported them after they were raised to power suddenly crumble, leaving them with no other means of support. Thatcher is the classic instance of this; and Major found that the pillars that seemed so sturdy after the unexpected Conservative victory in 1992 were in fact much weaker than he had imagined. The principle which allowed Churchill to replace Chamberlain back in 1940 remains unimpaired in the 1990s.

---

14   Foley, *The Rise of the British Presidency*, p. 121.

APPENDIXES

A

PARTY LEADERSHIP ELECTION RESULTS

The Conservative Party

An election system was first introduced in 1965. To win on the first ballot a candidate required an overall majority plus a 15 per cent lead over the nearest rival, calculated on the basis of the number of votes cast. To win on the second ballot an overall majority (of those voting) was required. If a third ballot were necessary, the three candidates who polled highest in the second ballot would be entered and an alternative vote system used. Voting was by secret ballot among Conservative MPs.

1965: RESIGNATION OF DOUGLAS-HOME

Heath	150
Maudling	133
Powell	15
Abstentions	6

After the result Maudling announced that he would not contest the second ballot. Heath's name alone was entered, whereupon he was declared the victor.

In 1975 the rules were slightly amended. For victory in the first ballot the required 15% margin was henceforth to be calculated on the basis of those eligible to vote rather than those who actually do vote. Also, candidates had to be proposed and seconded by MPs, but the names of proposers and seconders did not have to be made public.

1975: CHALLENGE TO HEATH

Thatcher	130	146
Heath	119	–
Fraser	16	–
Whitelaw	–	79
Prior	–	19
Howe	–	19
Peyton	–	11
Abstentions	11	2

243

1989: CHALLENGE TO THATCHER

Thatcher	314
Meyer	33
Spoiled	24
Abstentions	3

After the 1989 ballot it was decided that in future the names of the proposer and seconder of candidates would be made public.

1990: CHALLENGE TO THATCHER

Thatcher	204	–
Heseltine	152	131
Major	–	185
Hurd	–	56
Abstentions	16	–

To win on the first ballot an absolute majority (187) was required and a lead of 56 (15%) of the electorate. Thatcher's lead was four short of this requirement. On the second ballot Major was three votes short of an overall majority, but both Heseltine and Hurd announced they would not contest a third ballot, whereupon the chairman of the 1922 Committee announced that no third ballot would take place and declared Major elected leader.

The Labour Party

The Standing Orders of the Parliamentary Labour Party provided that when the party was in opposition the post of leader could be contested at the beginning of every parliamentary session. No provision was made for election when the party was in power. Successive ballots were held until one candidate had an absolute majority of votes cast. When the office of leader became vacant when the party was in power in 1976, this same procedure was used.

1955: RESIGNATION OF ATTLEE

Gaitskell	157
Bevan	70
Morrison	40

1960: CHALLENGE TO GAITSKELL

Gaitskell	166
Wilson	81

1961: CHALLENGE TO GAITSKELL

Gaitskell	171
Greenwood	59

1963: DEATH IN OFFICE OF GAITSKELL

Wilson	115	144
Brown	88	103
Callaghan	41	–

1976: RESIGNATION OF WILSON

Callaghan	84	141	176
Foot	90	113	137
Jenkins	56	–	–
Benn	37	–	–
Healey	30	38	–
Crosland	17	–	–

1976: RESIGNATION OF CALLAGHAN

Healey	112	129
Foot	83	139
Silkin	38	–
Shore	32	–

In 1981 Labour established an electoral college for the election of the leader and the deputy leader. Candidates for the leadership must be members of the House of Commons, and were required to have the support of 5% of the PLP. In the electoral college the votes were divided with 30% going to the PLP and 30% to the constituency parties, while 40% went to the trade unions. Percentages are calculated on the basis of those actually voting, not on those eligible to do so. Successive ballots can be held until one candidate has an overall majority of the votes cast. Voting was by open, not secret, ballot.

	PLP 30%	CLPs 30%	TUs 40%	Total 100%
1983: RESIGNATION OF FOOT				
Kinnock	14.8	27.5	29.0	71.3
Hattersley	17.8	0.6	10.9	19.3
Heffer	4.3	2.0	0.1	6.3
Shore	3.1	0.0	0.1	3.1

1988: CHALLENGE TO KINNOCK

Kinnock	24.8	24.1	39.7	88.6
Benn	5.2	5.9	0.3	11.4

After the 1988 ballot the rules were altered to require a challenger to have the support of 20% of the PLP rather than just 5%.

1992: RESIGNATION OF KINNOCK

Smith	23.2	29.3	38.5	91.0
Gould	6.8	0.7	1.5	9.0

After 1992 the rules were changed to give one-third of the votes to each section of the electoral college, and to adopt a 'one member one vote' framework. Henceforth all party members and all levy-paying members of trades unions were to be sent ballot papers. The PLP section was extended to include MEPs.

1994: DEATH OF SMITH

	PLP and MEPs	Party members	Affiliated organisations	Total 100%
Blair	60.5	58.2	52.3	57.0
Prescott	19.6	24.4	28.4	24.1
Beckett	19.9	17.4	19.3	18.9

B

GENERAL ELECTION RESULTS, 1945-1992

Election	Conservative seats / % of Poll	Labour seats / % of Poll	Liberal seats / % of Poll	Other seats / % of Poll	Overall majority	Prime minister
1945	213 39.8	393 48.3	12 9.1	22 2.7	Lab. 146	Attlee
1950	298 43.5	315 46.1	9 9.1	3 1.3	Lab. 5	Attlee
1951	321 48.0	295 48.8	6 2.5	3 0.7	Cons. 17	Churchill/ Eden
1955	345 49.7	277 46.4	6 2.7	2 1.2	Cons. 60	Eden/ Macmillan
1959	365 49.4	258 43.8	5 5.9	1 0.9	Cons. 100	Macmillan/ Douglas-Home
1964	304 43.4	317 44.1	9 11.2	0 1.3	Lab. 4	Wilson
1966	253 41.9	363 47.9	12 8.5	2 1.3	Lab. 96	Wilson
1970	330 46.4	287 43.0	6 7.5	7 3.1	Cons. 30	Heath
1974 (Feb.)	297 37.8	301 37.1	14 19.3	23 5.8	Lab. Nil	Wilson
1974 (Oct.)	276 35.9	319 39.3	13 18.3	27 6.5	Lab. 3	Wilson/ Callaghan
1979	339 43.9	268 36.9	11 13.8	17 5.3	Cons. 43	Thatcher
1983	397 42.4	209 27.6	23 25.4	21 4.6	Cons. 144	Thatcher
1987	376 42.3	229 30.8	22 22.5	23 4.4	Cons. 102	Thatcher/ Major
1992	336 41.9	271 34.4	20 17.8	24 5.8	Cons. 21	Major

C

SIZE OF GOVERNMENTS

	In paid government office			
	MPs	*Peers*	*PPSs in HC*	*MPs in Govt 'payroll vote'*
1940	58	16	25	83
1950	68	13	27	95
1960	65	17	36	101
1970	85	17	30	115
1980	86	21	28	114
1990	84	21	46	130

Sources : 1940-80: David Butler and Gareth Butler, *British Political Facts*. 6th edn, Macmillan, 1980. 1990: *Dod's Parliamentary Companion*; *The House Magazine*.

BIBLIOGRAPHY

EXCLUDING ARCHIVAL AND OFFICIAL SOURCES

Books

Bagehot, Walter, *The English Constitution* (1st edn 1867), Collins Fontana, 1963.

Baker, Kenneth, *The Turbulent Years*, Faber and Faber, 1993.

Barber, J., *The Prime Minister since 1945*, Blackwell, 1991.

Benemy, F.W.G., *The Elected Monarch: The Development of the Power of the Prime Minister*, Harrap, 1965.

Benn, Tony, *Out of the Wilderness: Diaries 1863-1967*, Heinemann, 1987.

——, *Against the Tide: Diaries 1973-1976*, Hutchinson, 1989.

——, *Conflicts of Interest: Diaries 1977-80*, Hutchinson, 1990.

Berkeley, Humphrey, *The Power of the Prime Minister*, Allen and Unwin, 1968.

Berrill, Sir Kenneth, *Strength at the Centre: The case for a prime minister's department*, University of London, 1980.

Black, Jeremy, *British Foreign Policy in the Age of Walpole*, J. Donald, Edinburgh, 1985.

Blackstone, Tessa, and William Plowden, *Inside the Think Tank*, Heinemann, 1988.

Blake, Robert (Lord), *The Office of Prime Minister*, Oxford University Press, 1975.

Boorstin, D., *The Image: A guide to pseudo-events in America*, Athenaeum, New York, 1961.

Brazier, Rodney, *Constitutional Practice*, Clarendon Press, Oxford, 1988.

Brewer, J., *The Sinews of War: War, money and the English state, 1688-1783*, Unwin Hyman, 1989.

Briggs, Asa, *Sound and Vision*, Oxford University Press, 1979.

Burch, Martin, and Michael Clarke, *British Cabinet Politics*, G.W. and A. Hesketh, Ormskirk, 1980.

Butler, David, and Gareth Butler, *British Political Facts, 1900-1984*, Macmillan, 6th edn 1985.

Butler, David, and Dennis Kavanagh, *The British General Election of 1979*, Macmillan, 1980.

Butler, David, and Michael Pinto-Duschinsky, *The British General Election of 1970*, Macmillan, 1971.

Butler, R.A., *The Art of the Possible*, Hamish Hamilton, 1971.

Butt, Ronald, *The Power of Parliament*, Constable, 1967.

Byrd, Peter (ed.), *British Foreign Policy under Thatcher*, Philip Allan/St. Martins Press, 1988.

Callaghan, James, *Time and Chance*, Collins, 1987.

Campbell, John, *Edward Heath*, Jonathan Cape, 1993.

Carstairs, Charles, and Richard Ware, *Parliament and International Relations*, Open University Press, 1991.

Carter, Byrum, *The Office of Prime Minister*, Faber and Faber, 1956.

Castle, Barbara, *Diaries*, Weidenfeld and Nicolson, 1980.

——, *The Castle Diaries, 1964-1976*, Macmillan, 1990.

Chapman, Brian, and Allen Potter (eds), *WJMM: Political questions*, Manchester University Press, 1974.

Chester, D.N., and Bowring, N., *Questions in Parliament*, Clarendon Press, Oxford, 1962.

Churchill, Randolph, *The Fight for the Tory Leadership*, Heinemann, 1964.

Clark, Alan, *Diary*, Weidenfeld and Nicolson, 1993.

Clarke, Michael, *British External Policy-Making in the 1990s*, Macmillan, 1992.

Cockerell, Michael, *Live From Number 10*, Faber and Faber, 1988.

Colley, Linda, *Britons: Forging the nation, 1707-1837*, Yale University Press, 1992.

Cosgrave, Patrick, *Carrington: A life and a policy*, Dent, 1985.

Crossman, Richard, *Inside View*, Cape, 1972.

——, *The Diaries of a Cabinet Minister*, Hamish Hamilton and Jonathan Cape, 1975, vol. 1.

Daalder, Hans, *Cabinet Reform in Britain*, Stanford University Press, 1963.

Denver, D., *Elections and Voting Behaviour in Britain*, Philip Allan, 1989.

Dickie, John, *Inside the Foreign Office*, Chapmans, 1992.

Donoughue, Bernard, and George Jones, *Herbert Morrison: Portrait of a Politician*, Weidenfeld and Nicolson, 1973.

Donoughue, Bernard, *Prime Minister*, Cape, 1987.

Drewry, Gavin, and T. Butcher, *The Civil Service Today*, Basil Blackwell, Oxford, 1988.

Drucker, H.M., *Doctrine and Ethos in the Labour Party*, Geo. Allen and Unwin, 1979.

Eden, Anthony, *Full Circle*, Cassell, 1960.

Fisher, Nigel, *The Tory Leaders*, Weidenfeld and Nicolson, 1977.

Foley, Michael, *The Rise of the British Presidency*, Manchester University Press, 1993.

Fulton, Lord, *The Civil Service:* Vol. 1 – Report, Cmnd 3638, HMSO, London, 1968.

Garner, Richard, and Kelly, Richard, *British Political Parties Today*, Manchester University Press, 1993.

Gilbert, Martin, *Winston Churchill*, Heinemann, 1988.

Goldie, Grace Wyndham, *Facing the Nation: Television and politics, 1936-1976*, Bodley Head, 1977.

Gordon Walker, Patrick, *The Cabinet*, Cape, 1970.

Gray, A., and W. Jenkins, *Administrative Politics in British Government*, Wheatsheaf, Brighton, 1985.

Harris, Kenneth, *Attlee*, Weidenfeld and Nicolson, 1982.

Harris, Robert, *Good and Faithful Servant: The unauthorised biography of Bernard Ingham*, Faber and Faber, 1990.

Haseler, Stephen, *The Gaitskellites*, Macmillan, 1969.

Hattendorf, John B., and Malcolm H. Murfett (eds), *The Limitations of Military Power*, Macmillan, 1990.

Healey, Denis, *The Time of My Life*, Michael Joseph, 1989.

Hennessy, Peter, *Cabinet*, Basil Blackwell, 1986.

——, *Whitehall*, Fontana, London, 1990.

Herbert, A.P., *Independent Member*, Methuen, 1950.

Heseltine, Michael, *Where There's a Will*, Hutchinson, London, 1987.

Hoffman, J.D., *The Conservative Party in Opposition, 1945- 1951*, MacGibbon and Kee, 1964.

Horne, Alistair, *Macmillan, 1894-1956*, Macmillan, 1988.

——, *Macmillan, 1957-1986*, Macmillan, 1989.

Howell, David, *A New Style of Government*, Conservative Political Centre, London, 1970.

Hurd, Douglas, *An End to Promises*, Collins, London, 1979.

——, *The British Cabinet*, Stevens, 1968.

Ingham, Bernard, *Kill the Messenger*, HarperCollins, 1991.

James, S., *British Cabinet Government*, Routledge, 1992.

Jenkins, Peter, *The Battle of Downing Street*, Charles Knight, London, 1970.

Jenkins, Roy, *A Life at the Centre*, Macmillan, 1991.

Jennings, Sir Ivor, *Cabinet Government* (3rd edn), Cambridge University Press, 1959.

Judge, D., *The Parliamentary State*, Sage, 1993.

Kavanagh, Dennis, *Thatcherism and British Politics* (2nd edn), Oxford University Press, 1990.

——, and Anthony Seldon (eds), *The Thatcher Effect*, Clarendon Press, Oxford, 1989.

Keegan, William, *Mrs Thatcher's Economic Experiment*, Allen Lane, 1984.

Kellner, Peter, and Lord Crowther-Hunt. *The Civil Servants: An enquiry into Britain's ruling class*, Macdonald, 1980

Kelly, Richard, *Conservative Party Conferences*, Manchester University Press, 1989.

King, Anthony (ed.), *The British Prime Minister* (2nd edn), Macmillan, London, 1985.

—— (ed.), *Britain at the Polls*, Chatham House Publishers, 1993.

Lever, Michael, and N. Schofield, *Multiparty Government: The politics of coalition in Europe,* Oxford University Press, 1991.

Lawson, Nigel, *The View from No. 11: Memoirs of a Tory radical,* Bantam Press, 1991.

Leapman, Michael, *The Last Days of the Beeb*, Geo. Allen and Unwin, London, 1986.

Leruez, Jacques, *Economic Planning and Politics in Britain*, Martin Robertson, 1975.

Leuchtenburg, William E., *In the Shadow of FDR: From Harry Truman to Bill Clinton*, Cornell University Press, Ithaca, NY, 2nd edn, 1993.

Linklater, M., and D. Leigh, *Not with Honour*, Sphere, 1986.

Louis, Wm. Roger, *Imperialism at Bay: 1941-1945*, Clarendon Press, Oxford, 1977.

Mackintosh, John P. (ed.), *British Prime Ministers*, vol. 2, Weidenfeld and Nicolson, 1975.

Macmillan, Harold, *At the End of the Day*, Macmillan, 1973.

Margach, James, *The Abuse of Power*, W.H. Allen, London, 1978.

McCallum, R.B., and A. Readman, *The British General Election of 1945*, Oxford University Press, 1947.

McKenzie, Robert T., *British Political Parties: The distribution of power within the Conservative and Labour Parties*, Heinemann, 2nd edn, 1963.

McKie, D. (ed.), *The Election: A voter's guide*, Fourth Estate, London, 1992.

Meyer, Sir Anthony, *Stand Up and Be Counted*, Heinemann, 1990.

Milne, Alisdair, *DG: The memoirs of a British broadcaster*, Hodder and Stoughton, 1988.

Minkin, Lewis, *The Contentious Alliance*, Edinburgh University Press, 1991.

Moran, Lord, *Winston Churchill: The struggle for survival*, Sphere, 1968.

Neustadt, Richard E., *Presidential Power*, John Wiley, New York, 1976.

Nicholson, R., C. Cunningham and P. Gummett (eds), *Science and Technology in the United Kingdom*, Longman, 1991.

Norton, P., *Dissension in the House of Commons, 1974-1979*, Clarendon Press, Oxford, 1980.

——, *The Commons in Perspective*, Martin Robertson, Oxford, 1981.

——, *Does Parliament Matter?*, Harvester Wheatsheaf, Hemel Hempstead; 1993.

Part, Anthony, *The Making of a Mandarin*, André Deutsch, 1990.

Peden, George, *British Rearmament and the Treasury, 1932-1939*, Scottish Academic Press, Edinburgh, 1979.

Pfeffer, Jeffrey, *Power in Organisations*, Pitman, 1981.

Pimlott, Ben, *Hugh Dalton*, Macmillan, 1985.

——, *Harold Wilson*, HarperCollins, 1992.

Plowden, William (ed.), *Advising the Rulers*, Basil Blackwell, Oxford, 1987.

Pollitt, Christopher, *Manipulating the Machine*, Geo. Allen and Unwin, 1984.

Prior, James, *A Balance of Power*, Hamish Hamilton, 1986.

Punnett, R. Malcolm, *Selecting the Party Leader*, Harvester Wheatsheaf, Hemel Hempstead, 1992.

Rhodes James, Robert, *Anthony Eden*, Weidenfeld and Nicolson, 1986.

Richelson, Jeffrey T., and Desmond Ball, *The Ties that Bind: Intelligence co-operation between the UK/USA countries*, Geo. Allen and Unwin, 1985.

Riddell, Peter, *The Thatcher Government*, Basil Blackwell, Oxford, 1985.

——, *Honest Opportunism: The rise of the career politician*, Hamish Hamilton, 1993.

Ridley, Nicholas, *My Style of Government: The Thatcher years*, Fontana, 1992.

Rose, Richard (ed.), *Studies in British Politics*, Macmillan, 1966.

——, *Influencing Voters*, Faber and Faber, 1967.

——, *The Problem of Party Government*, Penguin, Harmondsworth, 1976.

——, *Do Parties Make a Difference?* (2nd edn), Macmillan, 1984.

——, *Ministers and Ministries*, Clarendon, Oxford, 1987.
—— and E. Sulieman (eds), *Presidents and Prime Ministers*, American Enterprise Institute, 1980.
Sedgemore, Brian, *The Secret Constitution*, Hodder and Stoughton, 1980.
Seldon, Anthony, *Churchill's Indian Summer: The Conservative Government, 1951-1955*, Hodder and Stoughton, 1981.
Seymour-Ure, Colin, *The Press, Politics and the Public*, Methuen, 1969.
——, *The British Press and Broadcasting since 1945*, Basil Blackwell, Oxford, 1991.
Shay, Robert Paul Jr., *British Rearmament in the Thirties*, Princeton University Press, 1977.
Shell, D., *The House of Lords*, Harvester Wheatsheaf, Hemel Hempstead, 1992.
Short, Edward, *Whip to Wilson*, Macdonald, 1989.
Skidelsky, Robert (ed.), *Thatcherism*, Chatto and Windus, London, 1987.
Street, H., and R., Brazier, *Constitutional and Administrative Law*, Penguin Books, Harmondsworth, 1986.
Tebbit, Norman, *Upwardly Mobile* (2nd edn), 1989.
Thatcher, Margaret, *The Downing Street Years*, HarperCollins, 1993.
Theakston, Kevin, *Junior Ministers in British Government*, Basil Blackwell, Oxford, 1987.
Wakeham, John, *Cabinet Government*, Brunel University, 1993.
Walkland, S.A. (ed.), *The House of Commons in the Twentieth Century*, Clarendon Press, Oxford, 1979.
Whitelaw, William, *The Whitelaw Memoirs*, Aurum Press, 1989.
Williams, Francis, *A Prime Minister Remembers*, Heinemann, 1961.
——, *Nothing so Strange*, Cassell, London, 1970.
Williams, Marcia, *Inside Number 10*, New English Library, London, 1972.
Wilson, Harold, *The Labour Government, 1964-1970: A personal record*, Weidenfeld and Nicolson, 1971.
——, *The Governance of Britain*, Weidenfeld and Nicolson/Michael Joseph, London, 1976.
——, *A Prime Minister on Prime Ministers*, Michael Joseph, 1977.
——, *Final Term*, Weidenfeld and Nicolson, Michael Joseph, 1979.
Wilson, Stephen Shipley (ed.), *The Cabinet Office to 1945*, HMSO, London, 1975.
Woolton, Earl of, *Memoirs*, Cassell, 1959.
Young, Hugo, *One of Us*, Macmillan, 1989; 2nd edn 1991.
Young, Lord, *The Enterprise Years*, Headline, 1990.
Ziegler, Philip, *Wilson*, Weidenfeld and Nicolson, 1993.

Articles in Journals and Chapters in Edited Books

Alderman, R.K., and N. Carter, 'A Very Tory Coup: the ousting of Mrs Thatcher', *Parliamentary Affairs*, vol. 44 (1990), pp. 125-39.
Baker, Kenneth, 'The Ides of Margaret', *Sunday Times*, 30 August 1993.
Berrill, Sir Kenneth, 'Strength at the centre: The case for a prime minister's department' in Anthony King (ed.), *The British Prime Minister* (2nd edn), Macmillan, 1985.

Brand, Jack, 'Faction as its own Reward: Groups in the British Parliament, 1945-1986', *Parliamentary Affairs*, vol. 42, no. 2 (1989).

Brown, A., 'Prime ministerial power', *Public Law* (1968), pp. 28-51, 96-118.

Burch, Martin, 'Mrs. Thatcher's approach to leadership in government', *Parliamentary Affairs*, vol. 36 (1983), pp. 399-416.

——, 'Who organises what? The management of business in the British cabinet system', *Manchester Papers in Politics*, 3/90, Department of Government, University of Manchester, 1990.

Burnham, J., and George Jones, 'Advising Margaret Thatcher: The prime minister's office and the Cabinet Office compared', *Political Studies*, vol. 41 (1993), pp. 299-314.

Crossman, Richard, Introduction to Walter Bagehot, *The English Constitution*, Collins/Fontana, 1967.

Devereau, M., 'Do we need government information services?', *RIPA, Report*, vol. 13, no. 1 (1992).

Dunleavy, P., G.W. Jones and B. O'Leary, 'Prime Ministers and the Commons: Patterns of Behaviour, 1868-1987', *Public Administration*, vol.68 (1990), pp. 123-39.

Griggs, E., 'The politics of health reform', *Political Quarterly*, vol. 62 (1991), pp. 419-30.

Gummett, P., 'History, development and organisation of UK science and technology up to 1982' in R. Nicholson, C. Cunningham, and P. Gummett, (eds), *Science and Technology in the United Kingdom*, Longman, 1991.

Hunt, Lord, of Tanworth, Contribution in William Plowden (ed.), *Advising the Rulers*, Blackwell, Oxford, 1987.

Irwin, H., A. Kennon, D. Natzler and R. Rogers, 'Evolving rules' in M. Franklin and P. Norton (eds), *Parliamentary Questions*, Clarendon Press, Oxford, 1993, pp. 23-72.

Jones, George W., 'The prime minister and parliamentary questions', *Parliamentary Affairs*, vol. 26 (1973), pp. 260-73.

——, 'The Prime Minister's Power', *Parliamentary Affairs*, vol. 18 (1965), pp. 167-85.

——, 'The United Kingdom' in William Plowden (ed.), *Advising the Rulers*, Basil Blackwell, Oxford, 1987.

——, 'The prime minister's power' in Anthony King (ed.), *The British Prime Minister* (2nd edn), Macmillan, London, 1985.

King, Anthony, 'The rise of the career politician in Britain – and its consequences', *British Journal of Political Science*, vol. 11 (1981), pp. 249-85.

——, 'Margaret Thatcher as political leader' in Robert Skidelsky (ed.), *Thatcherism*, Chatto and Windus, 1987.

——, 'The British prime minister in the age of the career politician', *West European Politics*, vol. 14 (1991), pp. 25-47.

——, 'The Implications of One-Party Government', in A. King (ed.), *Britain at the Polls*, Chatham House Publishers, 1993.

Lee, J.M., 'Cabinet procedure', *Public Administration*, vol. 64 (1986), pp. 347-9.

——, 'Central capability and established practice: The changing character of the "centre of the machine" in British cabinet government' in Brian Chapman and Allen Potter (eds), *WJMM: Political questions*, Manchester University Press, 1974.

——, 'The ethos of the Cabinet Office', *Public Administration*, vol. 68 (1990), pp. 235-52.

Lewis, N., 'The Citizen's Charter and the Next Steps: A new way of governing', *Political Quarterly*, vol. 64 (1993), pp. 316-26.

Mackintosh, J.P., 'Harold Wilson' in J.P. Mackintosh (ed.), *British Prime Ministers in the Twentieth Century*, vol. II, Weidenfeld and Nicolson, 1978.

Norton, Philip, 'Government defeats in the House of Commons: Myth and reality', *Public Law* (1978), pp. 360-78.

——, 'Choosing a leader: Margaret Thatcher and the parliamentary Conservative party', *Parliamentary Affairs*, vol. 43 (1990), pp. 249-59.

——, 'The Organisation of Political Parties in the House of Commons' in S.A. Walkland (ed.), *The House of Commons in the Twentieth Century*, Clarendon Press, Oxford, 1979.

Parris, M., 'Prime minister's question time', *The Times*, 28 April 1989.

Rees-Mogg, W., 'Major fails the leadership test', *The Times*, 10 May 1993.

Rose, Richard, 'British government: The Job at the Top' and 'Government against sub-governments' in R. Rose and E.N. Suleiman (eds), *Presidents and Prime Ministers*, American Enterprise Institute, Washington, DC, 1980.

——, 'Parties, Factions and Tendencies in Britain', *Political Studies*, vol. 12 (1964); reprinted in R. Rose (ed.), *Studies in British Politics*, Macmillan, 1966.

Sainsbury, K., 'Harold Macmillan' in J.P. Mackintosh (ed.), *British Prime Ministers in the Twentieth Century*, vol. II, Weidenfeld and Nicolson, 1978.

Seldon, Anthony, 'The Cabinet Office and co-ordination', *Public Administration*, vol. 68 (1990), pp. 103-21.

Seymour-Ure, Colin, 'British war cabinets in limited wars', *Public Administration*, vol. 62 (1984), pp. 181-200.

——, 'Prime minister's press secretary', *Contemporary Record*, vol. 3, no. 1 (1989), pp. 33-6.

Shell, Donald, 'The House of Lords in context' in D. Shell and D. Beamish (eds), *The House of Lords at Work*, Clarendon Press, Oxford, 1993.

——, 'The British Constitution in 1984', *Parliamentary Affairs*, vol. 38 (1985), pp. 131-49.

——, 'The British Constitution in 1993', *Parliamentary Affairs*, vol. 47 (1994), pp. 293-309.

Weller, Patrick, 'Prime minister/prime ministerial government', in Vernon Bogdanor (ed.), *The Blackwell Encyclopaedia of Political Institutions*, Blackwell Reference, 1987.

Willetts, David, 'The role of the prime minister's Policy Unit', *Public Administration*, vol. 65 (1987), pp. 443-52.

Wilson, Craig V., and Andrea L. Bonnicksen, 'The British prime minister' in Taketsugu Tsurutani and Jack B. Gabbert (eds), *Chief Executive: National political leadership in the United States, Mexico, Great Britain, Germany and Japan*, Washington State University Press, Pullman, WA, 1992.

INDEX

257